THE NARROW LUTHERAN MIDDLE

Following the Scriptural Road

Daniel M. Deutschlander

NORTHWESTERN PUBLISHING HOUSE
Milwaukee, Wisconsin

Cover photograph: ShutterStock, Inc.

Library of Congress Control Number: 2008935156
Northwestern Publishing House
1250 N. 113th St., Milwaukee, WI 53226-3284
www.nph.net
© 2011 by Northwestern Publishing House
Published 2011
Printed in the United States of America
ISBN 978-0-8100-2344-4

CONTENTS

PREFACE

Some people say that the Bible is too hard for anyone to understand. They are both right and wrong. They are right if they expect to grasp and fathom with fallen reason everything that God has to say in his Word. Indeed, such an expectation should appear to us as foolish and irrational on the face of it. For what do we have in the Bible? Nothing less than God's revelation of his own mind and heart and will. If mere mortals could plumb the depths of the mind of God and fully comprehend it, they would be God's equals; they would in fact have achieved what Eve hoped to get when she imagined that with sin she could acquire the very essence of God and his wisdom. And we all know how that turned out!

So, yes, in one sense the Bible is indeed difficult to understand, since in it God shows us his own unfathomable being and wisdom. We will never fully grasp those things, even to the limited extent that God has revealed them in his Word. St. Paul admitted that too. He reminds us that while we are here on earth we know God, ourselves, and all truth only in part; we wait for heaven for our knowledge to become complete (1 Corinthians 13:12). But unlike the lazy person or the scoffer who dismisses the Bible because he cannot completely comprehend the mind of God revealed in it, St. Paul rejoices in what God reveals there. He can never get enough of it. He worships a God who is bigger than we are and wiser than we can comprehend (Romans 11:33-36). Could it be that even in heaven we will know and understand only as much as a creature can ever know or understand? Could it be that even in heaven the peak of our knowledge and understanding will consist chiefly in this, that in heaven we will be more fully in awe of the wisdom and knowledge of God?

God himself tells us that we should not expect to fully fathom his divine mind and way of thinking. He tells us through the prophet Isaiah: "'My thoughts are not your thoughts, neither are your ways my ways,' declares the LORD. 'As the heavens are higher than the earth, so are my ways higher than your ways and my thoughts than your thoughts'" (Isaiah 55:8,9). The really beautiful thing about this passage is that God speaks these words with special reference to the heart and core of the gospel: the almighty and the holy God calls pitiful, weak, sinful man to repentance; and he *wants* to forgive and receive mere mortals into his fellowship and blest communion—that is not the way *our* reasoning would go. But God's divine mind, his perfect and holy reasoning, most happily for us goes way beyond what we would ever reason! Most blessedly for us, his reasoning is as far away from ours as heaven from earth! God be forever praised and adored that it is so! So, yes, in a sense those people are right who say that the Bible is hard to understand.

But in another sense, those who say that the Bible is hard, too hard, to understand are as wrong as they could be. At the very beginning of Isaiah's book, God puts the heart and core of the Bible's message so simply, and he does so with an expression of his own divine reasoning: "'Come now, let us reason together,' says the LORD. 'Though your sins are like scarlet, they shall be as white as snow; though they are red as crimson, they shall be like wool'" (Isaiah 1:18). What could be more simple? It is as simple as John 3:16, as 2 Corinthians 5:18-21, as 1 John 2:1,2: God forgives sin because his own Son paid its dread penalty; God welcomes and embraces the penitent; God gives eternal life to those who believe that saving message.

There is nothing difficult or complicated about those sentences. They are within the grasp of the most simple among us, yes, of even an infant newly baptized. And at the same time, they are so profound that only the miracle of the Holy Spirit working through those very simple words could bring us to believe them. That is the way it is with the gospel that is the heart and core of the Bible, of the very mind and heart of God. It is, as one ancient church father said, a water so simple that a child can swim in it and, at the same time, so deep that an elephant could drown in it.

Others say that the Bible contradicts itself. Such people then dismiss the Bible altogether as the work of men with varying and inconsistent opinions, a book therefore worthy of no more respect than any other book. Or they try with their fallen reason to reconcile what they consider its contradictions and end up denying some truths and overemphasizing others to the point of turning even those into errors. Whichever path those go who contend that the Bible contradicts itself, they share in one common error: They begin with the conviction that the Bible is not the verbally inspired and therefore inerrant Word of God himself. Only with such a denial of the divine source of the Scriptures could they dare to declare that God doesn't quite know what he is talking about or that he contradicts himself and needs our help in straightening out the tangled web of his Word.

We, however, have the Spirit-worked conviction that the Spirit has worked through the Word itself, that the Bible is the very Word of God. The Holy Spirit through his Word has brought us to accept in childlike faith the truth that God has breathed the words of that holy, that unique Book. It is therefore, in everything that it says, profitable for doctrine, for faith, for life, and for life eternal (2 Timothy 3:15,16).

It is in that conviction that the following chapters and pages have been written. We want to examine some of those teachings of the Bible that so many have found either too difficult or have declared to be contradictory. We want to examine them in the light of all that God's Word says about those teachings. It will not be our purpose to resolve every difficulty to the satisfaction of fallen reason. It will not be our purpose to dismiss some things that the Bible says in favor of other things that seem more reasonable to us. Rather, this is our intent: We want to see how God himself in his Word balances truths and does that invariably to our advantage. We want to consider how one truth is made the more clear and blessed for us by another truth that at first glance may seem to be at variance with the first truth. We will do that in the confidence that God does not lie to us or deceive us in his Word. We will do it in the certainty that whatever God teaches us in his Word is in perfect harmony with who he is, what we are, and what we so desperately need for life and for life eternal. Like Mary, we wish only to sit at Jesus' feet and receive from him in his Word grace heaped upon grace (Luke 10:38-42; John 1:16). If this book accomplishes that purpose for you, then you will join its author in still more gladly singing with the church over the centuries:

How precious is the Book divine,
    By inspiration giv'n!
Bright as a lamp its doctrines shine
    To guide our souls to heav'n.

Its light, descending from above
    Our gloomy world to cheer,
Displays a Savior's boundless love
    And brings his glories near.

It shows to us our wand'ring ways
    And where our feet have trod
But brings to view the matchless grace
    Of a forgiving God.

This lamp through all the dreary night
    Of life shall guide our way
Till we behold the clearer light
    Of an eternal day. (CW 284)

1

So What's the Problem?

Aristotle (d. 322 B.C.) said in one of the most important and influential books ever written, *The Nichomachean Ethics,* that the goal of life is happiness. He defined *happiness* as the virtuous soul engaged in virtuous actions. But what is virtue? There are many virtues, said Aristotle, and most of them are in the middle between two opposite vices. The trick is to find and hold the middle between the two vices. The vices, he said, are often an overdoing or an overemphasis on some particular aspect of a virtue. Thus, for example, liberality or generosity is a virtue in the middle between stinginess on one side and wasteful prodigality on the other side. Find and practice the golden mean in the middle and, with respect to money, you will be happy—or at least that's what Aristotle thought.

In religion and theology there is something of a parallel to Aristotle's search for the middle between two false alternatives, between an overemphasis on some aspect of a truth at the expense of the rest of the truth. Any number of false doctrines are the result of falls off the narrow middle road into ditches on either side of the truth in the middle. See how clever the devil is: Often he does not make a frontal assault on the truths of God's Word. Rather, he prefers to take a bit of truth and distort it until it becomes a lie; he does that by emphasizing only one aspect of the truth at the expense of the whole truth. With the grain of truth that he has corrupted, a grain that he uses to make his lie believable, he seduces unguarded souls into error and even unbelief; he pushes them from the narrow middle into the ditches on either side of the truth.

He even tried that ploy with Jesus. In the temptation of Jesus recorded in Matthew 4:5-7, the devil quoted the Bible, from Psalm 91:11,12. The devil held before Jesus the truth that God promises to protect his children. He urged Jesus to put God's promise to the test by throwing himself down from the peak of the temple; if God was faithful to his promise, then no harm should come to Jesus. There was a grain of truth in what the devil said. But Jesus saw the perversion of truth that was at the heart of Satan's temptation. In the first place, Satan left out an important part of the passage that he quoted. God's promise in Psalm 91 is that he will guard you *in all your ways.* The assumption of the psalm is that our ways will be in accord with God's Word. God does not promise his help and protection for us when our ways are no longer his ways. He does not promise his protection so that we can sin boldly and successfully.

Jesus' answer to the devil was, of course, perfect. He declared the truth of God's Word in Deuteronomy 6:16. Jesus, on the basis of that Word of God, answered that we are not to test God's promises to see if God will be faithful; rather, we are to trust his Word as we go about doing *his* will *in accord with his Word.* Trust in the promise of God is the middle. Doubt, which holds only to part of the promise, is the ditch on one side of that middle. Presumption, which makes use of the promise in a sinful way, is the ditch on the other side. (We will consider this particular stretch on the narrow middle road in greater detail in the next chapter.)

Examples of temptations to overemphasize one aspect of the truth to the point that it becomes an error abound. Some, for example, so emphasize the grace and love of God that they deny the existence of hell and teach that all will eventually end up in heaven. They make God's love into a license to sin boldly[1]; it is as though God redeemed us by his blood so that we could continue comfortably in our sins without either repentance or any struggle against the flesh. For if we all end up in heaven anyway, why bother with the struggle against sin and temptation? Indeed, why bother with his Word and sacraments at all?

Others fall into still other ditches along the way. They overemphasize the justice and power of God to the point that they end up setting a limit on the grace of God. But if God's grace has a limit, how can I ever be sure that it extends even to me and covers all of *my* sin and guilt? Yes, and if God's grace does not extend to all, where can I look for some assurance that it extends to me? Despair of God's grace must be our lot when conscience accuses us; conscience should have no difficulty in convincing us that our faith and our works are never good enough to merit even the smallest particle of our salvation. The only alternative for those not satisfied with the Bible's teaching that salvation is altogether the gift of grace on account of Christ's merit is yet another ditch; if God's grace and Christ's merit are not sufficient to save me, then there must be something in me that must make up for whatever grace does not cover. I must add my works or my best efforts or my faith to Christ's work as causes of salvation. To put it another way, Christ has made my salvation possible; now I must finish the job. Both ditches are perilous indeed. Despair and self-righteousness alike are the opposites of faith.

So then, there is a narrow middle road between these two errors: the one which so emphasizes grace that it perverts it into a license to sin and the other which so emphasizes God's justice that it either places a limit on God's grace or requires me to do something to aid in my own salvation. (Despair and self-righteousness are, after all, two sides of the same coin.) Each of

---

[1] St. Bernard opines that this was the essence of Satan's fall: He did not doubt that God was almighty and could punish him for his pride; rather, he presumed that God was so gentle that he would not punish him, even though he could. Such presumption, Bernard says, is even worse than failing to love God; it repays God's love with hatred. (Cf. "On the Steps of Humility and Pride," in *Bernard of Clairvaux—Selected Works* [New York: Paulist Press, 1987], p. 127.)

those errors holds on to only part of a truth at the expense of the whole. Each error misses the middle and ends up turning truth into error to the great harm of both Christian faith and life. The truth in the middle is that there is no reason to despair since Christ has done it all; the truth in the middle is that our life is a grateful response to the gift of salvation, not an effort to complete it.

It is the narrow middle road that we will seek to find and travel in this book. We undertake such a search with the awareness that the task is urgent and that failure in our quest threatens our faith. Jesus bids us to enter on this task with his own warning of the danger to our souls if we fail to find and walk that narrow middle road. He warns against the ditches and points to the ease with which one can fall into them when he urges us to "enter through the narrow gate. For wide is the gate and broad is the road that leads to destruction, and many enter through it. But small is the gate and narrow the road that leads to life, and only a few find it" (Matthew 7:13,14).

As we begin our search and our journey, it may be well to ask a few basic preliminary questions. Why is it, for example, that so many fall into the ditches? How come so few find that narrow middle road that leads to life and life eternal? And just as important, how can we know that we ourselves are not already in one of the ditches? Or how can we be sure that we will not fall off the narrow middle road at some time in the future?

Why do so many end up in the ditches?

The short answer to the question of why so many end up in the ditches is this: They listened to their reason and let reason take control where the Word of God should have been in control.

Reason, to be sure, is one of the greatest gifts that God has given to us. It is second after the gospel in Word and sacraments with its faith-creating message of salvation by grace through faith in Christ and his work for our salvation. God wants us to use the precious gift of reason in our daily lives. He wants us to use it when we decide how to vote, how to spend money, how to find a spouse, how to raise children, how to carry out the work we have to do in this life. Without the use of reason, life descends into a swamp of disorder, then into a sea of chaos, and finally into certain misery. How many people do you know who, as the saying

4

goes, "never use their heads"? They have no grasp of the concept of cause and effect, no ability to see any further than the moment. Abandoning the use of reason, their attention spans are fixed on the fleeting and their lives are devoted only to the moment. They have the attention span of a gerbil! The result is a plunge from one mess into another. Sadly, no matter how miserable they make their lives with their irrational lifestyles and choices, they often never change. Nor does it occur to them that they need to. That's life without a good use of God's gift of reason.

In our religious life and in theology too there is a proper use for reason. We need it when we study the Scriptures. We use it, for example, to compare passages with other passages in order to see all that God has to say on a given subject. We use it to study the languages of the Bible. We use it to apply the truths of the Word to concrete situations in life. Indeed, many of the greatest of the church fathers made excellent and noble use of God's gift of reason. Among the most brilliant theologians who often (sadly, not always) knew how to use reason properly in theology we could mention St. Athanasius of Alexandria, St. Augustine of Hippo, and St. Anselm of Canterbury. Among the best and greatest Lutheran theologians who had a deep respect for the proper use of reason in theology we would put Martin Chemnitz and the other authors of the Formula of Concord at the top of the list.

What then is the problem with reason, that as great and good and useful a gift of God as it is, it nevertheless gets misused to the ruin of many? How is it that reason, so necessary in our daily life and in our religion, ends up singing a siren song that lures so many into a ditch that leads to destruction? The answer is as simple and as complicated as this: *In the temple of God, reason is the servant and the scullery maid; the Bible is queen!* As beautiful as the maid may be and as useful, even as necessary, as she may be, she must never be allowed to usurp the role of the queen.

Our reason however has been terribly corrupted by the fall into sin. Though reason still has vital uses, now, because of that corruption, she is never satisfied with her position as maid. While trying to hide the warts that cover her because of sin's corruption, she struggles with might and main to paint over the warts and then to steal royal robes for herself. If not controlled by the Christian's converted will, if not governed by the Word of

5

God, she will dethrone the queen and take control of both the secular and the sacred.

We see that already in the Garden of Eden. Eve allowed reason to rule over God's Word. After all, what could be more reasonable and on the surface more desirable and pious than to get what Satan promised? He promised wisdom equal to the wisdom of God himself! Wouldn't that be a good thing, to be even more godlike than she was at her creation? Eve's reason was seduced. In this instance there was but one ditch. And deep it was indeed. And Eve fell headlong into it by choosing to follow Satan's word instead of God's Word. She fell into sin when she enthroned reason and threw away faith in the plain and clear Word of God. But reason enthroned and the Word of God dethroned equals unbelief and its dread consequence of spiritual death.

Since the fall of Adam and Eve in the garden, little has changed. Satan still seduces us by urging us to enthrone a fallen and rebellious reason over of the clear Word of God. Few heresies and few sins are there that do not have a misuse of reason somewhere prominent in the evil.

No one can surpass St. Paul in the appreciation of this fundamental truth: The devil likes nothing better than to push our reason from the backseat into the driver's seat, from the broom closet into the throne room, when matters of faith and morals are at issue. Paul saw the conflict between fallen reason and the Word of God at its sharpest in the truth that our salvation is altogether the work of Christ on the cross—as is revealed in God's Word. The devil hates no truth of God's Word more than that one. Indeed, all of his attacks on the rest of God's Word have as their goal the destruction of this central truth of our salvation. Paul saw that and declared:

> The message of the cross is foolishness to those who are perishing, but to us who are being saved it is the power of God. For it is written: "I will destroy the wisdom of the wise; the intelligence of the intelligent I will frustrate." Where is the wise man? Where is the scholar? Where is the philosopher of this age? Has not God made foolish the wisdom of the world? For since in the wisdom of God the world through its wisdom did not know him, God was

pleased through the foolishness of what was preached to save those who believe. (1 Corinthians 1:18-21)

In the rest of the chapter, the apostle pursues the theme that the gospel is nonsense to fallen reason and to those who give their reason the throne and the deciding voice in spiritual matters.

But that doesn't mean that Paul had no appreciation for a proper use of the gift of reason, even in expressing the truths of the Scriptures. He demonstrates that best in the whole organization of the epistle to the Romans. He arranges the truths of God's Word—by the direction and the inspiration of God the Holy Spirit himself—in a perfectly logical order, and he argues them in a reasonable manner. But then, when reason wants to get in the way and raise an objection to God's reasoning, Paul puts reason in its place. (Consider, for example, Romans 3:5-8; it is interesting to note that even in this passage Paul uses reason to put reason in its place.) He knew where the narrow middle road is between contempt for God's gift of reason on the one hand and the enthronement of reason over God's Word on the other hand. Since the epistle is itself the verbally inspired Word of God, it is God himself who is giving us an example in this epistle of the proper use of reason.

Luther too appreciated reason for the great gift of God that it is in secular and temporal matters. But like St. Paul, he saw all around him the damage done to the church, to souls, and yes, to civil society as well when reason took control in spiritual matters. So great was the damage done by reason enthroned over the Word of God that Luther called reason the devil's own harlot.[2]

The sad fact that Luther experienced before the Reformation was that pastors and theologians knew Aristotle better than they knew Paul. Aristotle, of course, knew nothing of the revealed Word of God. For Aristotle, reason was queen, yes, even a god. In Luther's day, Aristotle's very reasonable-sounding philosophy was imposed on the Bible so that whatever the Bible said was

---

[2] Cf. Luther's treatise "Against the Heavenly Prophets," *Luther's Works,* edited by Jaroslav Pelikan and Helmut T. Lehmann, American Edition, Vol. 40 (St. Louis: Concordia Publishing House; Philadelphia: Fortress Press, 1955-1986), pp. 73-223 and his sermon for the Second Sunday after Epiphany, Vol. 51, pp. 369-380.

forced to fit into one of Aristotle's categories. The result was that church teaching often appealed to fallen reason but contradicted the apostles and prophets. As brilliant as Aristotle was—and arguably no one outside of the household of faith ever used reason more brilliantly than he—his philosophy has no place as queen in the temple of God. While Aristotle's use of reason in the formation of logical categories can be helpful in organizing the truths of the Scriptures, his philosophy is no substitute for the light of the gospel. Reason is not light but darkness when it rules as queen over the revealed Word of God.

Much of Luther's work was devoted to attacking the rule of reason both in the papacy and in the work of other reformers who wanted to get rid of the pope but not the rule of reason. Luther worked long and hard, for example, to purge the University of Wittenberg's curriculum for training pastors, to clean out Aristotle and replace his influence with the simple and clear Word of God. Luther recognized that as long as courses in logic and philosophy took precedence over the study of God's Word, pastors and their people would continue to fall into the ditches of faith-killing error. He made the study of logic and the rules of reason always subject to the authority of the Word. When God speaks in his Word, reason must say *Amen,* whether she wants to or not. If she objects, we must take the whip to her and drive the maid back behind the mop where she belongs! Again, many are the ditches that make up the broad roads leading to destruction; they are found on both sides of the narrow road that leads to life. Few there are who find and remain on that narrow middle road.

In the chapters to come we will consider a number of truths that turn into errors when reason takes hold of them and sits as judge over the Word of God. Most of the ditches we will be examining are subtle; Satan has hidden some of the ditches so cleverly that it is easy for us to miss them. Other ditches are not hidden at all; Satan has made these so attractive and appealing that the uncautious are tricked by their apparent attractiveness and run into them, totally unaware of the danger. Satan has made still other ditches so crude and obvious that it is difficult to understand why so many fail to recognize them and plunge headlong into them to their own destruction.

Since in the following chapters we will not be dealing with the most obvious and blatant attacks of the devil on the Word of God, we will spend a few moments now briefly noting some of them. These ditches Satan digs right out in the open, after people have already enthroned Dame Reason and consigned the Word to the broom closet; once that happens, there is no end to the follies contrary to the Word of God that people will embrace. These errors have no grain of truth in them at all; they are not on either side of a truth but are error and delusion from beginning to end.

Think of some of the more obvious and blatant examples of the perverse use of reason that people use who live in the ditch far from any narrow middle road. The thief reasons that he needs what he steals more than the one from whom he steals it. The murderer reasons that his own life and well-being are somehow threatened by the continued life of his enemy; therefore, it makes perfect sense to him that his enemy should die. The two people "living in sin" and the adulterer each in turn use reason as a see-through cloak to cover shame; with that cloak, each declares without shame, "But we love each other; how can that be wrong?"

In matters of doctrine as well, some errors are just ditches, without any element of truth at all. In these the devil dresses up Dame Reason so that her attempts to overthrow the Word of God will not seem as ugly as they are. He has Dame Reason pretend to be the helper of the queen, even though the queen is nowhere to be found. Reason subtly suggests that she only wants to make some doctrine more clear than it already is in the plain words of the Bible. For example, Jesus said in his institution of the Sacrament of the Altar, "This is my body, this is my blood given and shed for you, for the forgiveness of sins." Dame Reason confronts the host of problems presented by those simple and clear words of Jesus and objects that he could not have meant what he said so plainly. He must have meant that the bread and wine in the Sacrament are symbols that represent his body and blood. And he could not really have intended, she declares, that the Sacrament would actually convey forgiveness of sins and the life and salvation that come with forgiveness.

The simple truth that Jesus meant exactly what he said Dame Reason dismisses as beyond belief. And so she pushes the truth of God's Word aside, flatly contradicts it, and assumes for herself the role of queen in the church. In addition to shoving the Word off of its throne, she robs Christ of his glory as the giver of himself and of his grace and mercy in the Sacrament. And of course, whenever the Word is pushed aside and Christ is robbed of his proper glory, the sinner always ends up deprived of the comfort of the gospel that Jesus intends to give in his Word and sacraments.

At other times Dame Reason just ignores the Bible altogether and presents notions that seem to make sense but have no foundation at all in the Word of God. She says, for example, that it makes sense that there must be a place between heaven and hell. To such a place we (or at least some people we could mention!) should go after death to be purged of sins and made pure enough to enter heaven (the Roman Catholic doctrine of purgatory). Bold reason declares as well that it makes perfect sense that the mother of the Savior should be without sin. Why would the holy Son of God want to be enclosed in the womb of a sinner? Why not, the devil's reasoning continues, appeal to this supposedly sinless mother of God for help both now and even hereafter for rescue from the pain of the imagined purgatory? Would not her Son listen to the interceding prayers of his mother and be pleased as well when we seek his mother's help? And if he is pleased with our devotion to her, would he not also be pleased if we were likewise devoted to his friends in heaven: the saints and angels? Would he not listen to his friends in heaven if they interceded for us together with his mother? It all makes sense; it makes sense, that is, if the Word of God has been pushed aside.

But the Bible teaches us to rely on Christ alone for our salvation. It teaches us that all, even the greatest of saints, are in need of his saving work. The Bible has not one word about a purgatory; and in fact, the whole notion of purgatory flatly contradicts the gospel of salvation full and free. Additionally, the Bible contains neither a command nor a promise nor an example regarding prayers addressed to the saints. It tells us to address our prayers to God alone and reminds us as well that only God is present everywhere with power sufficient to hear and answer our prayers.

But none of that deters Dame Reason. All of these errors and all the others that spring from reason separated from the Word of God share in these attributes: They are all contrary to the clear Word of God in the Bible; they all rob Christ of his glory as our perfect and only Savior; they all deprive the Christian of certain comfort precisely because they are without foundation in the Word and push Christ and his work to the sidelines. Nevertheless, into the ditch of these superstitions plunge all of those who place faith in reason instead of in the clear Word of God. For superstition is best described as a faith based on lies and errors.

Sometimes Dame Reason is just a bit more subtle. She pretends to defend one truth of God's Word in order to dismiss another truth. She pretends that she wants to save us from one ditch by leading us into the ditch on the other side, with little or no regard at all for any truth in the middle. Thus, for example, she convinced Calvin and his successors (old-style Presbyterians and the Dutch Reformed) that they should defend the truth that God is almighty, just, and sovereign. In the interest of that truth, she convinced Calvin that the sovereign and almighty God has chosen some to be saved and that the rest he has chosen for damnation; that is the false doctrine called double or absolute predestination.

The Bible does indeed teach that those who are saved have only God to thank for it. It assures that God has chosen them from eternity and has so ruled over time and tide that they hear his Word, believe it, and die trusting in Jesus alone for their salvation. But the Bible likewise teaches that those who reject his Word and perish eternally have only themselves to blame for it. God neither asks nor expects us to blend those two truths; rather, through the power of his Word, he brings us to trust them both. Reason doesn't like that. And Calvin didn't like it either. Instead of simply bending his mind to receive what God had said and letting it go at that, he chose reason over the Word of God and came up with his false doctrine of double predestination.

Arminius, who came after Calvin, thought it was a terrible thing to say, as Calvin did, that God had chosen some to go to hell. But Arminius was just as infatuated with Dame Reason as Calvin was. So, he followed reason out of Calvin's ditch into the ditch on the opposite side of the road and thus perverted the truth just as much as Calvin had. Arminius and his followers (e.g., Methodists, Baptists, and most other non-Lutheran Protestants) believe that it's up to us to decide whether we go to heaven or to hell, up to us to decide whether we should believe or not. They deny what the Bible says about the results of original sin. They deny that by nature we are fallen, blind, dead, enemies of God and that as such we are incapable of any good in the eyes of God. Arminius and his followers teach instead that we are born either neutral or perhaps basically good, with the ability to contribute to our salvation by our own will and choice. They turn faith, at least in part, into man's work instead of God's gift through the gospel's power in Word and sacrament.

Dame Reason pretends in these examples to help our faith; but in fact she takes us on a road that, if followed to its reasonable end, leads to destruction. The follower of Calvin may cast about looking for some assurance that God has picked him for heaven and not for hell. Ultimately, he may trust that his good works prove that he is fit for heaven, even though that was the opposite of Calvin's intent. Or his temptations and his guilt may convince him that he must be one who has been predestined to hell. Thus, convicted by God's law and his own conscience, he may fall into despair. Both pride in one's own works as a cause of salvation and despair that salvation can never be mine are the opposites of saving faith.

The followers of Arminius, on the other hand, may become either proud that at least they made the right decision or else may doubt whether they really believe or believe enough to get into heaven. In either case, the Word is pushed aside, the glory of Christ the Savior is obscured, and faith is damaged or destroyed either by self-righteousness or by despair.

In contrast to Calvin and Arminius, Luther granted that many of the teachings of the Bible present fallen reason with problems. But Luther "reasoned": "When something in the Bible conflicts with my reason, I simply doff my doctor's cap and assume that the Holy Spirit (the ultimate author of the Scriptures) is a little smarter than Dr. Luther!" And so he took the narrow middle road laid out in the Bible. Only the narrow middle road of the truth so clearly taught in John 3:16; Romans 1–8; 2 Corinthians 5; Ephesians 2; and so many other places in the Bible will dispel both the self-righteousness and the despair that are the logical results of Calvinist and Arminian attempts to be reasonable.[3] Only the truth that Jesus alone is Savior and his Word alone creates the faith which trusts in him as Savior, only that will put us on and keep us on the narrow middle road that gives life and brings us at last to heaven. Only that teaching finds its source in the Word of God; only that teaching gives all glory to Christ; only that teaching gives all consolation to the penitent sinner.

Perhaps the previous but by-no-means-complete listing of examples of Dame Reason's more blatant and crude attempts at pushing us into ditches will suffice to encourage our further examination of the devil's more subtle attacks on the narrow middle road. In the chapters that follow, we will strive to find and stay on the narrow middle road while taking careful note of the ditches on either side of the road. We will do that by riveting our attention on the Word of God while we at the same time take note of the attempts of Dame Reason to lure us into one ditch or the other. If we do not watch out for those ditches, it will be all the easier for us to fall into them. Yes, it is the ditches and their dangers that should make us all the more attentive and devoted to the Word. That's Jesus' own methodology in teaching us. He warns against the ditches and then encourages and urges us on with his words: "I am the light of the world. Whoever follows me will never walk in darkness, but will have the light of life. . . . If you hold to my teaching, you are really my disciples. Then you will know the truth, and the truth will set you free" (John 8:12,31,32).

---

[3] We cannot help but note that all attempts to help God out by submitting his Word to the rule of reason end up in folly, in total "unreason": The false doctrines designed to be reasonable at the expense of God's Word are always themselves unreasonable in the end. And why is that? It is because the devil is incapable of sound reason; he lost the sound use of reason when he fell. Thus, all that he produces and suggests is ultimately irrational and leads to ruin. Consider, for example, the total irrationality of all that the devil says and inspires others to say in Mark 5:1-17.

2

The Narrow Lutheran Middle Between Doubt and Presumption

We begin our journey along the narrow middle road with a stretch of the road that is one of the most important. On either side of this stretch of road we will find ditches that have to be wide enough to accommodate the many perishing in them. Therefore, let us give careful attention to the narrow middle road that is paved with the promises of God. But on each side of that middle is an enormous and perilous ditch. The ditch on one side is *doubt. Presumption* is the ditch on the other side.

Consider the broad sweep and scope of God's promises

Of the many truths in God's Word that make Christianity unique among all the religions of the world, surely this is one of the most beautiful and delightful for the soul to ponder: Our God is a God of promises! Search and see if you can find a man-made religion where the promises are as sweeping and comforting as the promises made by the one true God in his Word. Just a sampler of his promises will leave us with eyes popping out and mouths hanging open.

He promises, for example, "Though the mountains be shaken and the hills be removed, yet my unfailing love for you will not be shaken nor my covenant of peace be removed" (Isaiah 54:10).

That's a promise from the God who made the mountains and fashioned the hills. He shakes them in earthquakes and sweeps them away as with a whisk broom when it pleases him. One day, at the sound of the last trumpet, when the Savior returns, all the mountains and hills will fall down in a heap and perish. But let them quake as they may. Let them fall into the midst of the sea. Let them be weak as water and unstable as melting wax. This truth will remain: God's love for his children will not change or depart. He who is truth itself, he who is Maker and Redeemer, he who is not a mere mortal that he should lie—he has promised it. Nothing in heaven or on earth is more reliable than his promise!

Or consider this promise: "Can a mother forget the baby at her breast and have no compassion on the child she has borne? Though she may forget, I will not forget you! See, I have engraved you on the palms of my hands" (Isaiah 49:15,16).

Love greater and more tender than a mother's love? Love that neither age nor the behavior of the child can dim or destroy? Age may dim the mother's love, and the behavior of the child could conceivably diminish it. But the love of God is greater, yes, incomparably greater. It is a love so fixed and firm that it is as though God carved our names, one by one, on his hand and keeps them there ever before his eyes. To carve a name on one's hand is painful; it is surely a mark of supreme, dare we say it, passionate love. But that's how God describes his love for us. And that carving was indeed painful and expensive. After all, it cost him the blood of his only begotten Son. Whenever he moves or lifts a finger to act, he first sees the name of each one of us in love; then he moves his hand in both grace and power to protect and help those whose names are ever before his eyes, yes, inscribed deep within his heart.

These promises are not empty words. They are not mere sentimental babblings. God proves his steadfast love with mighty acts in history. In both the Old Testament and in the New, we find countless demonstrations of his changeless love and of his faithfulness to his promises. He promised to rescue Adam and Eve from eternal death while they were still mired in rebellion. He rescued Abraham, Isaac, and Jacob from all their enemies, often before they ever even asked for his help. He took their descendants from the house of bondage in Egypt and carried them as on an eagle's wings in the wilderness for 40 years. And he did that in spite of their repeated failures to listen to him and to take his Word seriously. He brought their descendants into the land of promise by his own mighty arm. He purged them in the Babylonian Captivity and then kept his promise to bring them back home again. He saved them over and over again from their enemies. In the New Testament, he rescued the apostles from prison. He delivered them from the hands of those who wanted to kill them, until it pleased him to take them into glory by their deaths. Throughout the history of the church, for over two thousand years, God has frustrated and brought to nothing the attempts of men in alliance with the hosts of hell to destroy his church.

All of these acts that demonstrate his faithfulness to his promises are rooted and grounded in his grace in Christ. Christ is the center of all of his promises, the ultimate proof of his love. In Christ, in the manger, on the cross, at the empty tomb, we see the lengths to which God is willing to go to carry out his promises to us. That grace in Christ is the essence of the promise made in the Garden of Eden (Genesis 3:15). Immediately, without even waiting for Adam's and Eve's repentance, God promised a rescue that would come at a cost to him and at no cost to them. The cost would be the wounding of the Seed of the woman, a wounding that cut deep and pierced to the bottom of that Seed's body and soul. Read Psalm 22, and hear his cry. Read Isaiah 53, and see his agony. And then be forever astonished. Read again the Passion History in the gospels, and see these Old Testament writings fulfilled in all their horror: that Seed is none other than God himself, the Son of God in the flesh! All that he did for us and for our salvation he did without asking for the help of any of us. All alone he trod, as he tells us through the prophet Isaiah, the winepress of God's wrath against our sin (Isaiah 63:1-6). Is it not classic biblical understatement for God to tell us that he has our names "engraved . . . on the palms of [his] hands"?

17

St. Paul never stops being amazed at this ultimate evidence of God's love and of his faithfulness to his promise to redeem totally sinful, undeserving, doomed mankind. He marvels at it as he tells us: "Very rarely will anyone die for a righteous man, though for a good man someone might possibly dare to die. But God demonstrates his own love for us in this: While we were still sinners, Christ died for us" (Romans 5:7,8). Then he gives us his exultant conclusion on the basis of that perfect demonstration of God's perfect love and complete faithfulness to his promises: "What, then, shall we say in response to this? If God is for us, who can be against us? He who did not spare his own Son, but gave him up for us all—how will he not also, along with him, graciously give us all things?" (Romans 8:31,32).

But it doesn't stop there. God knows how weak and frail we are, how prone to listening to Dame Reason's voice in our conscience when it condemns us. Conscience attacks and suggests this horrible thought: What if those promises don't apply to me? What if they are only meant for the good and the noble, for the saints among men? No, no, a thousand times no! declares the Word of God. For Jesus himself declares that "God so loved *the world*" (John 3:16). He promises, "Whoever comes to me I will never drive away" (John 6:37). And Paul exults in the fruit of that love for the whole world when he tells us that "God was reconciling *the world* to himself in Christ, not counting men's sins against them" (2 Corinthians 5:19). St. John says so too: "[Christ] is the atoning sacrifice for our sins, and not only for ours but also for the sins of the *whole world*" (1 John 2:2).

There go all grounds for doubt and despair! If God loves the whole world, then he loves me too. If Jesus counts those who come to him as those given to him by his Father, then he will look at me that way too; me too he will never drive away. If God's only begotten Son willingly suffered the torments of hell in order to reconcile the whole world to God, then he has reconciled me too. If his sacrifice pays for the sins of the world, then it pays for my sins too. What could be more sure, more certain, more comforting and consoling to the sinner's guilty soul than that? (Notice that we are using reason here; but it is reason used in obedience to the Word of God, as a maid servant, not as queen over the Word of God.)

To put an exclamation point behind the promise that each individual is the object of God's grace and that the benefit of Christ's sacrifice is intended for each of us, God has given us the sacraments. They are seals and assurances meant for the individual, as distinguished from promises addressed to the whole world. In Baptism, God promises grace, pardon, and life eternal to one person at a time. Baptism unites the individual to Christ and all that he has done for our salvation (Romans 6; 1 Peter 3:21). While the individual may decide to turn his back on the promise in Baptism and reject its saving benefit, the promise stands. Should the fallen later hear the promise of the gospel and by its power return, the promise made by God in Baptism will remain firm and sure.

Just as firm and sure is the promise affixed to the Sacrament of the Altar. There we eat and drink the price of our salvation, Christ's true body and true blood. There one repentant sinner after another, one at a time, comes to receive under the forms of bread and wine the Savior himself. In receiving the Savior, one at a time, each receives the promise Jesus made: "This is my body; this is my blood; it is given, it is shed *for you* for the forgiveness of sins." When God sees us, he sees his Son. When God sees us, he sees the sacrifice that his Son made to win and redeem us. What could be more certain or more sure than the grace and love of God for those Jesus has washed in Baptism and fed with himself at the altar?

And still it doesn't stop. The promises of God's abiding love are not limited to his sacrifice for our sins. They are not meant only for our spiritual life or intended to come into effect only in the hour of death when we depart this world for life eternal in heaven. Those promises of God's love in Christ cover every moment of our lives. They cover, not least, those times in our lives when the consequences of our own sins have brought us to pain and misery. To a rebellious people who thought that their sacrifices to God were what delighted him most and who otherwise did whatever they wanted, God called out: "Call upon me in the day of trouble; I will deliver you, and you will honor me" (Psalm 50:15).

Often the trouble is of our own making. At other times it is the result of the sins of others. And at still other times we cannot trace a direct cause of our suffering to ourselves or others. How come the storm blew down my house and not his? How come I got sick, even after I did everything right to take care of myself? Whatever the cause of our pain or suffering, God promises to use the pain or suffering for our good. By it he wants to pull us closer to himself! He calls us to the worship of trusting him to help and deliver us even from the sorrows that our sins bring down on our heads. That's how God wants to be worshiped: he wants us to listen to his promises and trust him and live in that trust—not least in the days of sorrow and in the times of sadness.

Yes, especially in *the day of trouble,* we find our peace, even our joy, in Christ's presence with us through his promises in the Word and the sacraments. The suffering can, as already noted, be the result of our own sins. It can come from the sins of others. It can be the result of Satan's attacks, as it was in the life of Job. Luther rightly said that Satan is the source of much of our suffering in this life, that he is not happy when we have so much as a crust of bread to enjoy.[1] Whether we know or do not know of a precise reason for *the day of trouble,* the promises of God in Christ are sure and certain. St. Paul registers his apostolic coda to the Savior's promise to be always and in every circumstance with us and for us. He sings of it through all of Romans 5 and 8 and then concludes with this exultant chorus:

> I am convinced that neither death nor life, neither angels nor demons, neither the present nor the future, nor any powers, neither height nor depth, nor anything else in all creation, will be able to separate us from the love of God that is in Christ Jesus our Lord. (Romans 8:38,39)

Paul's confidence is rooted and grounded in the Savior's own words. At his ascension into heaven, Jesus promised his disciples of every age that his visible departure did not mean that he was abandoning them. Quite the contrary! Since he possesses all power in heaven and in earth, he can be present with each one of us—fully and completely present. Jesus does not divide himself into fractions when he promises, "Surely I am with you always, to

---

[1] Cf. Luther's Large Catechism, Fourth Petition, par. 81.

the very end of the age" (Matthew 28:20). Dame Reason may bring in the laws of physics, or new math or old math. Aristotle and his camp of followers may protest with the rules of logic; they may loudly object and insist that a person cannot be present in more than one place at a time, much less *fully* present in more than one place at a time. They will accomplish nothing with their objections. There is the beautiful promise of Christ, the risen Lord, who has all power in heaven and in earth. He will not lie to us or deceive us. He is where he has promised to be. He is there, the entire Christ, the God-man, with both his divine and human nature. He is with us just because he said so!

With such sweeping, such all-encompassing promises of God's love and care for us, for each of us, for us in Christ, for us in life and in death, for us in time and in eternity, what could be the ditches into which we might fall on the right and the left of those promises?

The ditch of doubt

The ditch of doubt lies on one side of the road. Doubt does not necessarily reject the promises of God in bold unbelief. It does not call God a liar outright. The ditch of doubt is dug for those whose eyes turn to the left to glance for a moment at the evidence that can be seen, evidence that seems to contradict the beautiful promises of God. Dame Reason rushes to take advantage of that sideways glance to make the feet run off the narrow middle road into the ditch. There the sight of Jesus gets blurred because he and his Word are no longer the sole focus of attention. Where the light of the Word and the accompanying vision of Jesus grow dark, there faith fades, fear enters, disaster threatens.

Think for a moment of the passages with which this chapter began. God promises through Isaiah (54:10) that even if the mountains shake and the hills tremble, God's love and his promises remain the same. Or think of the second passage referred to; God promises that our very names are engraved on his hand so that even if a mother can forget her child, he can never forget us or fail to act in love for us. Fallen reason quickly forgets God's powerful promises when it sees the mountains shake. Reason grabs hold of what it sees at the moment and leaves behind God's Word and all the proofs of God's faithfulness that we have experienced in the past. It focuses on the trouble of the moment, not on the face of Jesus in his faithful Word and sacraments.

Consider a few examples in the Bible of those who fell into the ditch of doubt. In Numbers 13 Moses, at God's command, sent men from the 12 tribes of Israel to search out the land of Canaan that God was about to give his people. They were to bring back firsthand reports of how rich the land was and how abundant its fruits. Such firsthand reports would encourage the people to enter the Promised Land and receive it as a generous gift from their most gracious God and Savior who had promised it to them.

But when the spies returned, what did most of them report? They reported that, to be sure, the land was just as God had said, beautiful and rich, a land that flowed with milk and honey. Nevertheless, they were not content with God's promise to give them the land. They took their eyes off the promise and looked at the strength of the inhabitants of Canaan. Their conclusion: "*We* are too weak and too small to face the giants of the land, to whom we will appear as grasshoppers by comparison." They forgot that God was the one who would give the land to them; forgetting the promise, they imagined that they would have to take it by their own strength, a strength that was weakness in comparison with that of the giants they saw.

Once the eyes stray to the side, once they begin to focus on what appears as distinguished from what God has promised, doubt easily turns into blatant unbelief. Doubt questions the promise of God: Could it really mean exactly what it says? Does it really apply in this situation? Doubt starts out as the first cousin of unbelief but quickly becomes its father if the soul does not fly back to the middle road of the Word of God. Doubt asks Dame Reason for answers instead of relying on the promises of God. That's what happened in Numbers 13 and with disastrous results. Reason insisted: it can't be done; we're ruined; we should have stayed in Egypt! The reports of most of the spies moved the people to rebel against God and to despise his promises. As a result, the people wandered in the wilderness for 40 years and all died there, except for the two spies who had trusted the promise of God.

Or consider the example of the disciples in Mark 4:35-41. The disciples had seen the evidence in Jesus' miracles that he was the almighty Son of God. His mighty and gracious Word had moved them to abandon their own interests and to follow him. And Jesus had made very great and very specific promises to them: they would become fishers of men (1:17) and would even follow him in preaching and have authority to cast out demons (3:15). But in chapter 4 a storm came up on the Sea of Galilee and threatened to sink their boat. Jesus himself was in that boat. But the eyes of the disciples shifted from Jesus to the evidence of the moment. With all their might and strength they tried to keep the boat afloat. All their own efforts, however, seemed to be in vain. They cried out in a prayer that was a mix and a muddle of both faith and doubt: "Teacher, don't you care if we drown?" On the one hand, there still was a confidence that Jesus could do something about the storm. On the other hand, the prayer expressed a fear that he might not want to help them. The eyes were divided. One eye was on Jesus and what they knew of him; the other was on the wind and the waves. Dame Reason had pushed the disciples into the ditch of doubt; and with that doubt, all peace is gone. Fear and confusion take control.

We can easily sympathize with the disciples' fear. Under similar circumstances it is unlikely that we would be calm and unshaken. But we cannot excuse the doubt that produced that fear. For, as already noted, Jesus had made very specific promises to them. He had promised that they would preach and be fishers of men. He had promised that they would cast out demons in his name. None of those things had happened yet, nor could they happen if the disciples would drown in this storm. If Dame Reason had behaved herself and stayed in her role as Maid Reason, she would have reminded the disciples of the promises and then drawn the appropriate, divinely inspired, and rational conclusion: "Since these promises of the almighty Son of God have not yet been kept, clearly we are not going to perish. For if we drown now, the promises will never be kept and Jesus will have lied to us—and that's impossible." Then their prayer would have been the simple cry, "Lord, save us!" But instead the disciples listened to the voice of reason based not on Jesus' promises but on what they could see from the ditch of doubt.

We see a similar dilemma in Matthew 14:22-32. In the middle of another storm, Jesus came to the disciples, walking on the water. The ever impetuous Peter called out to Jesus, "Lord, if it's you, tell me to come to you on the water." When Jesus bid him come, Peter, trusting in the Word of Jesus and his implied promise, jumped from the boat into the surging waves and began to walk towards Jesus. But then what happened? Initially Peter's eyes were focused on Jesus and his heart was fixed on the promise implicit in Jesus' call to Peter, "Come." But Peter took his eyes off of Jesus and his mind off of the promise. And what happened? Into the waves he fell! He began to flounder and flail in the water and was at the point of drowning. Only at the point of total disaster, when all seemed lost, did he look again to Jesus and cry out, "Lord, save me!" Jesus heard his prayer and rescued him from the surging sea. Then Jesus asked him, "Why did you doubt?" We hear no answer from Peter. But the answer was the same as it always is from that ditch of doubt: the mind was moved from the Word and the eyes of the soul were moved from the image of Jesus to what appeared on the surface. In the crisis of the moment, it was easier to trust the merely apparent and to listen to Dame Reason's conclusions about the merely apparent than to keep the eyes on Jesus and the mind fixed on his promises.

The most dramatic and most painful of all falls into the ditch of doubt for the disciples was the fall that occurred between Good Friday and Easter Sunday. How terrible for the disciples! In spite of all that they had heard and seen from Jesus, they were all in confusion. Already on Thursday they fled from him in the Garden of Gethsemane. On Friday we hear only of John's presence at the foot of the cross. Peter was in anguish of soul because of his denial of Jesus the night before in the courtyard of the high priest's palace. The other disciples were invisible. Jesus died. Jesus was buried. Jesus had told them repeatedly and in detail that he would suffer thus and die. Yes, and he had told them as well that he would rise again. Nevertheless, the sight of his suffering and death removed all recollection from their minds of what he had said about the saving purpose of his death. Gone as well from their memory was the assurance of his resurrection. Thus they were all surprised to hear of his resurrection when the women brought them news of it from the tomb.

Easter Sunday night they were still behind locked doors, in fear that they too might soon be arrested, tried, and executed as

Jesus had been. Jesus was still out of sight, and his Word was a fog of confusion in their minds. What else then could they have but fear and doubt to the point of unbelief? Only the faintest glimmer of faith could still be theirs. Indeed, the best we can say of their faith at that point was that it was confusion. The ditch is deep, its slopes steep; and the pain of the fall into it is great indeed. It was Jesus' Word that rescued them and refocused their minds' eye on him and his faithful promises. He greeted them in the depths of the ditch when he showed himself to them that first Easter night. He brought them to life again with his powerful "'Peace be with you!' . . . The disciples were overjoyed when they saw the Lord" (John 20:19,20).

We should not fail to note that not every instance of doubt in some specific promise of God is the same as the damning unbelief that rejects Jesus as Savior. The examples of the disciples in Mark 4 and of Peter in Matthew 14 are cases in point. The disciples and Peter in these instances still knew that Jesus was their God and the Savior promised throughout the Old Testament. The doubt that Jesus variously rebukes as "little faith" and "no faith" was not with reference to the promise of salvation but to other specific promises that Jesus made to the disciples: the promise, as already noted, that they would be fishers of men, and the promise implied when Jesus told Peter to come to him on the waves.

It is certainly likely that we too at times fall into the ditch of doubt without in every instance rejecting Jesus as our God and only Savior. When we, like the disciples, are overwhelmed by the sorrows and troubles of the moment, we may take our eyes off of his promises to us, just as they did. We may not see how his promise to be with us always in grace and love applies to the pain of the moment. We may cry out in the dark night of the soul: "Oh my God and Savior, where are you? Why do you not hear my cries and rescue me?"

Such anguish, yes, such doubt may not yet be gross unbelief. But if it is not cured and corrected by Jesus' call to us in his Word, it may ultimately lead to that unbelief which rejects the Savior and his work for our salvation. The slope of the ditch of doubt is steep and perilous indeed. If we continue the slide down that slope, we may finally lose sight of Jesus altogether.

That's what happened to Thomas, who rejected both the promise of Jesus to rise again and the words and eyewitness accounts of the disciples and the women on Easter Sunday. So deeply did Thomas fall that he even arrogantly set the conditions that Jesus would have to fulfill before he would believe. How dreadful! How shameful! The wonder is that Jesus still loved the apostle who had fallen from doubt into wicked unbelief. Jesus loved him so much that he came to Thomas and reclaimed him, even fulfilling the terrible conditions that Thomas had set. In the process Jesus pointed the rest of us to the only cure for doubt: "'Blessed are those who have not seen and yet have believed.' . . . These are written that you may believe that Jesus is the Christ, the Son of God, and that by believing you may have life in his name" (John 20:29,31). In these things written, Jesus seeks and finds us just as surely as he sought and found fallen Thomas. By these things written, he makes us blessed as he conquers unbelief and sweeps away doubt. He then is once more what he should always be—the light on the narrow middle road with his Word as the lamp for our feet.

Jesus comes to us still in his quiet Word, in his lowly sacraments. He calls us out of the ditch and rescues us from doubt and from gross unbelief as we hear his Word and ponder his promises. By that Word he brings us again to abandon ourselves to him and what he has said and to leave behind the doubt and the fear that focuses only on what is seen at the moment.[2]

Thus the stumbling into the ditch of doubt with respect to the specific promises of God to be our God of grace and help in every time of need is not necessarily or immediately the same thing as damning unbelief; it is nevertheless dangerous. Jesus points out the danger in his great parable of the sower in Mark 4:16-19. There he speaks of those who hear his Word and receive it with joy. But then when trouble comes, they take their eyes off of Jesus and his Word. They focus only on the trouble, not on its

---

[2] German students will remember that beautiful construction used so often by our forefathers: *sich verlassen auf.* The simple dictionary translation is "to rely on," but the more literal translation is much more expressive: "to abandon oneself on." Thus: *Ich verlasse mich auf Gottes Gnade, auf Christi Blut und Gerechtigkeit* ("I abandon myself on/to God's grace, on Christ's blood and righteousness").

solution in Christ and his promise to never leave or forsake them; and so, they fall into the ditch to their ruin. Doubt left to itself ends up as choking weeds that can kill faith altogether.

The only cure, the only poison for those weeds of doubt, is swift recourse again to the promises of God in Word and sacraments. It is the very essence of faith, whether the saving faith that embraces Christ alone as Savior or the faith that trusts him in every time of trial: Faith focuses on Christ and his promises. Faith in Christ as Savior casts aside the doubt and despair created when I look at my sins and hear the damning voice of both the law and conscience; it focuses on Christ's cross and his promise of forgiveness. Faith in days of trouble casts aside what is seen and fixes its attention on the promises of Christ to be with us in every trouble and to rule all things ultimately for our good here and hereafter. Do we see that always or at once? No; but so great is the power of Christ in his promises that he overcomes what is seen with what is unseen—the trouble of the moment with his sure and certain promise for the present and the future. The narrow middle road remains a focus on Jesus and a focus on his promises that refuses what seems to be true at the moment in favor of what always is true in Christ and in his Word.

The ditch of presumption

At least as common and equally disastrous is the ditch on the other side of the narrow middle road of simple trust in the Word of God. It is the ditch into which Satan tried to lure Jesus when he tempted Jesus to jump down from the temple peak (Matthew 4:5-7). It is a trust that takes God's promises of help and rescue, his promises of grace and love and mercy, as a license to sin.

The one who has fallen into that ditch listens to the luring voice of Dame Reason and concludes: "Since God loves me, since Jesus died to pay for all my sins, since God promises never to cast me out, I can do exactly as I please; I can sin boldly and to my sinful heart's content; I have been saved so that I can sin without fear or guilt!"

David fell into that ditch when he cast God's Word aside, when he took all of God's love and grace for granted (2 Samuel 11). He apparently was seduced into thinking that with all the evidences of God's goodness he could do as he pleased. And so, with reckless abandon, he committed adultery, then murder to cover up the adultery. For almost a year after that he hid from God. The results were disastrous not only for Uriah, whom David had murdered at the hand of others, but also for David—both in the short and in the long term (2 Samuel 12:9-14).

When the grace of God in the words of his pastor, Nathan, finally brought David to repentance and restored faith, the consequences of his sin nevertheless continued. David's family was tormented with grief at the death of the child conceived in adultery. Strife and bloodshed did not depart from David's house for the rest of his life. No one can cast aside God's Word and sin boldly without consequences. Not the least of those consequences for David was the abiding sense of guilt that he felt, a guilt whose torment David expressed so eloquently in the Psalms (for example, Psalms 6,51,130).

God uses the grief that follows a fall into the quicksand ditch of presumption to warn us not to take his Word lightly in the future. He uses the grief as well to remind us of the enormity of his grace when contrasted to the greatness of our guilt. Nevertheless, the pain of those consequences—whether outward pain and suffering or the gnawing of conscience that must battle against despair or both—can be severe indeed.

So earnestly does God warn us against the ditch of presumption that he gives us examples in his Word of those whom he destroyed for their presumptuous rebellion against his clear Word. Read about the rebellion of Korah, Dathan, and Abiram and their comrades in Numbers 16. They knew the truth that they were beloved children of God. But then they let Dame Reason convince them that since they were holy children of God, just as much as Moses was a holy child of God, they could set aside God's choice of Moses as his representative. They picked one aspect of God's Word, his choice of the people of Israel to be his own children, and then used that truth to reject another truth, the truth that God had expressly called Moses to be his spokesman and the leader of the people. For their presumption, the ditch into which they had fallen opened up wide and swallowed them: "They went down alive into the grave, with everything they owned; the earth closed over them, and they perished and were gone from the community" (16:33).

In the New Testament we have a similar example in Acts 5. Lest the newly converted imagine that all of God's grace and love meant that God did not take his will expressed in the law seriously, Ananias and Sapphira were struck down when they lied to the Lord in public. Perhaps their crime might not seem so serious to us. That would be a shame indeed! God takes all of his Word seriously, whether we do or not.

To be sure, the ditch that takes God's love and grace for granted can appear very appealing. The devil knows that. He is quick to urge Dame Reason to seduce us into presuming on God's grace. Powerful and sweet to our sinful flesh is the siren song that since we have been saved, we can sin all we want. For that very reason, the Bible is filled with warnings against the ditch of such godless presumption. St. Paul met the alluring temptation of Dame Reason head on. Even when he teaches most beautifully about the promises of God to save us by grace alone through faith, he attacks the temptation to presumption. He knew that Dame Reason would rush from behind the mop pail into the throne room and argue: "If our sins magnify God's grace, then why not sin all the more so that God's grace may be magnified all the more when he keeps on forgiving you?" St. Paul answered with just a few words, but words that say it all: "Their condemnation is deserved" (Romans 3:8).

If we want to employ reason properly, we could use an analogy that is apt. Let reason argue this way: What if a bride said to her husband, "Dear, I will always love you and would forgive anything!"? What if the husband on hearing those words then concluded, "Now I have a license to be unfaithful, to abuse my wife in every way, and when not abusing her, to ignore her"? What would even reason say of such a husband? Would not even reason declare, "He knows nothing of love; he has forfeited the love that his spouse pledged to him!"

That's the appropriate answer of reason the handmaid to the rebellious voice of Dame Reason who wants to lure us into the ditch and overthrow the Word of God. Those who despise the will of God revealed in his law do not love God. In fact, they throw away the love, grace, and, yes, the forgiveness of God's saving gospel when they are determined to live in their sins.

To be sure, our works and our obedience, no matter how good, cannot save us or contribute to our salvation in the least. And, certainly, we never get to the point in this life where we have reason to boast of perfection, as St. Paul also confesses (Romans 7:14-25). Always this side of the grave we will be in desperate need of grace and pardon. But to give up the struggle against sin and temptation and instead to embrace our sins and use God's love as an excuse to do so, that is perilous indeed. In point of fact, it is damning unbelief.

The Bible warns us against such presumption powerfully and often. St. Paul in Ephesians 5 exhorts us to be imitators of God as dear children; then he warns those who reject such imitation that the wrath of God will surely fall on them. In Galatians 5 he warns that those who practice disobedience will not inherit the kingdom of God (5:19-21). He follows that warning up with this simple summation: "Do not be deceived: God cannot be mocked. A man reaps what he sows. The one who sows to please his sinful nature, from that nature will reap destruction" (6:7,8).

As the Bible from beginning to end is beautiful and comforting in its promises, so too is it powerful in its pleadings that we avoid the ditch that presumes on that love and grace and uses them as an excuse for living in sins. Right up to and through the last book of the Bible, the narrow middle road is laid out for us with warnings against presumption. The risen and ascended Jesus portrays himself as walking in the midst of his people and holding their pastors close to his heart. But at the same time he warns that those who have started to grow cold and to embrace their weaknesses and temptations will soon perish if they do not repent (Revelation 1–3). In the very last chapter of the Bible, Jesus warns against tampering with his Word and threatens with destruction all who ignore his warning. He does this at the same time that he is promising to come and rescue his own and bring them to himself in heaven.

The narrow Lutheran middle

It should be clear and it should be obvious where the narrow middle road is between the ditch of doubt on the one hand and the ditch of presumption on the other. The narrow middle road is a steadfast clinging to *all* of God's Word.

Burdens may weigh us down. Uncertainty about health and wealth may press in on every side. Pain may torment us day and night. Just ask Job. Friends may betray. Just ask Jesus when Judas came to Gethsemane. Those we have served may spurn us. Just ask St. Paul. Ultimately, a little germ, a tiny virus, a little clog in an artery will bring most of us into the hands of the mortician. But God's promise stands firm! He has not forgotten us or forsaken us. In it all, in spite of it all, through it all, the cross of Christ and his resurrection guarantee his love and grace and mercy that cover us for time and eternity.

Will we always see and understand how that can be the case? No! But the promises of his Word and sacraments are so powerful that those promises can overcome all the outward evidence of the moment. So powerful is that Word that it can triumph over Dame Reason's pull into the ditch of doubt. So powerful is it that in spite of what we see, we can rejoice with St. Paul when he encourages us to rejoice with him even in suffering (Romans 5). Suffering is the devil's tool to drive us to doubt and then to despair. But it is God's tool for separating us from pride or from a love of the world that blinds us to his love in Christ. Indeed, suffering is one of God's ways of keeping us on the narrow middle road that leads to life eternal. However, only those who keep their eyes fixed on Jesus and his promises see and learn and appreciate that fact.

The Bible is not without wonderful examples of those who triumphed on the narrow middle road in the face of the most severe testing. Think of those long years of David's struggle and exile before he became king. God had promised that David would be king. But God appeared to be in no hurry to keep the promise. David fled from Saul and even lived in exile among the enemies of his people for a time. His friends urged him to look to the ditch of presumption on the side of the narrow middle road of trust in God's promises. They urged David to consider the apparent opportunities of the moment and to take matters into his own hands. "Kill Saul while you have the chance," they pleaded; that way God's promises would quickly come to pass (1 Samuel 24, 26). But David refused. He trusted that God himself would keep his promise when it pleased God to do so. God kept his promise, kept it in his own good time and, therefore, in the best possible way. In the New Testament, the writer of the epistle to the Hebrews piles example upon example when he lists the great heroes of faith (Hebrews 11,12). All of them kept their eyes fixed on the promise, no matter how hard the road or how long they had to travel it. The holy writer bids us to follow their blessed example and so share in their blessed outcome—the victory that is the gift of Christ the Savior.

As God takes all of his gospel promises seriously, so he takes all of his commands seriously. He declares that he loves the world enough to become man and die for it—to die, therefore, also for you. He declares with equal earnestness in the law, "Thou shalt . . . Thou shalt not!" These are not just pious preferences on God's part. He means them. Those who cast aside his commands from the ditch of presumption will ultimately cast aside his gospel promises as well and perish in their unbelief. For as noted previously, God will not be mocked.

Yes, the ditches are deep and perilous indeed. On the one side of the road, Dame Reason would like to grab hold of God's promises of grace and let go of God's commands. On the other side of the narrow middle, she would have us doubt that all of God's promises are true and that he remains forever faithful to them and to us in Christ. God does not ask or expect us to satisfy Dame Reason. He bids us hear his Word and keep it. In his Word he gives the faith that trusts the promises and the love that strives after obedience to his commands. He gives faith that despairs of earning salvation, and he inspires in us a love that longs to live up to the high calling of a child of God. He gives grace heaped upon grace so that even in disaster and in the hour of death itself, we desire to see Jesus only and thus give way to neither fear nor doubt. That's the narrow Lutheran middle between the ditches of doubt on the one hand and presumption on the other with respect to the promises of God.

3

The Narrow Lutheran Middle Between Carnal Security and Despair

If we walk a few steps further down the narrow middle road, we will notice again ditches on either side of the middle. These ditches are very closely connected to those discussed in the last chapter. They are perilous ditches indeed! The ditches are those of carnal security on the one side and despair on the other. And again, many fall into one or the other of these ditches. Still others spend their lives running from one ditch into the other, with only so much time on the middle road as it takes to get to the opposite ditch.

God's promise of forgiveness

The narrow middle road between despair and carnal security focuses on what God has to say in his Word about forgiveness and on what Christ has done to win forgiveness for us. The only change in the pavement on which we travel in this chapter is that the road is still more narrow than it was in the last chapter. There we were concerned with all the promises of God, promises that cover time and eternity, promises of grace and redemption for our souls as well as promises for help and rescue in every time of need. The pathway we travel in this chapter is concerned chiefly with just one promise, the promise of forgiveness.

Each day we show our trust in the promise of forgiveness when we pray the Lord's Prayer. It is Jesus himself who bids us pray, "Forgive us our trespasses." The simple fact that Jesus has taught us that petition carries with it an implied promise that God wants to forgive and will forgive. For why would Jesus invite us to ask for something that God did not want to give? Reason serves as a good handmaid when she grabs hold of the implied promise in Jesus' prayer and urges us to beg and then to ask again, to plead each day, "Forgive us our trespasses."

Reason rightly used may also infer that both the prayer for forgiveness and the trust that God really wants to and does forgive are not such easy matters. Jesus does not bid us to pray for easy or obvious things; he invites us to ask for those things which are beyond our power. That's true even when he tells us to pray for daily bread and all that belongs to daily bread.[1] Precisely because it is not such an easy matter, God in his Word repeats often both his urging that we cry out for forgiveness and the assurance that he wants to answer our repentant cries with pardon. His repeated calls to repentance and his many assurances of forgiveness are evidence that he knows how easily we find and fall into the ditches of despair and carnal security.

So let us consider some of his calls to repentance and some of the ways that he assures us of forgiveness. For a complete listing of passages, we can only urge the reading of the Bible each day. It is by the daily embrace of his Word that we come to grasp more fully the depth and the beauty and, yes, the earnestness and the passion with which God has paved this stretch of the narrow middle road. Consider the following passages as examples of the multitude of biblical references in which God urges us to heart-broken repentance and heart-bursting joy over his forgiveness.

---

[1] Cf. Luther's comments on the Fourth Petition in both the Small and the Large Catechisms.

In a lengthy discourse with the prophet Ezekiel (chapter 18), God calls on the ever stubborn and rebellious remnant of his people in exile in Babylon to repent. His people had tasted of God's goodness and mercy for generations in the land of Israel. But all of his goodness had only made them indifferent to his greatest gift, the gift of forgiveness. Instead, they were only greedy for more of this world's goods, heartless to the suffering of others, and ever ready to cheat one another and to take advantage of the poor. At the bottom of their sins against one another was their spiritual adultery, their chasing after other gods; they often reflected, as in a mirror, that spiritual adultery in their physical adultery with the neighbor's spouse.

As a consequence of their sin, God sent them individually and as a nation one humiliation after another, loss followed by loss, defeat heaped on defeat. The Northern Kingdom of Israel he destroyed altogether. He sent the Southern Kingdom of Judah into a dreary and disgraceful exile in Babylon. But even when God sent loss and frustration, exile and humiliation to the remnant of his rebellious people, he sent these things in order to call them back to himself. He sent them so they would see that their sins had consequences in this life which were but preludes to far worse consequences in eternity. Sadly, all of those afflictions that he had designed and sent in order to call them to repentance with the goal of forgiveness were met by most with a stubborn refusal to repent.

But how did God deal with their rebellion even in their exile? In Ezekiel 18 he shows his persistent and continuing ardor for his people and his earnest desire for their return to him. He lets himself be drawn into an argument with them. The case he makes in that argument demonstrates his own divine and perfect reasoning. Instead of casting them off altogether, as he had ample reason to do, he pleads with them to come back and be forgiven. While warning them again that those who cling to their sins and refuse to repent will surely die, he promises over and over again that those who repent will live. The evidence of their repentance—not the price they would pay for forgiveness—should be that they turn from their evil ways and live in the peace and joy of God's pardon. He concludes with the plaintive appeal of a heart that overflows with the desire to forgive: "'Why will you die, O house of Israel?

For I take no pleasure in the death of anyone,' declares the Sovereign LORD. 'Repent and live!'" (Ezekiel 18:31,32).

Jesus in the gospels so often and so enticingly repeats the theme of his longing for our redemption. "I am the good shepherd," he declares. "The good shepherd lays down his life for the sheep" (John 10:11). He gives new meaning to the word *good* and to the word *shepherd*! Sheep should exist for the shepherd, not the shepherd for the sheep. But divine reasoning goes in the opposite direction. In the sacred and gracious and loving heart of Jesus, no price is too high to pay for the sinner who has lost all worth because of his sin. And so he dies, the One worth more than all of them, more than all of us put together. He dies for those who have made themselves worthy of death by their sins. He dies, the innocent for the guilty. He dies, the ransom for the whole of fallen mankind that sold and continues to sell itself willingly into a slavery to sin, death, and hell. He dies, the payment for every sin that ever was committed or ever will be committed.

Note the stunning contrast throughout in the way that God deals with us: the omnipotent God pleads with the impotent sinner. The Holy One of Israel pursues as a lover the ever sinful and adulterous generation. The Ruler of the universe, who has no beginning and no end, lowers himself into the womb of the virgin and makes his bed in the feed trough of sheep and goats. Yes, he who knew no sin becomes sin for us so that we should be clothed with his own righteousness (2 Corinthians 5:21). These are but a handful of the many powerful pictures that God uses to illustrate his zeal and his ardor for our salvation.

So great and beautiful is the theme that it is difficult to keep from dwelling on it with the hundreds of passages and pictures which repeat it and give ever new sweetness and delight to the guilty, sad, and despairing soul.

Our Sunday morning liturgy reflects the longing in the heart of God for us. The call to repentance at the beginning of the liturgy invites us so warmly to do what our sinful nature does not want to do, either because it is proud and self-satisfied or because it is terrified and in despair. The first words of the call to repentance are "Beloved in the Lord!" Those already entice us and lure us to the overflowing heart of God. They invite us to ask that he pour out from his heart the forgiveness that fills it. The simple fact that this invitation comes to us week in and week out should thrill us. That's how God's heart always is toward us. It is the heart of God that cries out: "'Come now, let us reason together,' says the LORD. 'Though your sins are like scarlet, they shall be as white as snow; though they are red as crimson, they shall be like wool'" (Isaiah 1:18). It is the voice of Jesus in the last book of the Bible, with splendor laid by and glory hidden, that calls out: "Those whom I love I rebuke and discipline. So be earnest, and repent. Here I am! I stand at the door and knock. If anyone hears my voice and opens the door, I will come in and eat with him, and he with me" (Revelation 3:19,20).

Could there be a more compelling reason to repent and confess than that? So great is the banquet spread before us in his forgiveness that it is a meal which lasts forever with the Savior himself as our ever gracious host! Could there be a more delightful moment than that moment in his house when we plead for and anticipate forgiveness from the Almighty and All-Holy One? See and hear him in the liturgy! He can hardly wait to embrace you with the pardon and peace that he has won for us on the cross and that his servant announces and gives to you in the words of absolution. Look! There is the baptismal font where he adopted you and turned the promise made to the world into a promise just for you. Lift up your eyes! There is the altar with the holy meal spread out, the "medicine of immortality" as St. Ignatius of Antioch (A.D. 110) called it; it is the promise of his true body and blood, the very price he paid for your salvation. Could there be a richer sign of his love for you than the promise of his forgiving presence in your body and soul? We may well, and with good reason, be disgusted with ourselves because of our sin. But when God sees you, he sees his Son and the price he paid for your redemption; he sees you forgiven, a saint!

Yes, it is on the cross that we see most fully and most clearly the ardor of God for our repentance and our rescue. Even there, he who suffers the torments of the damned prays for the forgiveness of his tormenters. Less than a week earlier, he had seen in all its horror the kind of death that awaited him. Did he run away? Did he complain about it? Did he lash out at least with his tongue against mankind, the reason for his coming suffering? No! This is what he said: "Now my heart is troubled, and what shall I say? 'Father, save me from this hour'? No, it was for this very reason I came to this hour. Father, glorify your name!" (John 12:27,28). Exactly that was his desire and his Father's glory, that he should suffer and die to win our forgiveness. Earlier still he wept over Jerusalem because he knew that even such love and such a price would not move most in her to cry out for the forgiveness that he came to win at so high a price (Luke 19:41-44).

The ditch of carnal security

As ardent and earnest as God's promises and Jesus' yearning for our forgiveness, those over whom he wept in the last passage cited wanted none of it. They had fallen into the ditch of carnal security and refused the outstretched and blood-spattered arm that Jesus extended to lift them from it. Let us then consider this ditch of carnal security into which so many plunge headlong, in spite of Jesus' death for them and his ever-serious and fervent call to them. If the ditch of carnal security was a broad and easy one to fall into in Bible times, it is these days an even broader and more popular ditch. Those in it have hearts that feel no twinge of guilt at the sound of the law and the sight of the cross. Whenever conscience raises its feeble voice to condemn, the glib answer is close at hand: "Well, nobody's perfect! At least I don't do . . ."—and there follows a list of sins never committed. The sins not committed are always held up as the only ones that really count; the sins committed are just little ones, mistakes, someone else's fault, or outweighed in any event by imagined virtues of far greater importance. So the gossips boast that at least they are not adulterers, and the adulterers brag that at least they aren't like one of those hypocritical gossips.

When the "At least I'm not like . . ." doesn't work, there is the ever popular, "Who are you to judge?" That line works well for those who have decided that there is no such thing as absolute truth and, therefore, no way to know what is right and what is wrong, what is sin and what is virtue. It's all up to the individual and his feelings at the moment. *Sin, guilt*—we have risen above and outgrown those old-fashioned notions.

Also in this ditch we find those we saw in the last chapter. We find those for whom the death of Christ for the sins of the world has become a license to sin. "Since he died, since all sins have been paid for, it no longer matters what I do; I can do exactly as my flesh pleases because it has all been forgiven anyway." In their security, not to say arrogance and ingratitude, they go off like the pig who has been washed to wallow again in the filth of their choosing.

Those in the ditch of carnal security may hear Jesus calling from the narrow middle road on Good Friday, calling with the plaintive cry of Jeremiah: "Is it nothing to you, all you who pass by? Look around and see. Is any suffering like my suffering that was inflicted on me, that the LORD brought on me in the day of his fierce anger? From on high he sent fire, sent it down into my bones. He spread a net for my feet and turned me back. He made me desolate, faint all the day long" (Lamentations 1:12,13).

The sermon may declare: "And all this he did for you, in your place. All this he suffered because you deserved it. All this he endured so that you would not endure the same forever in hell." On Easter Sunday they may hear the great glad tidings that are the result of Jesus' anguish for us, also from Jeremiah: "Because of the LORD's great love we are not consumed, for his compassions never fail. They are new every morning; great is your faithfulness." But they will not answer as did Jeremiah: "I say to myself, 'The LORD is my portion; therefore I will wait for him'" (Lamentation 3:22-24). Instead, they will yawn and utter the cry of the bored: "We've heard it all before, know it all already. Tears of sorrow in repentance and songs of joy in forgiveness are for the really guilty or the merely silly and sentimental!" Even the very simple but richly instructive warning from Proverbs does not move such a one: "If anyone turns a deaf ear to the law, even his prayers are detestable" (28:9). He will go on mumbling his prayers when he feels like it, imagining that he is doing God some enormous favor and that God, therefore, is ever in his debt to bless and keep him.

In the gospels we see the Pharisees often stuck in this ditch of carnal security. For many of them repentance and confession were mere forms, devoid of any anguish in the heart or sincerity in the soul. Consider one of the most telling displays of their self-confidence and, at the same time, a display of their actual condition, of their desperate need for forgiveness. Read Matthew 9:9-13. Jesus had just called Matthew to be his disciple. Matthew was from that class of people always lumped together as "tax collectors and sinners." The tax collectors made their money by collecting tolls and taxes for the Roman government. They bought their position from the government. Once in office they were required to remit a fixed sum in tolls and taxes to the state; but there was little or no limit on what they could collect. They got rich by gouging their countrymen. They were hated because of their greed and dishonesty. They were despised because their job supported the government of the hated Romans. They were loathed because with the Roman army behind them, they could bleed their victims at will. Tax collectors were generally excommunicated and excluded from the synagogue. Tax collectors were usually lumped together as one in class with sinners. "Sinners" were those whose whole lives were public scandals and disgraces, i.e., prostitutes and adulterers, the openly immoral and indecent.

When Jesus called Matthew, the tax collector, to be his disciple, Matthew heeded that call. He showed his repentance, his joy in forgiveness, and the desire to leave behind his sin-dominated life by preparing a banquet for his fellow tax collectors and sinners with Jesus as the honored guest. The banquet must have been quite an event! It was not the normal gathering of tax collectors and sinners, a gathering during which the tax collectors would gloat over their dishonest gains and the sinners would flaunt their vices. Oh no, not that! Quite the opposite was the aim of this banquet. Matthew invited his friends because he wanted to share Jesus. He called them together to make public his confession of faith in the Savior, no doubt with the earnest desire that those invited would come to share in his confession and in his joy in forgiveness.

What was the response of the good people, the best people, the Pharisees to this whole spectacle? Always on the lookout for an excuse to criticize Jesus, they were sure they had him on the hook this time. Not daring to approach Jesus directly, they asked his disciples this question: "Why does your teacher eat with tax collectors and 'sinners'?" (9:11). It was not an innocent query. It contained this implied accusation: Birds of a feather flock together.

Listen to Jesus' answer: "It is not the healthy who need a doctor, but the sick. But go and learn what this means: 'I desire mercy, not sacrifice.' For I have not come to call the righteous, but sinners" (9:12,13). The Pharisees were so sure that they were "healthy." They were so confident that their participation in the liturgy of the temple sacrifices in and of itself made up for any slight lapses of which they might be guilty. But what was the reality as Jesus revealed it in his answer to their criticism?

Look at that first line carefully: "It is not the healthy who need a doctor, but the sick." On its simplest level, that answer justified what Jesus was doing. Who could deny that the tax collectors and sinners were sick, sin sick, in desperate need of healing grace and forgiveness? But go one step further, and see the arrow that Jesus shot at the hearts of those who thought themselves to be most healthy. Who really are the most sick and the most needy? It is not those who recognize their illness and long for the healing hand of the Physician. Rather, those who show no mercy are the most sin sick. Those are most needy who not only do not recognize their own sickness but who prevent the Physician from going to those who seek his help. It was bad enough that the Pharisees did not see their own need. But it was far worse that they wanted to keep the Physician away from those who longed for help and healing.

Jesus' words must have thrilled many at Matthew's banquet. Jesus wanted to heal them, not cast them into hell. He wanted to rescue them from their past and for a future in his blessed fellowship. But Jesus' words were just as much intended to call the carnally secure Pharisees up from their ditch. The Pharisees should have felt in his words the stinging arrow of the law that damned their cruelty, their heartlessness, their pride in themselves, and their contempt for those so obviously in need. If only they would have seen themselves as sick, they would have been ready for the remedy of the Great Physician. Then and only then would they have delighted in him who ate with tax collectors and sinners, in whose number they should have included themselves.

So Jesus addresses all in the ditch of carnal security—those who think they have no need of repentance and confession: "I have not come to call the righteous, but sinners." If you don't know that you are a sinner in desperate need of his call and his pardon, then you are stuck in the tar pit of carnal security. If you imagine that there is anything at all in you that does not need his grace, then you too are still stuck in that ditch.

The ditch of carnal security must be a well-populated one indeed, given the frequency with which Jesus warns against it and calls us from it in the gospels. There is the account of the tax collector Zacchaeus in Luke 19:1-10. Again, the carnally secure murmur against Jesus because he has gone to be the guest of a sinner. And again, Jesus answers with words of richest comfort to the anguished penitent and with words that should have shocked the self-righteous into an examination of their own souls: "The Son of Man came to seek and to save what was lost."

These words of Jesus bid me to cry out: "O Savior of the lost, I did not sin with the same sins as those of the tax collectors and sinners. These are my sins: I covet the wealth of the tax collector; I share the lust of the sinner; I enjoy looking down on those who appear to have fallen while my fall is secret; I love the praises of men, praises that you and I know are undeserved; I rejoice not in your merit and goodness but rather in the fact that no one sees my heart; with my heart out of plain view, I can delight in the illusion that somehow I am better than the one whose sins are on shameful and public display."

Luke 18 is a rich chapter for those who want to be on guard against this ditch of carnal security. It is a chapter of warnings against it and of markers that reveal its often camouflaged but still slippery edge. In Luke 18 we have the parable of the Pharisee and the tax collector praying in the temple. In contrast to the tax collector, whose outward sins everybody knew about, the Pharisee was outwardly a model citizen. Indeed, even in his prayer he rejoiced in God's own law, which it was his fervent desire to keep. His prayer at first blush seems noble indeed. He was thanking God. What could be wrong with that? But closer examination of his prayer reveals a heart that had more pride in self and contempt for everyone else than thankfulness to God.

So "thankful" was he that he saw no need to bow low and smite on his breast in anguish over his sins. He simply didn't have any to confess. Or if he was aware of sin in his life, he was confident that his goodness more than outweighed it. The confession of Isaiah was as far from his heart as the cry of the tax collector was from his lips. Isaiah pleaded with God:

All of us have become like one who is unclean, and all our righteous acts are like filthy rags. . . . Yet, O LORD, you are our Father. We are the clay, you are the potter; we are all the work of your hand. Do not be angry beyond measure, O LORD; do not remember our sins forever. (Isaiah 64:6-9)

That is the constant cry of the Christian on the narrow middle road.

Yes, this too is the cry even of those who have been rescued from the most horrible sins of the flesh and live in them no more. It is surprising sometimes to find that people who are no longer coarse sinners have become refined Pharisees. They may remember their past sins. But more than that, they congratulate themselves that they no longer commit them. Now they look down their newly pious noses on those who still do, who still need the Physician so desperately. It is a sad truism that pietism/Phariseeism is sometimes the final refuge of the guilty conscience. Their last state is worse than the first. Sometimes the most unforgiving can be those who have been forgiven most, a point that Jesus makes so eloquently in the parable of the unmerciful servant (Matthew 18:21-35).

Also in Luke 18 we have the story of the rich ruler (verses 18-27) who thought that he had kept the law. Yet there was the nagging thought in his soul that something was still wrong with him. He was secure, and yet. . . . So, he asked Jesus what he was still lacking. Jesus' answer was striking: "You still lack one thing. Sell everything you have and give to the poor, and you will have treasure in heaven. Then come, follow me." The rich ruler went away sad. We cannot help but wonder if he ever came back. We cannot but wonder if he ever got the point that Jesus made with this unusual command, a command which he never gave to anyone else. The words of Jesus were designed to yank the rich young ruler out of the ditch of his security. Jesus wanted this young man to see that for all his goodness and piety, he had miserably failed to keep the First Commandment. Jesus' words bring it to light: he did not love God above all things; he could not, he would not leave his wealth; he loved that more. He was, therefore, in absolute, desperate need of forgiveness. Crushing were Jesus' words to him. They were words that should have brought him out of the ditch and onto the narrow middle road that would plead with the tax collector in the temple, "God, have mercy on me, a sinner" (18:13).

But just as noteworthy is the end of this story. At its conclusion, Jesus remarked on how difficult it is for the rich to enter into the kingdom of heaven: "It is easier for a camel to go through the eye of a needle than for a rich man to enter the kingdom of God." The disciples expressed shock, yes, despair, when they heard those words: "Who then can be saved?" Why did they ask such a question? They were not rich. By the standards of the day, we would probably consider them middle class. But their expression of dismay brings to light the hidden longing to be rich, or at least their own lingering excessive attachment to whatever wealth they had. Indeed, their words hint at the possibility of running from the ditch of security to the opposite ditch of despair when they cry out, "Who then can be saved?"

Jesus' answer is, of course, perfect: "What is impossible with men is possible with God." And that's the sum of it! Jesus' word in the law hauls us up from the ditch of carnal security when we recognize that we cannot possibly be saved; we have not even for a moment kept the First Commandment, let alone any of the others. For us, salvation is surely impossible. It is impossible, that is, except for the One who came to seek and save sinners. It is impossible, except for the One who not only makes my salvation possible but who has already accomplished it for me.

But what if one's life is so peaceful and respectable that his conscience does not stir from its repose and drive him to his knees in confession that longs for the forgiveness we all so desperately need? There is no better advice for such a one than that which Luther gives. In his Large Catechism, he encourages us to seek the grace and pardon so richly offered in the Sacrament of the Altar and addresses those who feel no need for it:

> If you cannot feel the need, at least believe the Scriptures. They will not lie to you, since they know your flesh better than you yourself do. Yes, and St. Paul concludes in Romans 7[:18], "For I know that nothing good dwells within me, that is, in my flesh." If St. Paul speaks this

way of his own flesh, let us not wish to be better or holier. But the fact that we do not feel it is all the worse, for it is a sign that ours is a leprous flesh, which feels nothing although it rages with disease and gnaws away at itself. As we have said, even if you are so utterly dead in sin, at least believe the Scriptures, which pronounce this judgment upon you. In short, the less you feel your sins and infirmities, the more reason you have to go to the sacrament and seek its help and remedy.

Again, look around you and see whether you are also in the world. If you do not know, ask your neighbors about it. If you are in the world, do not think that there will be any lack of sins and needs. Just begin to act as if you want to become upright and cling to the gospel, and see whether you will not acquire enemies who harm, wrong, and injure you and give you cause to sin and do wrong. If you have not experienced this, then take it from the Scriptures, which everywhere give this testimony about the world.

Moreover, you will surely have the devil around you, too. You will not entirely trample him underfoot because our Lord Christ could not entirely avoid him. Now, what is the devil? Nothing else than what the Scriptures call him: a liar and a murderer. A liar who entices the heart away from God's Word and blinds it, making you unable to feel your need or to come to Christ. A murderer who begrudges you every hour of your life. If you could see how many daggers, spears, and arrows are aimed at you every moment, you would be glad to come to the sacrament as often as you can. The only reason we go about so securely and heedlessly is that we neither imagine nor believe that we are in the flesh, in the wicked world, or under the kingdom of the devil.[2]

---

[2] The Large Catechism, *The Book of Concord,* edited by Robert Kolb and Timothy J. Wengert (Minneapolis: Augsburg Fortress Press, 2000), pp. 474, 475. Cf. also "Personal Preparation for Holy Communion," *Christian Worship: A Lutheran Hymnal,* p. 156.

The ditch of despair

Jesus does not rescue us from the ditch of carnal security without warning us against the ditch on the opposite side, the ditch of despair. It is a ditch deep and dark. In a way, those in it are remarkably like those in the ditch of carnal security. Those in both ditches look at themselves instead of at the cross of Christ. They listen to their own voices rather than to his in Word and sacraments. Those in the ditch of carnal security think that they are so good that they do not need forgiveness; those in the ditch of despair think that they are so bad that forgiveness cannot reach them.

But let us examine that ditch of despair and those in it a bit more closely. They lead tragic lives of anguish. The despair may be the result of a terrible sin known to all. It may be the sin of the drunk driver who killed someone as the result of his drunkenness. It may be the sin of the gambler who squandered the security of his family by his reckless greed. It may be the sin of the adulterer whose ruined marriage is a constant reminder of his lust. But just as likely, the sin of the one in despair may be a secret, known only to God and the sinner. The very fact that the sin is secret makes the anguish of this one in despair all the more acute; he feels that he has added to his guilt by what he counts as the hypocrisy of his outward uprightness. He may even wish that his guilt were known, so at least he would not feel like a hypocrite.

Some of those in despair may try to drown their fear and self-loathing with alcohol or lose it in a drug-induced fog. Others may abandon themselves to work or pleasure in the hope that they may somehow forget their guilt. They struggle to still the accusing voice of conscience and the nagging sense that in the eyes of God they are doomed. But all their efforts only increase their anguish.

Whether their sin is secret or known to all, many in the ditch of despair carry their grief hidden and alone. In the stillness of the night, they may turn their faces to the wall and weep. In the light of day, they get dressed and go about their business, but always with the arrow stuck in the heart: "If people really knew! But God knows, and I know; he has cast me off because that is what I deserve; because of what I did, because of what I am, I am forever cursed and lost. It is just a matter of time before I get what I deserve."

Some in despair may struggle with might and main to emerge from the always black cloud that envelops their souls into the clear sunlight of a peaceful conscience. They may try again and again to better themselves and become worthy. The most tragic aspect of their despair may well lie exactly in those efforts. What they really want to do is get into the opposite ditch, the ditch of carnal security. They long for the day when they can be not forgiven but righteous by their own efforts and works, without any further need of forgiveness. If they succeed in this striving, they will be at least as bad off as before. The only difference will be that whereas before they knew their need, now they will choose to forget it. In either case, left to themselves they are still doomed.

Indeed, some of those in the ditch of despair come to it fresh from the ditch of carnal security. They may have been very comfortable in their skin the day before. But then something happened. There was a sudden and dramatic fall from respectability and virtue into some horrible sin. Now overwhelmed with guilt, despair stalks the corridors of their souls and dread darkens their hearts only recently so self-assured and merry. They do not grasp that the need for grace and mercy is always absolute and total. They needed forgiveness just as much yesterday as they do today.

That is not to say that the fall which has brought them to despair is unimportant. The sin may well have some very painful consequences in life and certainly in the soul. It needs repentance. Of course, tears of sorrow and anguish over what was done will not wash away the sin, even though such tears are altogether appropriate. The flood of tears serves a good purpose if it lifts us out of the ditch of carnal security; it is counterproductive if it drowns us in the ditch of despair. Here we observe the devil's favorite trick: First, he minimizes sin when he tempts us to it; then, he exaggerates it when we have fallen into it. But God uses our fall to demonstrate our need for grace and to exalt his own mercy and love for us in Christ. And that's where the narrow middle road is to be found: in Christ, in God's grace for the fallen, in mercy always desperately needed and always full and free at the cross and so generously poured out on us in the Word and sacraments.

Though the exact causes of despair are many and varied, the ditch for each person in it is dark and dreary indeed. We have in the gospels a striking example of one on the brink of the ditch of despair. His cry of despair was so sudden and so desperate that one may suspect that he had been at or in that ditch a time or two before. It was the cry of Peter in Luke 5:8. Overwhelmed by the power and the holiness of Jesus occasioned by the miracle of the catch of fish, Peter fell on his knees and cried out, "Go away from me, Lord; I am a sinful man!" This cry came from a man who had already shown his devotion to the Word of God as a disciple of John the Baptist. He had already shown his trust in Jesus only moments earlier; Jesus had told Peter and his fellow disciples, these professional fishermen, to do the opposite of what they knew to be good fishing practice. Peter had responded beautifully: "Master, we've worked hard all night and haven't caught anything. *But because you say so,* I will let down the nets" (verse 5).

But what merit did even this good confession of faith have before the One who sees all, who knows the heart and the wickedness that dwells there? Peter recognized that fundamental truth. In his awareness of his own heart and the sin that dwelt there, he cried out as he did. Who dares to stay long in the presence of the One who knows exactly what lies hidden in the deepest recesses of the soul? And more than that, who wants to tarry with the One who knows all of that and who at the same time demands perfection and can punish any lack of it?

Others in the Bible also knew a good deal about the ditch of despair, either because of time spent there or because of the frequent sight of that ditch close by. One of the two thieves with whom Jesus was crucified certainly knew about that ditch. It was from it that he spoke in those dread hours when he made confession of his guilt and what he deserved for his sins. His fellow criminal mocked Jesus, just as he himself had done earlier. But as his tortured soul saw the jaws of death and hell opening to swallow him, his sense of not just the present torment but of what laid before him pressed in on him. He first acknowledged what he deserved: "We are punished justly, for we are getting what our deeds deserve." Then in the anguish of one who knows that he should soon storm through the gates of hell, he cried out in his pain, "Jesus, remember me when you come into your kingdom" (Luke 23:41,42).

For the dying thief there were no excuses. Promises to do better in the future were out of the question. The presentation of evidence that somehow he had done other things that were good and that, therefore, he might have at least a shred of merit could not even come to mind. All that he could do was despair of himself. All he could do was plead for grace and beg for mercy. Prompted either by what he had known about Jesus earlier or by Jesus' earlier words of grace from the cross, that was exactly what he did. What grace that Jesus in the midst of his own torment, a torment far greater than that of this one criminal, looked on him, even on him, with pity. In the midst of his own misery, Jesus rescued the despairing from eternal ruin with his work and his word: "I tell you the truth, today you will be with me in paradise" (Luke 23:43). And by those words, he snatched the soul from the ditch of despair and transported him to the narrow middle road. Soon thereafter Jesus kept his promise and snatched the guilty soul up into the paradise of the blessed saints and angels.

As in the case of the thief on the cross, so very often it may happen that outward misery has dragged someone from the ditch of carnal security to the brink of despair or all the way into the ditch. The thief, after all, had been quite secure before his encounter with Jesus at the approach of death. He had thought nothing of those he hurt by his crimes and had cared nothing for the judgment of God or man. He had demonstrated exactly that when earlier he had joined the other thief in mocking Jesus. But now in the hour of death and at the gate of hell, God ripped the thief from the jaws of Satan by just that agony of death and the anticipation of the far worse misery yet to come in hell. To put it another way, God in love sent the thief on the cross and sends many others a foretaste of hell in order to rescue them from hell.[3] Only in torment or terror will some listen to words of divine love and mercy.

We have another example of just such a jump from one ditch to the edge of the other in the case of King Manasseh, one of Judah's worst kings (2 Chronicles 33). In addition to the sins mentioned in the Bible, tradition has it that Manasseh had the prophet Isaiah killed by having him sawed in half. Only after God sent him

---

[3] Luther's translation of Isaiah 28:19 is particularly interesting on this point: *Denn alleine die Anfechtung lehret aufs Wort merken* ("For only tribulation/testing [which is always of the most severe kind] teaches one to pay attention to the Word").

misery did Manasseh recognize his sin and humble himself before the Lord. With a hook in the nose and bound in chains, Judah's most wicked king had time to remember his crimes and how he had despised the Word of God in favor of his own will and pleasure. As with the thief on the cross, Manasseh, and anyone else in the ditch of despair, only the Word of grace and forgiveness is powerful enough to rescue and save from despair.

Death in despair is exactly the end result for those who turn away from the only possible rescue in Jesus' Word of forgiveness. At its most extreme is the death of the unrepentant suicide. Saul despaired of any help from God either for this life or for the next and killed himself, and so he went to his eternal doom (1 Samuel 31). So too did Ahithophel during the rebellion of Absalom (2 Samuel 17:23). Judas did the same. Overwhelmed by guilt, Judas spurned the grace of his Savior. Even in Gethsemane, in the very hour when Judas' crimes reached their zenith, Jesus called Judas to repentance with his word of reproach so gently spoken, "Judas [in Matthew's gospel, Jesus in this hour even calls Judas 'friend'!], are you betraying the Son of Man with a kiss?" (Luke 22:48). When Judas finally realized what he had done, he thought not of Jesus' words to him even in Gethsemane. He thought only of his crime and so went and hanged himself and thus entered into eternal despair (Matthew 27:1-5; Acts 1:18). Tragic indeed is the end of the unrepentant suicide for this life and the next if even in that last terrible hour he is unable to lay hold of the cross of Christ that has the power to cleanse even from this dread deed.

Those who do not carry out their despair in the way that Saul and Judas did often find their lives crushed by two heavy burdens. The one we have already mentioned is the fear that God cannot forgive them, that their sin is too great for his blood to wash it away. A second kind of dread, one closely related but not quite the same, is this: the inability to forgive oneself. Such a one may hear of the love of God and his eagerness to forgive. He may even come to believe that God could indeed forgive him. But the mercy of God, his grace and pardon, give no peace to the one who cannot forgive himself. He is still tormented by his guilt that has morphed into self-loathing. That lack of peace, that inability to let go of the guilt once God has let it go can so crush the soul that it finally turns back again to total despair. On the way back to the bottom of the ditch, such a person may find that his disgust with himself draws him back again and again to the very things that disgust him most. Sick to death of the result of his earlier drunkenness, he seeks to forget it by more drunkenness. Disgusted with his immorality and despairing of rescue, he falls again into immorality. In the process, he turns his back on the mercy of God and ends up considering it irrelevant.

Tragic indeed is the lot of those in the ditch of despair.

The narrow Lutheran middle

How shall we get out of and stay out of these two perilous ditches of carnal security and despair? If we are to find and stay in the middle, we need at least briefly to look at the role of reason in pulling us into one or the other of those ditches. The role of reason is a strong one indeed. In the ditch of carnal security, however, one might think that her voice is a little ridiculous. If ever she is the painted harlot that Luther calls her, it is there in the ditch of carnal security. All dressed up, she minces and winks and poses before the fool to convince him that he can do exactly as he pleases without regard to the law of God. Smooth as silk are her words, and her tongue drips with honey as she whispers in the ears of the self-righteous: "You are so good and so right; you need not trouble yourself with any sense of guilt or with repentance. God is lucky to have you on his side, and he favors you with good reason." She sits on the throne of the *opinio legis,* that wicked and perverse notion that stirs in our souls from the moment of conception; it is the notion deeply rooted in us that we are, after all, not so bad and, truth to be told, pretty good; we are certainly not desperate sinners like so many others. But empty is the head and shallow the soul that listen to Dame Reason from the ditch of carnal security.

In the ditch of despair, however, Dame Reason takes to herself some powerful allies. She lays hold of the law of God. She brings along the voice of conscience that God himself has planted in us as a judge. The one who honestly looks into the law, the one whose conscience is alive and well, quite reasonably may despair. Dame Reason is right to declare that we merit only God's wrath and judgment. If anything, she does not go far enough. For unknown to reason, known only from the Word of God itself, is the plain fact that we are conceived and born in sin (John 3:6). And the plain fact is that we have not a single moment in a whole lifetime that is not stained by sin (Romans 7:14-25).

The problem, however, with Dame Reason's arguments from both the ditches is that she hangs on to only half of the truth as she lures the unwary to their ruin.

The half-truth for the secure is that they may look good on the outside. What's left out is the fact that the outward appearance only masks the inherited corruption of our nature and the hidden idolatry of self.

The half-truth for those in despair is that they indeed deserve nothing but wrath and punishment. What's left out is that God's grace is for the undeserving and his mercy is for those doomed to death and hell.

Jesus tells Nicodemus in John 3:6 that all mankind born according to nature is doomed and damned. That should shatter Nicodemus' carnal security. It should send him running toward the ditch of despair. But Jesus does not leave Nicodemus to despair. He points to himself as the divinely sent Savior who would be lifted up to draw all to himself by his work for our redemption. He speaks the gospel of God's love for all of the fallen, not one excluded. He proclaims that the way of salvation is the way of trust in him alone for that salvation (John 3:14-18). St. Paul does the same thing in Romans 7. After he has graphically set forth the hopelessness of our condition in the flesh, he bursts out in a song of triumph: "Thanks be to God—through Jesus Christ our Lord" (Romans 7:25).

There is no better example of one who kept to the narrow middle road than Paul. Few knew more from experience about these two ditches than Paul. But Jesus knew well how to keep Paul on the narrow middle road. He did it not least by making Paul fully aware of the ditches on both sides of that road. Jesus let Paul remember how little he deserved of God's grace and mercy. A return to the carnal security in which Paul had lived before his conversion was ruled out for Paul by the memory of the monstrous crimes he had committed: "I am the least of the apostles and do not even deserve to be called an apostle, because I persecuted the church of God" (1 Corinthians 15:9). By God's grace and in spite of his past, Paul became an apostle. Indeed, as he himself testified, he worked harder and more effectively than all the other apostles. But it was grace, not success, that saved him from the abyss of despair. Paul acknowledged the same when he declared, "By the grace of God I am what I am, and his grace to me was not without effect. No, I worked harder than all of them—yet not I, but the grace of God that was with me" (1 Corinthians 15:10). There's the middle road. With eyes that saw clearly the desperate need of forgiveness and saw just as clearly grace heaped upon grace in Christ, Paul did not fall into the ditch of despair because of his sin.

Could, however, Paul's labor and his sufferings for the sake of the gospel end up still putting him back again in the ditch of carnal security? Jesus saw to it that that did not happen. Paul tells us about it in 2 Corinthians 11,12. Matching the greatness of God's gifts to Paul in the ministry was the gift, yes the gift, of what Paul called his "thorn in my flesh" (12:7). He doesn't tell us exactly what the thorn was. Whatever it was, it was exceedingly painful. His pleas that God would take it away received only the answer, "My grace is sufficient for you, for my power is made perfect in weakness" (12:9). Once again, there is the narrow middle. The pain of the thorn would keep Paul from ever thinking that his "success" was due to his own hard work or genius. It would keep him out of the ditch of carnal security when things went well. So painful was the thorn that only the grace and mercy of God could enable him to survive it. And that grace and mercy was always sufficient.

Paul, therefore, is someone we would want to listen to as we struggle to avoid the ditches of carnal security and despair. Just what advice does he have for us? He gives us brilliant and divinely inspired advice in Philippians 3. Those in the ditch of carnal security should listen as Paul describes all of his own virtues and good deeds. But what does he declare of all of it? He says that his works apart from Christ are nothing but rubbish (3:8). The only thing that matters is gaining the Christ who gives himself freely in the message of his death and resurrection. The only thing that counts is the Christ who gives his own righteousness to those who have nothing but rubbish for merit. And that perfect righteousness Christ gives through faith alone.

Then Paul follows with words of special encouragement for those struggling with the temptation to despair. When the demons grab us by the throat and are ready to drag us into that ditch, we do well to answer with Paul: "I do not consider myself yet to have taken hold of it [i.e., perfection in my life of faith]. But one thing I do: Forgetting what is behind and straining toward what is ahead, I press on toward the goal to win the prize for which God has called me heavenward in Christ Jesus" (3:13,14). A perfect narrow middle road! Let go of the imperfection and the sin of yesterday, remembering only that Christ has fully paid for it. And then press on, striving with might and main to be the redeemed child of God that you are. There is no license to sin. There is no cause for lazy security. There is no reason for despair. There is only Christ. There is only the goal that he has set before us. There is only a striving to reach that goal in the knowledge and assurance that he has already won it for us. That's one of the many remarkable truths about the gospel: *we lose every battle to at least some extent because of the sin that always stains us, but we win the war because Christ has won it for us!*

To Dame Reason, all this is nonsense. It just doesn't fit the way she looks at things. Either we should boast of our goodness or sin with reckless abandon; either we should arrogantly wallow in our self-righteous pride or despair in our guilt. But Paul shows us the way that God looks at it. Ultimately, God's reasoning is the only reasoning that counts. It is God's reasoning that puts us on the narrow middle road. It is God's reasoning that rejects Dame Reason's sweet mincing from the ditch of carnal security as well as her ugly demons grabbing at our throats from the ditch of despair.

As we labor and even grow weary in the effort to recognize and shun both ditches, we are cheered on by the compassionate and inviting voice of Jesus our Savior: "Come to me, all you who are weary and burdened, and I will give you rest. Take my yoke upon you and learn from me, for I am gentle and humble in heart, and you will find rest for your souls. For my yoke is easy and my burden is light" (Matthew 11:28-30). Exhaustion is in the ditch, whether the one or the other. Refreshment and new strength, strength sufficient for the day, is under the yoke of Christ made easy by his presence, by his carrying it with and for us.

For further instruction on the narrow middle road between these two ditches, we can but encourage the reading of the epistles. Read them, and you will see in every one of them strong and clear warnings against both ditches. In Paul's epistles, the antidote to despair is usually found in the earlier chapters and the warnings against carnal security in the later ones; that's easiest to see in Galatians and Ephesians. In John's first epistle, the warnings against both ditches are close together, woven tightly, especially in chapters 1–3. The same is true in Peter's first epistle, especially in chapter 1.

Those who walk blindly or with eyes closed along the narrow road that leads to life eternal will stumble and fall into the ditches and never reach the goal. Those who walk in the light that comes alone from the Word of God and Christ its center will recognize the ditches and their danger. Let us then walk wisely as in the day as we press toward the goal that Christ has prepared and won for us at the end of the day. He has put us on the road by bringing us to faith in and through his Word. And he will keep his Word of promise to bring us safely to the end of the journey through that same Word and not apart from it. Yes, he will remain faithful to his Word and keep calling us back by it even when in our folly we have stumbled into the ditch. Through it all, there will be no doubt about it at the end of our traveling days: Jesus Christ alone was our Savior yesterday, is our Savior today, and will receive all the praise and glory for our salvation in heaven forever!

4

The Narrow Lutheran Middle Between an Exclusive Emphasis on God's Providence or on God's Promises Concerning Prayer

We enter now onto a very beautiful and interesting stretch of the narrow middle road. One side of the road affords rich comfort and sweet refreshment for the weary traveler. On this side of the road, we see and hear a beautiful doctrine from God's Word, the doctrine of the *providence of God*. Of the pleasure in the sunshine and shade of this doctrine, there is no end. In the sweet refreshment from its fruit, there is constant delight.

The opposite side of the road, likewise, is so attractive and appealing that to leave it would seem a shame indeed. On that side we hear the gracious voice of Jesus inviting us to pray and promising to hear us. So pleasing is his voice in those promises, so enchanting is the prospect of kneeling before him in prayer, that for all the world we could not imagine ever wanting to leave this side of the road either.

On this stretch of the road, the ditches on either side lie hidden behind the evident beauty at the edge of the road. The ditches consist chiefly in a failure to pay due attention to the promises of God found on *both* sides of the road. God wants us to have in rich measure the blessings he offers in both doctrines. But as we should expect, Satan is ever busy in his efforts to spoil the beauty and the blessings of God's Word concerning these two doctrines. The devil uses his dear agent, Dame Reason, to hide some poisonous fruits on one side and to stick thorns in the midst of the roses on the other side.

So then, let us consider on this beautiful stretch of the narrow middle road the delights that God offers in both doctrines without overemphasizing one or neglecting the other. Let us consider in each their turn what God has to say in his Word about his providence and then what he has to say about prayer.

The providence of God

The doctrine of the providence of God deals with what the Bible says about God's gracious rule over history for the benefit of his children. It covers his protection of the church and of his Word and sacraments for the creation and preservation of faith. It covers as well and in detail the life, the history, of each individual Christian who trusts in Jesus for salvation and eternal life. It is a doctrine rich in comfort and endless in its application to the life of the church and to the life of each Christian.

Eloquent and beautiful indeed are the passages in the Bible that speak of God's providence. St. Paul, for example, sings the praises of Jesus our ascended King in Ephesians 1. He glories in this truth that all of our lives are in the hands of our ascended Savior. He prays that each person may "know the hope to which [God] has called you, the riches of his glorious inheritance in the saints, and his incomparably great power for us who believe" (1:18,19). That hope is a sure and confident hope both for our ultimate salvation in heaven and also for God's ever-gracious rule over our lives in the here and now. Our hope is sure and secure because of the almighty power of God,

> which he exerted in Christ when he raised him from the
> dead and seated him at his right hand in the heavenly

realms, far above all rule and authority, power and dominion, and every title that can be given, not only in the present age but also in the one to come. *And God placed all
things under his feet and appointed him to be head over
everything for the church,* which is his body, the fullness of
him who fills everything in every way. (1:20-23)

Could there be a more rich and comforting assurance of Christ's
care for us than that?

Christus pro nobis! Christ for us! That has ever been the great
and jubilant cry of the church as she contemplates the *providence
of God.* God's providence is his gracious rule over everything, rule
that he has handed over to Christ our Savior. Christ is exalted on
high. Total, complete, and full is his rule over time, over history,
over governments, over sickness and death and hell itself.

And the authority that he has over everything in this world
and the next he exercises, as Paul says, *for the church.* The
church is not merely an organization with clergy and laity, offi-
cer holders, managers, and buildings. No, the church is "his
body, the fullness of him who fills everything in every way." His
rule is not that of an absent monarch or a distant and disinter-
ested governor. Rather, his rule has each individual fully in his
sight as a member of his own mystical body. His attention and
his care are not divided into fractions so that you and I have perhaps a billionth part of his attention, and that only for a moment.
No, it is his undivided attention that we enjoy every moment of
our lives. Indeed, the apostle reminds us in an earlier part of the
chapter (1:4) that Christ's eye and his mind, his heart and his
attention were devoted to us as individuals even before the
world began, in eternity!

Jesus himself tells us the same thing in his parting words to
the disciples shortly before his ascension to this exalted position
at God's right hand. He, the almighty and risen Lord, spoke
words that echo down through the centuries. They are words
directed to us collectively as his church; but just as much, they
are words addressed to each individual believer: "All authority in
heaven and on earth has been given to me. . . . And surely I am
with you always, to the very end of the age" (Matthew 28:18,20).
Again, Jesus does not dole out his attention in fractions. When he

promises that he is with you, with me, always, to the very end of the age, that promise is absolute. He is with me; he is with you according to both his divine and human natures. He is with you; he is with me with all of his attention, with all of his power, with all of his love and grace and protecting care!

In the Sermon on the Mount, Jesus underscores the truth that these promises of his providence are meant for each of us as individuals. After reminding us that God provides for the birds of the air and the lilies of the field without their worry or concern, he tells us:

> Will he not much more clothe you, O you of little faith? So do not worry, saying, "What shall we eat?" or "What shall we drink?" or "What shall we wear?" For the pagans run after all these things, and your heavenly Father knows that you need them. But seek first his kingdom and his righteousness, and all these things will be given to you as well. (Matthew 6:30-33)

Could there be a more complete, more generous, more reassuring promise of his providence than that? He knows and he provides for our greatest need, the need for forgiveness and eternal life. He knows and provides as well for the smallest need, our need for our next meal and change of clothes.

The providence of God is not always obvious

The doctrine of the providence of God clearly is not some abstract notion without any real or practical benefit for us as we travel the road from here to heaven. Quite the contrary; it is a doctrine that is especially useful to us as we stumble along on that road under the painful realities of a life stained by our own sin and marred by the sins of others. As a result of our sinful condition, we suffer in body and soul. We get sick. We endure the frustration of disappointed hopes for health and wealth, for family and friends. We, even in our life of faith, march one step forward only to fall back two steps a day later.

Who isn't acquainted with these facts of life? Just when we thought we had conquered one set of temptations, a new set rises to torment our souls and, when we fall, to torture our consciences.

Just when we thought all was going well, we get sick. Just when we thought our family lives were stable, someone dies. Or the marriage that was supposed be a dream come true turns into a sin-stained nightmare. Or the child who was the apple of the eye instead fills the eye with tears. Just when we thought our professional lives were on the right track, we get laid off. Just when we thought our finances were finally in order, a storm comes and rips a hole in the roof that insurance will not cover. Just when we thought that friends were worthy and true, one of them betrays us and leaves.

Whose life has not been touched by at least some of these plagues and so many others that the number is beyond counting? Yes, how many times are there in our lives when this thought creeps in: "Oh God, I thought you loved me and would take care of me. Where are you now when I seem so hopeless, helpless, and alone? Where is the promise of your providence?"

We seem to spend much of life in what seems to be little more than an endless cycle of ups and downs on the yo-yo of some mindless *fate.* So too the church seems one day strong and secure and the next, about to perish. In fact, in every age of her history, the church has seemed to be on the brink of complete destruction. Persecution from the outside has threatened her ruin when violent governments raised the sword against her. At other times the godless philosophy of the world wedded to nothing greater than personal fulfillment and the pleasure of the moment has threatened to seduce entire generations away from her doors. At still other times the moral or doctrinal corruption within her own walls has become so pervasive that any thought of her survival has seemed naïve at best.

It is at just such times, times of suffering—whether it be the suffering of the individual or of the church as a whole—that the doctrine of the providence of God is most comforting and reassuring. God's Word reminds us again and again that we are not in heaven yet and that in this life we must, because of sin, expect suffering (Psalm 90:10; John 15:18–16:9; Acts 14:22). But God assures us that his kind and gracious and providential hand is stretched over us each moment and leaves us never. Yes, it is the hand of Christ our Savior, who is our head, that remains in control and gives us so many days of gladness. And it is the same Christ who is in control and gives or permits so many days of distress and sadness. Both come from his kind, his gracious, his always loving heart and remain ever under his providential control.

It is only in his Word that we can make any sense of this truth, that it is in grace that he both sends joy and also permits suffering. That he is kind and gracious to us when we prosper may indeed be easier for us to understand, especially since we know that we deserve none of his blessings. But how will we find the sense in suffering? How will we trust that suffering too is an evidence of his love, even of his providence, of his divine rule over all things for our benefit? We will not learn that from Dame Reason. Nor will our own feelings and emotions bring us to understanding. And certainly the world's philosophy will be of no help at all. Only in God's own mighty Word will the Christian soul gain peace from God himself and even joy in suffering. In his Word, God explains suffering to us and then also gives us the grace and courage to see his kindness and goodness in it.

God's providence in suffering

A good deal, though not all, of the suffering we endure comes to us as a result of our own sin. When suffering is the result of our own sin, God sends the suffering to us to warn us against continuing in sin. To continue in deliberate sin is to bring eternal ruin to our own souls and often great harm to others as well. There is perhaps no better example of the kind of suffering that is the result of one's own sin than that which came to David as a result of his affair with Bathsheba (2 Samuel 11,12). The child who came out of that adultery died; though the child was rescued by that death and taken up into the arms of his heavenly Father, David and Bathsheba certainly never forgot the loss.

And God did not allow David to forget the seriousness of his sin. The loss of the child was followed by a succession of tragedies in David's family. But that suffering was necessary. It was even an evidence of God's loving providence. It was necessary as a reminder to David and to us as well that God takes sin seriously. It was necessary as a reminder that forgiveness is not a license to sin. Yes, the suffering was necessary, most important, as a demonstration of how great God's grace is: The suffering was a constant reminder that the eternal suffering was gone because

the sin was forgiven. How strange that must sound to fallen reason: Present suffering is a reminder of forgiveness; present suffering reminds us to give thanks for our release from eternal
suffering; present suffering is a warning sign against the danger
of future sin. Had there been no consequence for his sin, David
could have become bold in sinning even further and that to his
eternal ruin. That David got all of these points is evident in many
of the psalms that he authored, for example, in Psalms 6, 51, 130,
139, 143, to mention just a few. God in grace gave David the
strength to endure and the wisdom to recognize God's gracious
hand, no matter how deep the pain of the moment.

David, therefore, had good reason, and so too do we, to give
thanks, deep and heartfelt thanks for the suffering that we
endure. Suffering is sometimes God's kind hand calling us back
from our sins, calling us to repentance, warning us of the far
greater and eternal suffering that comes to those who embrace
their sins rather than repenting of them and struggling against
them. The chastening hand of the Lord is no less an evidence of
his providence than the hand that pours out obvious blessings
over us every day and hour of our lives.

As was the case with David, so too with us: If God ignores our
sins and sends us no chastening hand to call us back from them,
we will harm ourselves eternally and perhaps harm others as
well. David didn't just hurt himself by his sin; he also hurt God's
people by the horrible example that he had set. If he had suffered
no consequences for his sin, then people would have thought that
God doesn't care about sin, that we have a license to do just as
our corrupt nature pleases. Such an attitude and life can have the
effect of turning others away from the Word of God and making
the church an object of ridicule. Nathan, David's pastor, says as
much to David: "By doing this you have made the enemies of the
LORD show utter contempt" (2 Samuel 12:14).

St. Paul says (Romans 2:24), and he is quoting the prophets
(Isaiah 52:5; Ezekiel 36:22,23), that this was the great crime of
the Jews through so much of their history, that because of their
sins the Gentiles mocked God and were not interested in listening
to the Word of God. The souls of how many children are scarred
beyond healing when parents pretend at being Christians but live
like heathens? How many neighbors of church members never

darken the door of a church because they can say, "If that's what church members are like, I want nothing to do with the church." But if God sends suffering that causes such offenses to cease, that calls back the one acting the part of a hypocrite, there will be eternal thanksgiving for such suffering! Such suffering will certainly be an evidence of the providence of God, of his kind and gracious rule over history, over our history, if it removes one of the many obstacles that keeps people from hearing the saving message of the gospel.

It is in his providence that God sends both good days and bad

Read the Old Testament. Read the history of Israel in Exodus, the book of Judges, and the rest of the history of Israel and Judah in 1 Samuel through 2 Chronicles. It is an unbroken record of a loving and gracious God who poured out blessings on top of blessings. It is as well the record of his love and grace in sending suffering. In his providence he sends obvious blessings to move us to thanksgiving and grateful service. He sends suffering also from his providence to call back the sinner from his sin. He sends it in consequence of sin to remind the sinner of his seriousness in the law and of his surpassing grace in the gospel. So great is his ardor for our salvation! Read as a summary example Isaiah 9:8–10:19. Those verses are an eloquent testimony from the mouth and mind of God himself about his providence when he judges sin and then rescues those who suffer as the result of his judgment. Let men use their reason and their might as they will. It is God who rules and brings to nothing all of men's plots against his judgment. Let them try to rebuild what he tears down; he will tear it down again. He lets nations rise to punish the arrogance and the pride of his fallen people and then in his own good time destroys the destroyers for their pride and arrogance. Wondrous indeed are his ways as he judges in anger in order to rescue in grace!

So let the one chocked by greed suffer loss. Let the one who thinks that God's gift of time is his own to do with as he pleases experience sickness. Let the one who has begun to worship pleasure endure some pain. Let those who imagine that they are in control of their lives see unexpected tragedy. And then, let us with David fall to our knees in thanksgiving to the God who does not cast us off. Let us raise our voices in thanksgiving to the God who loves us enough to call us back to himself through suffering. It is in grace and love beyond measure that he sends suffering so that he can forgive and rescue our blood-bought souls for all eternity. The writer to the Hebrews put it well: "God disciplines us for our good, that we may share in his holiness. No discipline seems pleasant at the time, but painful. Later on, however, it produces a harvest of righteousness and peace for those who have been trained by it" (12:10,11).

A point worth remembering, even when our suffering can be traced to our own sins, is that God in his providence limits the suffering he sends; it never reaches the measure of our desert. Even in the case of David, his pastor pointed that out to him. As soon as David confessed his sin, Nathan declared: "The LORD has taken away your sin. You are not going to die" (2 Samuel 12:13). In his providence God disciplines us with a measure designed to accomplish his gracious purpose of calling us back to himself. Unlike the parent whose patience is finally exhausted and who then visits blows on his children in anger out of all proportion to their crimes, God measures all things carefully in justice that is always tempered with grace.

Many a Christian could write the book on such evidences of God's providence. And certainly, in considering our lives under Christ's providential rule, each of us has reasons beyond counting for saying to God, if to no one else: "Yes, O Lord, it is true; never have you dealt with me as I deserved; even in deepest sorrow, even when I could not see it or fully appreciate it, your hand preserved me and put a wall of protection around me. You saved me from the full weight of crushing that my sins deserved. Otherwise, I would have perished in my sins and in my despair a thousand times over!"

It is in the book of Psalms, the Bible's hymnal, that we hear the song of the church and of each believer in endless praise to God for his providence in ruling over all of history for the benefit of his own. Just to consider three of the many psalms that confess and praise God for his providence, for the triumph of grace over deserved justice, look at Psalms 66, 103, and 136.

In Psalms 66 and 103 the believing child of God looks with wonder and awe at all the goodness of God. He shows his goodness day by day in permitting trouble and sickness that come without explanation; and he shows it no less in the suffering and sorrow that come as a result of the believer's own sins. And what does God seek and accomplish in all of it? He rescues. He redeems. He restores. He gives songs of gladness and shouts of thanksgiving. These psalms are not just giddy and shallow expressions of happiness on good days. They are filled with deep thanksgiving precisely because the believer knows that in all his days, both the easy and the difficult, the merry and the painful, God rules. God gives all in love and kindness, in his infinite grace, not according to our miserable merit. And so the soul rests in the arms of the Savior and is content to sum it all up in this way: "Praise the LORD, all his works everywhere in his dominion. Praise the LORD, O my soul!" (103:22).

Likewise in Psalm 136, the child of God looks at all the works of the Lord in the history of his people. And what does he see? Nothing but the goodness, the kindness, the grace of God. Over and over again at the consideration of all God's mighty acts, the believer is moved to raise his voice in song: "Give thanks to the LORD, for he is good. His love endures forever." And in everything that he does, whether in the history of the church or of the individual believer, God proves it. His providence is ever active in crowning our lives with days of joys and in blessing us with days of sadness.

When suffering comes without any obvious connection to our sins, when it comes straight out of the malice and sins of others, even then God's providence rules over all for our good. Isaac was richly blessed by God in crops and flocks; he dug wells to water his flocks; but his neighbors, envious of the Lord's blessings to Isaac, destroyed the wells (Genesis 26:12-22). David was anointed by Samuel to be king in Israel instead of Saul, but he had to endure years of persecution and suffering at the hands of Saul before God installed him on the promised throne of Israel (1 Samuel 16, 18–26). Job had done nothing to bring down God's anger on him; nevertheless, he suffered a time of severe testing.

But in all of these instances where people suffered without it being the direct cause of their own suffering, God ruled over history. He replaced again and again the lost wells of Isaac. God waited for the time he considered best to bring David to his throne—best both for David and for his people; in the end God kept his promise and gave even more than he promised. For Job too the time of testing came to an end; when it was over, Job acknowledged what he had learned about God and his goodness, God and his might. Perhaps earlier he had known those things more in his head than in his heart. But once he was rescued from all his misery and even blessed as never before, he worshiped with a different level of gratitude than he had known previously.

In the book of Acts in the New Testament, we read of one persecution after another that resulted in suffering and even death for innocent believers. St. Paul describes his own suffering at the hands of unbelievers and, yes, his suffering even from the malice of those who considered themselves Christians. According to tradition, all of the apostles except for St. John died as martyrs. Eusebius (d. 339) wrote *The History of the Church From Christ to Constantine*; in it he recounts in graphic detail much of what the church endured in the years from Pentecost to A.D. 324. The church suffered from all the bloodthirsty tyrants in government. She suffered as well from false teachers who arose within her own ranks. In his first letter, St. Peter told the church of his day what remains forever true: "Dear friends, do not be surprised at the painful trial you are suffering, as though something strange were happening to you" (1 Peter 4:12).

But what do Peter and Paul have to say about the trials and tribulations that come as the result of the sins of others? What do they say of the persecution that happens whenever and wherever Christians faithfully hold to the truth of God's Word and strive to live according to it? The apostles point us to the providence of God! Peter tells us that we should just be sure that our suffering is not the result of our own wrongdoing; when it has the evil of others as its source, he tells us: "Rejoice that you participate in the sufferings of Christ, so that you may be overjoyed when his glory is revealed. . . . If you suffer as a Christian, do not be ashamed, but praise God that you bear that name. . . . So then, those who suffer according to God's will should commit themselves to their faithful Creator and continue to do good" (1 Peter 4:13-19).

Innocent suffering at the hands of others points us always to the saving hand of God and to a renewed confidence that we are in his ever-gracious care—that we do not see that in the moment does not change the fact. The fact is rooted and grounded in God's Word and promise. St. Paul sums up his attitude toward all that he endured at the hands of enemies of the truth beautifully:

> We do not lose heart. Though outwardly we are wasting away, yet inwardly we are being renewed day by day. For our light and momentary troubles are achieving for us an eternal glory that far outweighs them all. So we fix our eyes not on what is seen, but on what is unseen. For what is seen is temporary, but what is unseen is eternal. (2 Corinthians 4:16-18)

Thus, even when sorrow seems unjust and when Dame Reason loudly objects that evil has triumphed over God and the devil has won out over Christ, even then God is ruling. Even then Christ is head over all things for the benefit of the church. Even then God's providence holds sway over the life of each of the members of Christ's mystical body, the church. In it all the Christian has the assurance from God's Word that the sufferings of the moment, no matter what their source, point us away from excessive love for the world.

Yes, such suffering even keeps us from becoming too attached to the earthly blessings that God himself has given us to enjoy in this world. The momentary loss of some of God's earthly blessings can remind us again of the far greater blessings of forgiveness and the promised help of the Savior in every hour of need. Suffering and sorrow as well point us to the never-ending glory of heaven. Sorrow and loss bid us to trust in the providence of God promised in his Word and won for us by the Savior through his own innocent suffering in our place. The simple truth of the matter is that without earthly loss, we fall too much in love with earthly gain; without pain, we become too addicted to pleasure; without days of sorrow, we never really appreciate days of laughter.

Thus, the providence of God is made manifest as he rules over history, the history of the world and our own personal history. It takes time to appreciate that truth. A couple of examples from the Scriptures may serve to encourage our patience. Consider the life of Joseph in the Old Testament. His brothers wanted to kill him. Their evil was held in check by the providence of God, so that

Joseph was *only* sold into slavery. What providence was there in that? In slavery Joseph's condition went from bad to worse. He was falsely accused of rape and imprisoned. For years he endured one humiliation after another. But in time it all became clear: His suffering was preparation for a great work of rescue for his family, as undeserving as his brothers were of rescue.

Yes, and the famine in Palestine that caused such suffering to his brothers and their families, what a blessing that was! The famine brought them down to Egypt, where Joseph could save them. It brought them down to humble repentance, where Joseph and God could forgive them. Would anyone say that the sufferings of Joseph and his family were pointless? They were *providential* acts of God, who limits the evil that men can do and uses it in his own ways for his own *ever-providential purposes*. It took time for those lessons to become evident and to sink in. But Joseph certainly got the point and made the point clear to his family (Genesis 50:15-21).

Or consider the flood at the time of Noah (Genesis 6–9). What misery it caused—a misery occasioned by the great wickedness of men. They wanted so much to be rid of God and his rule that God finally in just judgment rid himself of them. Where was the providence of God in all that destruction and woe beyond measure? God's providence was abundant in the flood; by it the church was rescued. Had there been no destruction, the wickedness of unbelief would have grown so powerful that the church would have perished. Indeed, it had almost perished as it was. After all, Noah preached law and gospel for over one hundred years. He called out the message of God's providence, of God's yearning to forgive and reclaim the fallen human race. What did he have for all of his preaching? Only the souls of his own immediate family!

Small as it was, the church was saved by the destruction of the flood. St. Peter makes the point in such an interesting way when he uses the waters of the flood as a point of comparison for the Sacrament of Baptism: Just as the flood of Noah's day saved the church, so now the water of Baptism saves us (1 Peter 3:20,21). What an intriguing way God has of pointing us to his providence. He promised Noah that he would never again destroy the world by such a flood; and so, instead, he saves people by the mini-flood of the water in Baptism!

The epistle of James makes the point also in an especially interesting way. St. James tells us: "Every good and perfect gift is from above, coming down from the Father of the heavenly lights, who does not change like shifting shadows. He chose to give us birth through the word of truth, that we might be a kind of first-fruits of all he created" (1:17,18). Look at the passage carefully. What are God's good and perfect gifts? Why, everything that he sends us! It is all sent in his providence. There is no change in his sacred heart that always loves us and looks for ways to prove it. He does not shift like the shadows.

Since there is no change in him, good and perfect gifts are the only kinds of gifts that he knows how to give! Whatever he sends is a good and perfect gift that matches his love and fits our need. When we need health and wealth and family and friends and such other joys as may for a time delight us, he gives them. When we need peace for a troubled mind and a happy conscience, he gives that too—and most generously through Word and sacraments. Yes, and when we need chastening to bring us back from our sins, that too he sends as a good and perfect gift appropriate to his love and our need. For, again, with him there is no change.

His providence extends over all our days. He proves it by giving us the new birth, by giving us the faith that trusts in him in days both good and ill. That new birth came at Baptism, and it is nourished and sustained by the Water of Life, by Christ in his Word and in the Sacrament of the Altar. He does it all so that all our days we may bear the fruit of thanksgiving and service to him who in his kind providence does all things well for us.

So pleasant is this side of the road, the consideration of the providence of God, so full of peace and joy, so instructive for every day of our lives, that it is difficult to leave off thinking about it. Every event of life, from the most beautiful to the most painful, has the providence of God stretching over it. Every facet and phase, wherever we turn, has God's protecting hand blessing us, drawing us to himself, keeping us in his care, so that we reach the goal of eternal life purchased for us by him at so great a price.

St. Paul best summed it all up in Romans 8. Read the whole chapter. From beginning to end, it is a hymn of praise and thanksgiving to God for his providence; in his providence, God triumphs over the perversity of man, whether that is perversity in our own sinful flesh or in the wicked actions of others. Paul sums it all up so perfectly in the middle of his hymn of praise to God for his providence: "We know that in all things God works for the good of those who love him, who have been called according to his purpose" (8:28). Those who love him do so because he first loved them (1 John 4:19). In the gospel he has called them to life and for life eternal. They bask in the sunshine of this assurance that he rules over all things for their benefit, as Paul declares from the beginning to the end of Romans 8.

And so Paul concludes his great hymn of praise: "I am convinced that neither death nor life, neither angels nor demons, neither the present nor the future, nor any powers, neither height nor depth, nor anything else in all creation, will be able to separate us from the love of God that is in Christ Jesus our Lord" (8:38,39). It cannot be said any better. All praise and thanks to God for this wonderful truth of his Word, for all that his Word has to say to us about his providence!

The doctrine of God's providence is indeed a beautiful and most comforting one. But it is time to look at the other side of the road. There we find another beautiful and comforting doctrine: the doctrine of prayer and the promises that God has made with respect to prayer.

God's promises concerning prayer

But wait just a minute. Why leave the doctrine of God's providence to talk about prayer? This is the right place to begin talking about prayer precisely because all that God has to tell us about his providence raises an unavoidable question. In the question we can see Dame Reason again throwing off the maid's dress and sneaking out from behind her mop and pail. The question is this: If everything that God does is for our good, if he has designed and planned and rules over all of our history for our benefit, then what's the point in praying? It would seem (do you hear Dame Reason moving in to push the Word aside?) that if all things happen under God's providence, there would be no need to pray. After all, no matter what, it is all going to come out according to God's plan for our good and his glory. Isn't that the whole point of what we heard concerning the providence of God?

Why then ask him for anything? Why ask for help in trouble if the trouble is for our good? Why even ask for help in temptation if by temptations we learn all the more that both the strength to stand as well as our ultimate rescue in heaven are by grace alone? Yes, it would even seem that there is not much point in planning or in thinking about what we should do with our lives if it is all going to come out under his providence anyway.

So Dame Reason throws a whole host of obstacles in the way of prayer and reasons why we should not bother much about it. She starts, as we have just noted, with, "Since God rules over everything and does as he pleases, prayer will accomplish nothing." If that doesn't deter us from prayer, she will go in another direction and flatly contradict all that God's Word says both about prayer and about God's providence: "God is far away and cannot be bothered about your trivial concerns." Or she contradicts the gospel itself with the thought: "Don't you dare pray! You will only draw God's attention to your sins. At the very least, wait until you are better and more worthy to be heard!" Or she takes the opposite course: "Why should you pray? Only the weak look for crutches like that. You're strong enough to handle whatever life throws your way. Prayer for you is an unnecessary waste of time."

If those obstacles do not turn us away from prayer, the devil and Dame Reason, the devil's favorite preacher, have a long list of other obstacles to toss our way that distort and pervert God's promises concerning prayer. The devil may set up in our minds his own doctrine of prayer. He may suggest that prayer is really a means of grace, that as long as we pray, God is happy with us and we need not bother about doctrine or lives that conform to his Word.

We hear thoughts like that expressed quite often these days. Some people want to consider themselves Christians without the bother of either biblical doctrine or Christian lives. They pray without any notion of repentance for sin. They pray with no intention of listening or submitting to anything in God's Word that doesn't suit them. Such people foolishly imagine that they can define faith and Christianity any way that they please and that God should be satisfied with it: "See, I believe in God, just like you do. See, I even pray, maybe more than you do! So surely God is satisfied and won't be upset just because I don't carry out

all the little rules that you bother yourself with. After all, I'm
not some sort of fanatic!"

Others in their prayers imagine that God somehow owes them
his help when they deign to seek it. In the day of trouble, their
prayers go something like this: "O God, I know that I haven't spoken to you much lately or thought much about you. But see here!
Now I'm in trouble. Show me that you are really a God of love,
and do what I ask!" They may even add this threat: "If you don't
do what I want, how can you expect me to go on believing in you?"
Some might even add a little bribe to help God decide matters in
their favor: "If you just do thus and such, I promise I'll be a better
person; I might even go to church!" The petition of the Lord's
Prayer "Thy will be done" is as far from their thoughts as the
earth is from the moon.

What unimaginable gall! What arrogance that we who are dust
and ashes should think God's happiness depends on our believing
in him. What folly that sinful man should approach God and
make demands of him, as though man were the almighty and God
some dim-witted servant, easily intimidated and easily manipu-
lated to fallen man's purposes. Here Dame Reason really shows
her weakness and fallen man the depth of his corruption that he
could hold to such utter nonsense!

More subtle, but likewise damaging, are errors that may
ensnare even well-intentioned Christians: "I really did pray as a
Christian should. But no help came. I don't understand it. Does
God really hear and answer?" When troubled by such thoughts, the
devil or a heretic may suggest one of two false solutions to the
problem. The doubter may be driven to despair by this counsel:
"You just didn't believe enough or pray hard enough; if you had,
then you would have gotten what you asked for." That the Bible
nowhere suggests that God's answers depend on the depth of our
faith or the fervor of our prayers is not mentioned. To be sure,
many times Jesus says, "Your faith has saved you." But that is a
faith which he himself provided in his Word, a faith not weighed by
him or measured by some divine or human scale. It is the simple
trust that called to him in time of need; and from the same grace
that gave the faith, God gave what the one praying asked for.

Still others seem to think that if they just get enough people
praying for the same thing in a prayer chain and they all "pray

really hard," then God will give what they are praying for. To be sure, the Bible encourages us to pray for one another. We do that both privately and together in the intercessory prayers offered in church. But the notion that God is counting the number of prayers and weighing their intensity before he decides to answer is very much a mistaken notion. The one who cries out alone in the dark of the night and in the solitude of his closet should not fear that his prayer is of less importance to God than the common or public prayer of the many. Nor should the many imagine that their joint prayer weighs more than that of the individual. It's really a matter of both/and, not of either/or; that is, the private prayer of the individual and the public prayer of many are both heard by God. When offered trusting in his mercy and in the merit of Christ, the one is as good as the other; neither kind of prayer should be discouraged.

Another false solution for the problem of prayers that *seem* to go unanswered goes something like this: "Prayer really is chiefly for our psychological benefit; we pray, and then we feel better because we have unloaded our troubles on God; that should be a good enough reason for praying, but don't expect much more to come from it." Such a solution casts aside everything that God promises when he teaches us about prayer in his Word. Never does he suggest that we should just pray so that we feel better or that ultimately he has no intention of dealing with our prayers, taking them into account, or answering them.

Finally, there is the ever-popular error by which well-intentioned but deluded Christians make prayer a sort of second bible. "I pray, and God speaks to me in my prayers and tells me what I should do; I ask him if I should marry this person/get a divorce/take this job/buy this house; then I listen for his answer as I pray." The sad truth of the matter is that prayer as a second bible always ends up pushing the first and only Bible to the side. Where people imagine that God is whispering in their ears, they soon see little need of listening to him speak where alone he has promised to speak: in the Word, in the sacraments. God nowhere promises to speak to us in our prayers. We are the ones who speak in our prayers; that's what prayer is by definition: talking to God.

So, we pray for wisdom, and he answers us and gives it in the Word. We pray for direction about marriage and listen to what his Word says about marriage; that's where he answers such a prayer. To be sure, he may answer our prayer even as we are praying it—but not apart from his Word. We may, for example, pray for a cure for our despair; as we pray, he may call to our minds passages like 1 John 1:7: "The blood of Jesus, his Son, purifies us from all sin." But even then, it is not the prayer as such that is God speaking but his Word. So we ask for wisdom in deciding matters of vocation and the stewardship of our time, talents, and treasure. It is not in the prayer itself that God answers but in what his Word says about time, talents, and treasure.[1]

As already noted, too often those who imagine that God answers prayers by blowing in their ears or whispering (apart from his Word) into their inmost beings end up pushing aside the Word and sacraments. It is so much easier to wait for an inner voice and call it God's voice than to search the Scriptures and ask God to bless our search as we apply passages to our particular situations in life. Besides, inner voices are often much more agreeable to our fallen nature than God's Word is. Our fallen nature might not really want to know what God actually says in his Word. The attitude of those who want God to speak to them directly and apart from the Word is not unlike the attitude of the Pharisees that Jesus rebuked in Matthew 12:38-40. They too wanted signs from Jesus, outward and visible and measurable demonstrations of his deity. And they wanted it on their own terms, for their own purposes, according to their own wishes. But what did Jesus say in answer? He called them a "wicked and adulterous generation" and then pointed them to the Word, specifically to the promise of his own resurrection.

But didn't God speak directly to Abraham, Isaac, Jacob, Moses, Isaiah, and so many others in Bible times? Yes, he did. But we need to remember that the Bible, that book in which God promises to speak to all of us, had not yet been completed at that time. We need to remember as well that the times when God spoke even to these great saints of old were rare, not everyday occurrences. And God did not speak to everyone that way or ever promise to speak to anyone that way.

---

[1] We will consider this point further in the next chapter.

David is a good case in point: God spoke to him directly in the inspiration of the many psalms that he wrote. But otherwise, in the conduct of his life both before and after he became king, God did not speak to him directly, as far as we know. What we do know is that God spoke to him through the prophets Samuel and Nathan. That very fact, that God did not speak directly to David but through his prophets, David's pastors, is what makes it so remarkable that God did speak directly to David's son Solomon. But again, that was a rare occurrence indeed.

Now that we have God's Word in the Bible, we have a sure and certain, a constant and infallible message from God to us. There is no need to look for him where he has not promised to be but every reason to bend heart and ear to where he has promised to be, to his written Word. Those not satisfied with that Word, who look for him elsewhere, lean on broken reeds which provide only the illusion of support. They end up listening not to God but to their own imaginations and relying on their own will rather than on his revealed Word.

When considering the matter of prayer, one can scarcely help but call to mind this old German proverb: *Wo Gott eine Kirche baut, baut der Teufel eine Kapelle daneben!* ("Where God builds a church, the devil builds a chapel next to it!") Many and frequent are the attacks that the devil and Dame Reason make on the doctrine of prayer and the Christian's practice of prayer! What threads tie together all the previously mentioned temptations and delusions about prayer, be they coarse or subtle?

1. They all contradict the Scriptures.
2. They all detract from the glory of Christ.
3. They all encourage the impenitent to remain as he is while robbing the penitent of the assured consolations of God's promises in the gospel.

Those are the three characteristics of all false doctrine and certainly of the many false doctrines that cloud the beauty of God's promises concerning prayer. But we want to bring our every thought into subjection to the Word of Christ. Instructed by the Word of God, we can put Dame Reason back behind the mop pail and use her in the role assigned to her. In his Word, God has attached rich and beautiful promises to his command that we should pray. And those promises make it very clear indeed that prayer matters. God's Word makes it clear that prayer is not just a fruitless babbling which perhaps makes us feel better and which ultimately doesn't really accomplish anything.

We will consider first God's commands to pray and his promises to hear and bless our prayers. And then we will look at some of the many striking examples in the Bible of times when prayer made a difference.

Commands and promises

All of the saints of the Old Testament and the New, all of the great church fathers too, were men of prayer. Luther commented more than once that sometimes he was so busy with so many problems that he had to spend hours in prayer just to get through the day. These believers of old did not pray simply because God held a stick over their heads and demanded that they pray. Nor were they merely looking for some psychological relief. Far less were they sitting around all day waiting for God to blow some mystic answers into their ears. Oh no, never that!

They prayed because God not only commands it but as well adds rich promises to hear and answer our prayers. He puts the command and the promise so simply and yet so richly, for example, in Psalm 50:15: "Call upon me in the day of trouble; I will deliver you, and you will honor me." The command and the promise put the child of God in a never-ending circle of listening to God in his Word—speaking to God in prayer—awaiting God's rescue—giving God honor—and then starting the circle all over again with listening to him in his Word.

Read the whole of the psalm. It is a beautiful blending of God's providence and the promises he attaches to prayer. It is a fulsome answer to many of the obstacles to genuine prayer discussed earlier. The command assumes that we have troubles in this life and needs that we cannot meet by ourselves. The command has behind it the love of God that delights in speaking to us in his Word and answering our prayers in every time of need. The command has the promise of an answer that will move us to wonder, to awe and adoration, as we go back to listening yet again to God in his Word.

Or think of Jesus' own and oft-repeated exhortations to us that ours should be a life of prayer. So often the exhortation has attached to it the most abundant promises of God's gracious and speedy answers of help and rescue. In Luke 11, Jesus draws the comparison between God and a friend inconvenienced by a request for help in the middle of the night. The friend will help because of the very boldness of an inconvenient request. Will God be less provident in answer to the cries of his friends? Then he adds the comparison of God to a good father who gives his children good things and not evil, making this striking point: "If you then, though you are evil, know how to give good gifts to your children, how much more will your Father in heaven give the Holy Spirit to those who ask him!" (Luke 11:13).

Note Jesus' assumption here: He assumes that we understand that our greatest need is for the gifts which the Holy Spirit gives, that is, for forgiveness and faith in time of temptation, need, and struggle. And where does the Holy Spirit give those gifts? Where else but in the Word and the sacraments! At the same time we may conclude this from all that the Bible says about prayer: Jesus is making an argument known as an argument from the greater to the lesser; that is, if the Father is eager to grant the greatest gifts, those the Spirit gives in Word and sacraments, why should we doubt that he will give us all the other gifts that we need for this body and life?

In Luke 18:1-8 Jesus tells the story of the unjust judge who finally gives justice to a widow just to get rid of her. And then, again in such a striking way, Jesus makes his point about God and our prayers: "Will not God bring about justice for his chosen ones, who cry out to him day and night? Will he keep putting them off? I tell you, he will see that they get justice, and quickly" (18:7,8). But notice that little phrase "who cry out to him day and night." Now we are getting to it! That little phrase neatly sums up what we find in almost everything that the Bible has to say about prayer: *We are always in need, needs that only God can satisfy, needs that he promises to satisfy in answer to our prayers!*

Perhaps that point is made in the most stunning way in what Jesus says about prayer in his discourse just before his Passion. He is about to suffer and die, and he has promised the disciples that they too will suffer persecution and that those who kill them will think that they are doing God a favor! In that context, he says: "I tell you the truth, my Father will give you whatever you ask in my name. Until now you have not asked for anything in my name. Ask and you will receive, and your joy will be complete" (John 16:23,24).

The point could not be more striking: Prayer is not some magic bullet by which we instruct God to make sure that our lives are trouble free, without pain, without temptation, without suffering. What Jesus says about prayer assumes that in our lives we will have troubles aplenty, temptation on every hand, suffering this today and that tomorrow. What Jesus says about prayer makes it very clear that our trust in the providence of God will always be put to the test by what we experience in our bodily and in our spiritual/religious lives from day-to-day.

The disciples in all of the promised suffering should constantly hear his Word and should without ceasing trust that in good days and in bad, in life and in death, they are safe and secure in his hands. That's how, as Jesus promised, their joy will be complete. Whatever they experience, the experience will not be a proof that God has abandoned them. Rather, in everything they will have the assurance of his Word, yes, of his promised providence, that they are safe and secure. And trusting in his promised providence, they should pray for him to fulfill the promise. Do you see how it works? *The providence of God and the promises he attaches to prayer are like two hands folded together; they are different but always together.*

Paul showed that he got the point. In Acts 14, as his first missionary journey was coming to an end, Paul encouraged the converts to hold fast to the faith. Why? Because then they would have a soft life? Hardly! He gave the encouragement to them after they had seen Paul kicked out of their cities and almost killed by those who hated the gospel and wanted to prevent its proclamation. In the face of all that, Paul and Barnabas assured their members that "we must go through many hardships to enter the kingdom of God" (14:22).

That believers of every age also get that point is demonstrated in the ancient prayer that we sing at Matins, the *Te Deum Laudamus.* Note this line in the prayer: "The noble army of martyrs praise you!" Not: "The noble army of martyrs demand an explana-

tion for unanswered prayers seeking rescue from martyrdom."
That line in the *Te Deum* no doubt traces its origins to the question and then the song of the martyrs and all the saints in heaven
recorded in Revelation 6:9-11 and 7:9-17.

The Lord's Prayer, that most perfect and beautiful of all
prayers, makes exactly the same point. Why do we need to beg
God that his name be hallowed, his kingdom come, and his will be
done? Because on every side, in the world and in the church, in
my life and my flesh, God's name is always under attack. Judged
by outward appearance, it always seems that God's name, his
revelation of himself in his Word, is being thrown aside and
under the bus in favor of unbelief, doubt, and indifference. It
seems that his kingdom, that is, his rule in our hearts and lives
by his Word, is always on the brink of being overtaken by the rule
of the devil, the world, and our own sinful flesh. It always
appears as though the will of evil men and of the evil that lurks
within the shrine of my own heart and soul is about to win the
total victory. So day and night we cry, "Hallowed be thy name,
thy kingdom come, thy will be done!"

Then in recognition of the fact that the devil threatens to rob
us of even a crust of bread and to destroy all order in family, in
church, and in state, we beg without ceasing: "Give us this day
our daily bread." It is sad that so often we let these petitions fall
mindlessly from our lips. That we are not starving to death, that
we still believe the gospel, that the Word and sacraments are
still in our midst, all of that is proof that God answers prayer.
Without his answer to this, his own prayer, we would have perished long ago. That he answers the prayer so richly, even when
we mindlessly pray it, even when we have forgotten to pray it, is
yet further testimony to the richness of his grace—yes, and of
his providence.

Then, wonder of all wonders, after God has answered those
first four petitions, we still have to pray *"Forgive us!"* God in his
providence, in answer to our prayers, and in spite of our past
sins, preserves his Word among us; thus, he hallows his name
and preserves his kingdom. Thereby he accomplishes richly his
good and gracious will among us. In answer to our prayers and in
spite of our past ingratitude, he also gives daily bread and a measure of order in family, church, and state. Since he has answered

those four petitions so richly, how can it be that we still sin and
that we still, therefore, need to pray this petition? All of the
excuses we might have for sin are gone! Will we sin through doctrinal error or perversion? Not where God's Word is preserved by
him in its truth and purity and we cherish that gift of his Word
and grace. Will we sin by greed or envy or worry about tomorrow
and the day after? How silly, no, how perverse that would be. We
know that our heavenly Father answers the prayer Jesus taught
us to pray and has rescued us from war and famine, from terror
by day and calamity by night. We need not fear the devil or his
hosts. We need not worry about tomorrow. We have no reason to
complain about anything in the present or dread anything in the
future. But still, after God has done all of that, we still cry day
and night: "Forgive us; we have not treasured your gift of the
gospel nor your preservation of it in our midst. Forgive us; we
have neither appreciated your abundant gift of daily bread, of
peace in our land, of order in your church; nor have we permitted
your gift of these treasures to so capture our minds that we trust
you for them; instead, we worry and fret as though you have
never given us anything; instead, we grab and gripe as though we
were lords and you, but our bond servant!"

That petition and its place in the Lord's Prayer is a most hum-
bling recognition of the depth of our need. In spite of all he does
in his Word, in his Sacraments, out of his providence, and in
answer to our prayers, there will never be a moment in our lives
when that cry for forgiveness is out of place. But even more than
an acknowledgment of our constant need, it is an evidence of his
far greater grace. Jesus knew when he gave that petition that
perfection in us would always be a distant and an illusive goal
which we would reach only in heaven. Nevertheless, he bids us to
pray *"Forgive us!"* And by inviting us to pray such a petition, he
promises that he will hear, that he will answer, and that, yes, he
will still forgive! And again, he promises those things even after
he has taken away any possible excuse in us for sin by answering
the first four petitions!

Lest we forget that our whole lives, each hour and every
moment, depend on him and his grace, he further bids us to pray
"Lead us not into temptation, but deliver us from evil!" He knows
us so well and, nevertheless, loves and cares for us. The simple

fact of the matter is that without his answer to our prayer, we would run into one ruinous temptation after another and finally fall totally into the clutches of the devil. And so we cry in expectation of his gracious answer: "Put a wall around me so that I am not tempted beyond all possibility of rescue; then, deliver me from the evil one and his snares, snares that I am too weak and foolish to escape on my own; and finally, in the hour of death, rescue me from every peril and all evil and take me to yourself in heaven."

In recognition of the fact that what we ask for in his prayer is high and holy and utterly beyond our reach, we close it in worship and adoration: "For thine is the kingdom and the power and the glory forever!" We will leave it to others to argue about the canonicity of that line. The truth it expresses is, however the argument comes out, fitting and sublime: Only God is big enough, mighty enough, and gracious enough to satisfy these needs of ours that surround us our whole life long. And as we sigh "Amen," we call to mind again the promise implied in the fact that Jesus himself has taught us so to pray: If God were not willing, even eager, to answer this prayer, Jesus would not have told us to pray it; God does not joke with us in his Word or play mind games with us.

St. Paul sums up the matter so succinctly when he tells us, "Be joyful always; pray continually; give thanks in all circumstances, for this is God's will for you in Christ Jesus" (1 Thessalonians 5:16-18). Why should we always be joyful? Because God in his providence has promised to rule over all things for our eternal good. Why should we always be joyful? Because God has commanded us to pray always in every circumstance, need, and condition of life and has promised to hear and answer us. See! It is God's will. See! It is God's will in Christ Jesus, who proved his love on the cross and assured us of his eagerness to answer prayer by himself teaching us to pray.

Notice that this passage together with all of the other passages in God's Word which teach us about prayer see no contradiction or conflict between God's providence and the command to pray. Again, they are like two hands folded together—each distinct, but always together.

And so, we pray. We pray for spiritual blessings, for true repentance, for the forgiveness of sins, for a more confident faith, for help in resisting temptation. To these prayers God always says an unconditional *"Yes!"* He does it in the gospel in general as we hear that gospel applied in the absolution pronounced each week in the liturgy. He does it as we ponder the life and death of Christ for us in our private devotions. He does it as we call to mind his promises to us in our baptisms: the promises to adopt us as his children, to forgive all our sins, and to keep us members of his own family. He does it in the Sacrament of the Altar as he feeds us with himself to assure us again and again of our forgiveness and of his real and substantial presence in our bodies, in our lives. He does it as he in Word and sacraments heaps upon us his love and grace to give us the incentive of his love to grow in love and devotion to him and to his Word. In short, let those who want spiritual blessings draw ever closer to him as he speaks those blessings to us in his Word and sacraments. For there and there alone he has promised to give such blessings, and that in richest measure.

And so, we pray. In every time of need, we call to him for help. In sickness, we ask for health. In poverty or its threat, we beg him for relief. In worry about the future, we cry to him to save us from despair and needless depression. In loneliness, when we are sure that no one understands or cares, we ask him to send an angel of compassion in the person of someone near to us. Or we ask that he fill us with the assurance that his companionship and that of the holy angels is sufficient until such a time as he may be pleased to provide us with someone who will help us carry our load. When we feel useless, we ask him to show us opportunities to serve him by serving those around us. In days of toil that exhaust us but seem to afford little reward, we ask that he give us contentment in the knowledge that in our work we are really serving him. In days of helplessness when we have to rely on others to help and serve us, we pray for gratitude to replace grumpiness, for patience to endure without complaint.

All these and so many other prayers he answers by giving us what serves our true and best interests. Maybe he lets us wait a while for his answer, but that is also an answer: "Not just yet; learn patience; learn to trust me; learn to marvel at my generosity when I do give you your heart's desire!" Maybe his answer to a specific request will be this: "I have something better in mind for you; look for it! No prayer comes to me in vain, and no cry from my dear child goes unheard or unanswered." Yes, and who cannot recount times when God gave what we asked for, gave even more than what we asked for or could have imagined possible.

The prayers, of course, that ask for a life of ease and a soul free of every temptation, a successful outcome to our greed, or an escape from the consequences of our willful sins he answers like this: "That is never what I promised you; if I gave it, you would worship ease; and without temptations you would become a self-righteous Pharisee. If I gave you success in your favorite sins, you would wallow in them and perish eternally. So, see, I have something better for you: enough good things so that you do not despair and enough troubles and temptations so that you do not forget me and my Word. Indeed, the greater the blessings that you consider good, the greater too shall be the troubles and the temptations, so in all things you may remember my grace that matches your weakness, my forgiveness that covers your sin, my help that humbles the proud and raises up the fallen." Jesus said it all when he told us not to worry: "Seek first his kingdom and his righteousness, and all these things will be given to you as well" (Matthew 6:33). And St. Paul understood it too when he prayed for relief from his thorn in the flesh and received something better: Grace to endure, and with that grace the reminder for himself and for those he served that everything comes from God as a gift of grace (2 Corinthians 12:7-10).

And so, we pray. We pray not just for our own spiritual and temporal needs. We pray as well for others. It is as impossible to overstate the value of these prayers, as it is to overstate the value of the other prayers we have considered.

Jesus himself urges us to pray for the church. He looked out over the crowds of his day and the multitudes in our day; with a heart overflowing with the compassion that soon would take him to the cross, he told his disciples and he tells us: "The harvest is plentiful but the workers are few. Ask the Lord of the harvest, therefore, to send out workers into his harvest field" (Matthew 9:37,38). He himself prayed for the church, for its growth, for its steadfastness, and for its purity in doctrine. Think of it: He was praying *for us,* only hours before his death, and prays for us still (John 17:6-26). He even prayed for individuals; for example, he prayed for Peter, who was contradicting him at that very moment and was about to deny him (Luke 22:31,32).

Mindful of the value of others' prayers, St. Paul often asked that his members pray for him and for the work he was doing in preaching the gospel. In 2 Thessalonians 3, for example, he urges the Thessalonians: "Pray for us that the message of the Lord may spread rapidly and be honored, just as it was with you. And pray that we may be delivered from wicked and evil men, for not everyone has faith" (3:1,2).

Are these not remarkable prayers, both those of the apostle and of Jesus himself? They bear witness to the value and the power promised to prayer, even prayer for the church, which is always God's great concern. Again we have to note it: There is in the mind of God no contradiction between his providence and prayer. In prayer we trust the promise and count on God's providence. Dame Reason will just have to scratch her head in wonder while the Christian smiles and abandons himself to what God promises, to what God says.

But there is still more. The Bible encourages us to believe that our prayers even make a difference in the course and direction of history. On one occasion Jesus encouraged his disciples to pray that the destruction of Judea and Jerusalem would not come during the winter or on the Sabbath, lest the suffering of those fleeing be even greater than it would be as the result of the destruction itself (Matthew 24:19-21). Paul urges us to pray for the government and its officials (1 Timothy 2:1-4). He knew full well that the rulers of his day were godless tyrants, ripe for God's judgment. But he urged prayer that God's hand of judgment on them may be delayed and held back for a time. Peace and order in society was useful to God's people in their daily lives, useful especially for the easier carrying of the gospel throughout the vast Roman Empire. And those prayers were effective! The Roman Empire lasted for almost four hundred years after the time of Paul, by which time the gospel had been preached in almost every corner of that vast empire. By that time the wickedness of that empire had filled up the cup of sin to overflowing. And so the ailing, corrupt, violence-plagued empire perished.

We too pray for the state, for rulers whose lives or whose agendas may flatly contradict the clear Word of God. To this day, in spite of the growing godlessness of the world, God hears the prayers of his people. Peace, sometimes a troubled peace, prevails where the gospel can still be preached. In sum, it is for the sake of the church and for those who pray that God restrains his judging hand and holds back his wrath for a time.

What an astonishing thing! Does the immovable, unchangeable God permit himself to be moved by the cries of simple mortals, as Jesus implied when he told the disciples to pray that the destruction of Jerusalem not happen in winter or on the Sabbath? Does he who rules the great moments of history according to his pleasure allow himself to be turned in answer to our cries for peace and order when the nation has turned its back on him and his Word? Oh yes! The whole of the book of Jonah says so. The promise to turn aside his wrath even from Sodom and Gomorrah under set conditions and at the prayer of Abraham says so (Genesis 19). And our own experience to this very day argues the same. Who then will say that prayer is just a psychological crutch that accomplishes nothing? The Bible and all of history testify to the contrary. On your knees, O Christian! God waits for your prayer and is eager to answer it!

And so, we pray. We pray for all sorts and conditions of men. We pray for help in our own need. We pray for the church and for the state. We pray for friends and family. We pray, trusting in the promise of God to hear and answer. We pray, trusting God to so order affairs in things both great and small in his providence and in answer to our prayers.

As an interesting side note, it is worth observing that often God answers our prayers by using us to accomplish that for which we pray. We pray, for example, for good order in the state and in society. Then God moves us to obey the laws of the land; that serves the peace and order of society in our small corner of the world. We pray for the success of the gospel as it is proclaimed in our midst and throughout the world. Then we faithfully share it in our own homes, in our parish lives, in society in general as the Lord himself gives us opportunities to do so. And we support as well the work of our congregations and our churches as collectively we preach and teach his Word when and where he gives us such additional opportunities. Clearly the one who prays for the success of the gospel but then hides it under a bushel basket, never defends or tries to share it, or never supports its proclamation through the work of the church is not serious with his prayer. Or we pray for those around us in need. Then God gives us the means and the opportunity to help those in need. Is it not a good day when at its end we can say or see that God has used us as part of his answer to our prayers?

It is clear that God has over centuries answered the prayers of his people for the well-being of the church. It is clear that he has answered the prayers of his people for the well-being of the state so that we may live peaceful lives and the church may with less difficulty proclaim the gospel. When the church has been troubled and the state afflicted, was it because Christians failed to pray? Could it be that in times of trouble in church and state, God shows his providence by reminding us of our need for him and of the usefulness of being more on our knees? Is it not a blessing in the end when we learn that lesson, though painful it may be, and come anew to find in him our all in all, our only real help in time of need?

And could not the same point be made with reference to our own private lives? When we prosper and things go well, it is evidence of God's providence and his answers to our prayers. When we are in trouble and afraid, could it at least some of the time be the result of ingratitude for his earlier answers to our prayers when we were in trouble or in need? Could it be because we came to think that we were entitled to his providential answers to those earlier supplications? Could it be that he is teaching us again, and that in his providence, that all our help is in him alone?

Further encouragement to a life of prayer
from the miracles of Jesus

In the gospels many of the miracles of Jesus provide a wealth of encouragement and instruction about prayer. To be sure, the miracles of our Lord in the gospels have a purpose beyond giving answer to prayer; Jesus performed them as demonstrations of his compassion and especially also to prove that he is indeed the Son of God, the promised Messiah. But there are a few things to be learned from them besides that. Consider for example Luke 8. There we hear of a number of Jesus' miracles, each with its special point. Much could be said about each of them. We will content ourselves with the following:

1. Jesus calmed the storm (verses 22-25). The disciples prayed and knew in their prayer that without Jesus' rescue they would perish. But Jesus rebuked them for their lack of faith, for a prayer that was offered more in fear than in trust, more in despair than in confidence. It's comforting to know that he does not cast off our prayers when, through lack of attention to his Word, we too sometimes cry out in weakness, fear, and doubt. He looks instead on his own providence, not on the depth of our faith, as the cause of his rescue. He answers the prayer and wants thereby to pull us back again to trust in his Word and thereby to heal the weakness that he rebukes.

2. Jesus healed the demon possessed (verses 26-39). There are so many interesting things in this account. Here Jesus first rescued a man possessed, and that out of his providence alone, without any prayer or possibility of a prayer from the man possessed. But after the miracle of expelling the demons, the man did pray. When Jesus was about to leave, he asked that he may go with Jesus. Jesus' answer to the man's prayer was most interesting. In essence it was this: "No, I have something better in mind for you; stay where you are, and share the good news of what *God* has done for you." That was an especially interesting answer to the man's prayer; Jesus answered thus in the context of another prayer, the prayer of those who witnessed the miracle in the first place. They had asked Jesus to go away! What grace, what astonishing grace, there was in Jesus' answers both to the request of the multitude and the prayer of the man healed! He went away, as the crowd had asked, instead of striking them down for their pernicious unbelief. But he left behind an apostle to the obstinate: this man who had been possessed body and soul by the devil and now was free. This man went about and told everyone, whether they would hear or not, of what *Jesus* had done for him—he got the point that Jesus is God and the additional point that Jesus' will was better than his own. So, Jesus rescues at times without our prayer, rescues even those in the clutches of the devil so that they will hear his Word. His answer to the prayer of the man formerly demon possessed might well be kept in mind by the pastor who prays for a different call, the

spouse who prays for a different mate, and any who complain about their station in life. "Stay where you are, and tell what great things God has done for you."

3. Jesus healed the woman with the issue of blood (verses 43-48). Notice her humility, her lowliness. Notice Jesus' superabundant love and grace. He raised her up and gave her far more than she asked for. All she wanted was a physical healing. But he called her *"daughter"* and bid her to think of herself not as the outcast her sickness had made her but as a dear child of God, the object of his tender affection. She had counted herself unworthy to pray to him openly. He healed her and then said, "Your faith has healed [better translation: helped, saved] you" (8:48). How so? Her faith, after all, was his gift; on the basis of what she had heard about Jesus, she trusted in both his power and his kindness. The Word created faith; however, Jesus here as so often elsewhere praised faith! In short, that is Jesus' way: We hear his Word, he gives faith to believe, and then he praises the act of believing for which he alone deserves the credit. No less, in his providence and in answer to our prayers he gives health and time and wealth and then praises us on the Last Day when we use them aright (Luke 19:11-19; Matthew 25:34-40). And then to seal and crown the whole matter for this woman, he bid her to go in peace, tormented no more by her sickness or by her overwhelming sense of unworthiness: She had been made worthy by the touch of the Savior! Let all take note who think themselves too lowly or unworthy to pray. Let them touch the hem of his garment and see in his Word and in his answer how he loves best the lowliest and the most unworthy! See how it is?

4. Jesus raised Jairus' daughter (verses 49-56). He did that in answer to Jairus' pleading, without which, of course, the miracle would not have taken place. But notice again how Jesus gave more than was asked of him. After he had raised her from the dead, he told her parents to give her something to eat. Couldn't they have figured that out by themselves and done it without Jesus telling them to do it? Of course. But the point is that Jesus takes note of our needs down to the smallest, even the most self-evident detail. What a beautiful encouragement for us in our prayers! He hears what we ask for and is eager to provide what we didn't think to ask for.

Of course it is true that Jesus has not promised to raise the dead at our prayers. Nor has he promised that he would give us miraculous healing for all our sicknesses. Normally he answers our prayers through very ordinary means. Our sickness he heals through physicians and medicines. Or else, he in his good time, the time best for us, takes us to himself in heaven. Nevertheless, it cannot be denied that he does at times still heal and help with what to our eyes may seem very much like miracles. The sick patient thought incurable and at the point of death lives for ten more years. The desolate and the lonely cry in despair, beyond all hope of help. Then, unnoticed by any but the one who prayed, help comes, help better than that hoped for. It may well be that each Christian, at least in his own heart, could write a diary of times that God rescued when rescue seemed impossible. It may be that each Christian, at least on his knees in prayer, should recount times when God gave more than what was asked for.

Would things have turned out differently had our prayers not come before the throne of the Almighty? That's what St. James implies when he speaks of blessings that people do not receive. He says: "You do not have, because you do not ask God. When you ask, you do not receive, because you ask with wrong motives, that you may spend what you get on your pleasures" (James 4:2,3). Then (5:13-15) he urges us to pray for God's help in every need, for things spiritual and for things temporal; he tells us to trust in the providence of God to answer in accordance with his good and gracious will (cf. 1:5-7). Lest we think that such prayers are really of no effect, he points to the example of the prophet Elijah. Elijah's prayers prevented rain for three years and then brought it again. It's a remarkable example, but one that James uses for our encouragement nonetheless.

Finally, let those who still doubt the value of prayer or who merely mumble prayers in a mindless mechanical repetition because "we're supposed to pray" make a pilgrimage. Go to the Garden of Gethsemane, and learn there about prayer! There we see with what fervor, with what inexpressible ardor, Jesus teaches us about prayer by his own example. Just before entering the garden, Jesus tells us (Luke 22:31,32) that he had prayed for Peter, who was about to deny him. He had prayed that Peter would be converted and not perish. He had prayed that Peter, who even at that moment was contradicting his God and Savior, would finally get it right and then strengthen his fellow disciples. What love! What grace! What a consolation for us too, that Jesus prays for us even when we have abandoned the narrow middle road and are falling into a ditch. He prays and, as with his prayer for Peter, he is heard so that we do not perish. He prays so that we too have our times when we "get it right" and can strengthen our brothers and sisters. Yes, and his prayer for us continues to this day. In heaven he pleads for us. He serves as our defense attorney and holds before God's justice the price that he has paid for our forgiveness (1 John 2:1,2). How can anyone hear of such a thing and then still think that prayer is a waste of time or in vain?

But back to Gethsemane. Watch and see with wonder and in awe: The most holy Son of God, "God from God, Light from Light, true God from true God," fell on his face. He cried. He begged. He pleaded with sweat falling from his sacred face as great drops of blood. He, in whom all the fullness of the Godhead dwells bodily (Colossians 2:9), was praying. Seeing all the agony of that night and of the next day that he would experience in body and soul, in the utter lowliness of his human nature, he prayed that the cup of hellish suffering may pass from him.

What answer did he receive? It was not possible for our salvation to be accomplished unless he drank the cup of suffering to the very bottom of the cup. And so, his ultimate prayer, the prayer "Your will be done!" was answered at once. God's will would be done, and that for us. And that will was also now Jesus' own will. He had to drink the cup, drink it in all its bitterness and woe, drink it until in his inmost being he had felt all the sting and poison of the whole world's sin. He had to drink it until his sacred person had endured the unendurable—the horror, the curse of being forsaken by God! He had to drink it until he had tasted sin's ultimate consequence of separation from life in death and the grave. But even then his prayer that the cup may pass from him did not go unanswered. The cup did pass from him three days later when he rose in triumph from the grave for us and for our salvation, so that now and forever in heaven he still prays for us (Hebrews 5:1-10)!

In Gethsemane he urged his disciples to pray. Because they had not been paying attention either to what Jesus had said earlier or to his prayers, they were unaware of the peril that soon would threaten their own souls. So Jesus urged them to pray (Luke 22:40), lest they fall into the temptations soon to come. How differently things would have turned out for them had they listened to his Word earlier. How differently things still could have turned out for them had they listened to Jesus in Gethsemane and prayed with heart and soul for rescue in the hour of temptation. They would have conquered over the despair of Good Friday, the desolation of Holy Saturday, even the doubt of most of Easter Sunday. But they didn't listen to the Word. They didn't pray either. And so they afflicted themselves deeply, and as needlessly as deeply.

Verbum sapiens satis est! ("A word to the wise is enough!") Those who will learn nothing of the importance, the value, the effectiveness of prayer from a pilgrimage to Gethsemane will never learn it. Those who make the pilgrimage often will not have to be taught much more about prayer than they can learn in that holy place, that place of prayer, stained with the blood-filled sweat of the Savior!

To conclude, it is a wondrous and mysterious thing indeed how God's providence and his promises to answer our prayers fit together. Could it be that already in eternity God's providence has taken into account the prayers that we will offer in time? Perhaps that's how it works. But the mind and soul, the heart and the faith of the Christian need not break themselves in trying to unravel the mystery. God never asks us to do that. As so often, he tells us *the what* of a mystery but not *the how*; the how he often reserves to himself.

So the Christian with humble heart and mind bends rejoicing and bows with a smile before the always greater mind of his Maker and Redeemer. In his simplicity he may ask this question: How do these things fit together? But when God's Word is silent, then the Christian accepts the answer implicit in God's silence: "O child of God, that's my problem, not yours; your concern is to hear my Word and trust it." And so we do. He tells us that in his providence, he rules all things for our good. He promises at the same time to hear our prayers and to answer them. We rejoice on both sides of the narrow middle road. We delight to rest in the sunshine and the shade of his providence. We rejoice as we enjoy the fruit of his promise to hear our prayers and answer them. We see his grace in abundance on both sides of the narrow middle road. But we will not give up any of the blessings from either side by trying to put the two sides together. Instead, we will trust in his always good and gracious rule while we pray without ceasing.

That's the narrow middle road between what God says about his providence and what he says about prayer. Thank God for it![2]

---

[2] For an excellent example of the many things that Luther has to say about prayer, we refer the reader especially to Luther's comments on the Lord's Prayer in his Large Catechism. There, in a very succinct and engaging way, Luther disposes of so many of the reasons people have for not praying, while encouraging us with God's rich promises to hear and answer our prayers. Additionally, we refer the reader to the Appendix for our translation of some especially appropriate remarks of C. F. W. Walther from a sermon that he wrote for Rogate Sunday.

5

A Pause Beside a Pool

We need to take a slight detour before we continue along the narrow middle road. It's a detour to look into a pool beside the road. The pool is at first glance not at all clear but cloudy. It is a pool with questions swirling around in it, questions provoked by the last stretch of the narrow middle road. It's not so much the questions that make the pool murky; rather, it is the many and popular wrong answers to the questions that make it so cloudy and confused. Among the questions are these:

- If God works all things for our good in his kind providence, does that mean that everything which happens in our lives is preordained or predestined?

- Is it right to say that since God is almighty as he exercises his providence, nothing happens except what God wills?

- If everything that God does is for the best, does that mean that nothing could have happened in history or in our lives differently than it did?

Even Dame Reason hides out when these questions come up. She too finds the pool made murky by a host of answers that conform no better to reason than they do to the Word of God. And so, she is inclined to leave the scene and let people mutter mindless clichés in answer to the questions. We hear such answers often these days. A man-caused disaster occurs; a drunk driver has an "accident" and kills the innocent passengers of the other car while he walks away without a scratch; the wicked rob and cheat the innocent; the vile slay the hapless bystanders and escape punishment. But someone will say, "Well, it must have been the will of God; otherwise, it couldn't have happened."

Such an answer betrays an unwillingness to examine either the Bible or reason. If everything that happens happens because God willed it, then sin too must be the fruit of God's will. Sin happens. That it could be the result of God's will is on the face of it utter nonsense. Indeed, it is a monstrous notion that recalls the ancient heresy of the Manicheans. They taught that there are two principles at war in the universe, one good and one evil. To the Manicheans, these two principles often appeared to be of equal strength, sometimes one gaining the upper hand and sometimes the other. In effect, Manichean thinking makes God and the devil equals.[1]

Others try to clear the murkiness from the pool by saying instead, "Well, then, everything that happens, except sin, is the will of God; otherwise, it couldn't have happened." That answer is likewise nonsense on the face of it. There is nothing in this life, at least nothing that man wills or does, that is not stained or affected somehow by sin. Since that is the case, to say that only things untouched by sin are the result of God's will is to say that nothing is the result of God's will except perhaps the weather.

How then shall we clear away the cloud in the pool? How else but to search the Scriptures to see what God has to say about his

---

[1] Anyone interested in pursuing the battle against the Manicheans will want to reference the works of St. Augustine of Hippo, especially his *Answer to Faustus, a Manichean* written around the year 400; St. Augustine knows whereof he speaks in this battle, since he himself had at one time been associated with the Manicheans. This particular work is invaluable as well for its examination of early Christian hermeneutics.

will and the will of man? How else but to see how God relates the sublime truth of his providential will to the reality of the sin in man that is by definition a contradiction, a defiance of God's will?

The will of God

Moses sings in Psalm 90: "Before the mountains were born or you brought forth the earth and the world, from everlasting to everlasting you are God. For a thousand years in your sight are like a day that has just gone by, or like a watch in the night" (verses 2,4). God lives in eternity. Before anything happens, he already knows its end. When a thousand years have passed by, nothing has been added or taken away from his might or his knowledge.

St. Paul sings his great hymn of praise to the all-wise rule and will of God in Romans 11:33-36: "Oh, the depth of the riches of the wisdom and knowledge of God! How unsearchable his judgments, and his paths beyond tracing out! 'Who has known the mind of the Lord? Or who has been his counselor? Who has ever given to God, that God should repay him?' For from him and through him and to him are all things. To him be the glory forever!"

His hymn is an echo and a summary of Isaiah's beautiful hymn in Isaiah 40:12-31. Again Paul bears witness to God that he "alone is immortal and [he] lives in unapproachable light, whom no one has seen or can see. To him be honor and might forever" (1 Timothy 6:16).

Psalm 139 is one of the most beautiful hymns in the Bible in its expression of the greatness of the mind and will of God. The psalmist sings of God's presence everywhere at the same time and of his complete and detailed knowledge of all that happens before it happens. Yes, the psalm exults in God's control over all that happens. Note the exquisite detail of the psalm, bearing in mind that God himself inspired and revealed these things to the holy writer: "O LORD, you have searched me and you know me. You know when I sit and when I rise. . . . You discern my going out and my lying down; you are familiar with all my ways" (139:1-3). What an amazing thing, not just that God should be so completely present but that he should care one way or the other about even the most trivial details of my life!

But there's more: "You perceive my thoughts from afar. . . . Before a word is on my tongue you know it completely, O LORD" (139:2,4). Lest anyone miss the point that God's knowledge encompasses every corner of creation and every detail of life, that God knows always the end of a thing before its beginning, the psalmist goes on: "My frame was not hidden from you when I was made in the secret place. When I was woven together in the depths of the earth, your eyes saw my unformed body. All the days ordained for me were written in your book before one of them came to be" (139:15,16).

Then, overwhelmed by the whole subject of God's knowledge, of his wisdom and the connection of these with the individual, the psalmist sings in wonder and in awe: "How precious to me are your thoughts, O God! How vast is the sum of them! Were I to count them, they would outnumber the grains of sand" (139:17,18). And then the blessed, the most happy result of God's thoughts: "When I awake, I am still with you" (139:18). Is he talking about waking up from sleep in the morning? Or is he talking about waking up from the sleep of forgetting the constant presence of God and God's care for him every moment of his life? Why not both? After all, whatever we do or think or say that is unaware or ignorant of God's gracious presence is a work, a word, a thought akin to that done by the sleepwalker.

In a certain sense, all of these passages and so many others like them are inspired commentaries and reflections on the creation account in Genesis 1. God gave these reflections to mere mortals that they might be forever in awe of their almighty and all-wise Maker. Genesis 1 states the facts in such a matter-of-fact manner: "In the beginning God." There never was time when God was not. Before there was a *there,* before there was a *before,* God was. Nor since creation has there ever been a place where God is not. In the creation account, we hear that God spoke and it was done. Wherever his voice went out to say, "Let there be . . . ," there God was; God cannot be separated from his voice. In response to his word, all that is came into being. Matter and energy; sun, moon, and stars; all the plants and animals exist in their wholeness and in their detail in response to God's speaking. Where they are, there his voice is and has been; there he is, not in fractions but wholly and entirely. God cannot be broken up into fractions or parts.

And so, there we have it: God is so great that he is in every-thing, while nothing holds or limits him. He is in time and space but not limited by time or space. He is present in all that is cre-ated but beyond the control of anything created. He is separate and distinct from all that he has created. Creation is not, as the pantheists imagine, a part of God. All created things have time and space and limits in time and space. Way out there, some-where in space, space ends and so too does time. But not God. God is above all space and beyond all time, absolutely without limits of any kind—totally other and unique.

As great as his creating power is, just as great and beyond limit is his wisdom and knowledge. God is so great that he knows all things perfectly, down to the smallest detail, and knew it already in eternity before anything except God even existed. Jesus says that God knows the number of hairs on our heads and when a sparrow falls. He knows and feeds the birds and clothes the lilies of the field (Matthew 6:25-34). And it is all present to him in what we call *the eternal now*. As the psalmist said, it is all too wonderful for us. For mere mortals to completely comprehend the mind of God is on the face of it impossible. The psalmist put it so simply and so completely: "Our God is in heaven; he does whatever pleases him" (Psalm 115:3).

But, even though it is impossible for us to fully comprehend the mind of God, what he has revealed about himself and as much as he has revealed we can know with certainty, precisely because he is the one who has revealed it. Obviously, God knows himself; and we know of him what he has been pleased to reveal of himself in his Word. His creation, nature, and all its wonders tell us some things about God. They testify to his might and wisdom as the psalmist declares in Psalm 19. Conscience too bears witness to God's existence and to his justice as Paul tells us in Romans 1. But it is in his Word that God makes himself known to a far higher degree than nature alone could ever show us. In nature and in our conscience we but poke after him in the dark. It is in his Word that we have his own voice, his infallible revelation of himself, of his attributes, of his purposes and intentions, and yes, of his sacred and saving heart and will.

When we examine his Word and peer into his revelation of himself, we are struck with wonder and awe at who and how he is. What he shows us makes us the more eager to search out and discover what his almighty power and his perfect and unlimited knowledge have to do with us.

To put it another way: Given his unlimited power, perfect wisdom, and complete knowledge of everything, how much happens because he knows and wants it to happen? How much happens that he knows will happen but not because he wanted it to happen? Just knowing that something will happen doesn't by itself mean that the one knowing caused it. For the sake of simple and admittedly imperfect analogies: The teacher knows that lazy Fritz will fail the course, but the teacher's knowledge doesn't cause the failure. You know that your spendthrift and wayward son is on the brink of ruin, but your knowing it doesn't cause it. So then, how much of what God knows does God make happen or will to happen?

Already in Psalm 139, cited previously, there is a hint of the distinction between what God knows and what God's knowing causes. The psalmist says that God knows of his sitting down and his getting up, of his coming and going, even of his thoughts before he thinks them. But he does not say that God caused him to sit down or to get up, to come or to go, to think this rather than to think that or not to think at all. And still he declares that God has ordained the days of his life, each one from beginning to end. So then, some things God wills and causes and some things not.

What then does God tell us about the difference between the things that he wills and causes and the other things that happen even though God did not cause and did not want them to happen? Are there things that God knows will happen but that happen against his will—in spite of the fact that God is almighty? Can God's Word get the murkiness out of the pool for us?

Things that God wants to happen and that, therefore, must happen

We can sum up much in this category in one word: *gospel*. Everything that has to do with your salvation and mine God willed and God brought to pass. That is clear already in Genesis 3:15. There God promised a Savior who would crush the head of the serpent and thus rescue fallen mankind from the dread consequences of sin. God willed the redemption of the world. And the redemption of the world, therefore, had to take place in just the way that God said it would in all of the promises of the Savior in the Old Testament. Read Psalm 22 and Isaiah 53, the most complete of the many pictures of the Savior's work in the Old Testament. They are written in the past tense, as though the work of Jesus had already taken place! They and other promises of the Savior are written in the past tense because his work described there *must* take place; God willed it, and it could not fail to take place just as he said.

To be sure, the events described in Psalm 22 and in Isaiah 53 are inseparably connected to the acts of sinful men: Wicked men counted his bones on the cross and mocked him; wicked men despised and rejected him. Their wickedness, however, was their own; God did not will or force those individuals to behave as they did. But, nevertheless, his intent of redeeming the world through the suffering of his Son at the hands of the wicked was accomplished—and again, that without God being responsible for their wickedness.

The point is that God would rule over all of history to see to it that his divine and saving purpose was carried out. He would carry it out in spite of the wickedness of men, even if that meant turning the wickedness of men to his own purposes. That's what St. Paul is telling us too when in Galatians 4:4 he speaks of the coming of the Savior and of his work taking place "when the time had fully come," i.e., just when God willed it, just when God had so ruled over history that the timing was perfect; the place was just right; the way the world was governed suited his purposes; the language in common use; the prevailing philosophy in the world and thinking in the Jewish world—all of it would suit and serve God's purpose in the work of redemption.

Likewise, the preservation of faith, of the church, is something that God wills and causes, something that must take place and cannot fail to take place. Jesus himself assures us of that. He tells Peter in response to Peter's great confession of faith that even the gates of hell cannot overcome the church (Matthew 16:18). His descriptions of his coming on the Last Day assure us as well that he will keep his promise to preserve the church until he returns (Matthew 25). Let the world rage against it, let men mock and scorn to their hearts' content; God laughs (Psalm 2).

Let heretics come and go and do their worst, as indeed they always will (1 Timothy 4:1-3); God's mighty power will still accompany his Word and sacraments for the preservation and extension of the church.

God does not leave us in any doubt about the way in which the church is and must be created and preserved. He wills it, and he sees to it that it all takes place through the preaching of the gospel and the administration of the sacraments and not apart from them. He ruled history so that the redemption of the world was accomplished and completed by Jesus Christ alone, without anyone's help or cooperation. That all happened just as he had promised already in Isaiah 63:3 and most beautifully as Jesus himself had promised it in John 3:16. And through that message and not apart from it, sin is forgiven, saving faith is created, sin and death are overcome, hell is vanquished, and heaven is filled with the company of the saints, as Paul tells us (1 Corinthians 1:18-31). Jesus so often compares the preaching of the gospel to the sowing and growing of seed: God's power was present and powerful in his Word at creation to make seed grow and produce after its kind (Genesis 1:11-13); just so, God's power to create faith rests in the seed of his Word proclaimed to one individual at a time (Mark 4:1-20,30-32). The only difference would be that the seed in the ground grows as a result of his almighty command; the seed of the Word in the gospel prospers as a result of his powerful grace. Shortly before his ascension, Jesus told us that that is the way it would be (Matthew 28:18-20); because he has all power in heaven and in earth, he would see to it that disciples would be made until the end of time through Baptism and the teaching of his saving work for the world.

The apostles understood that. In Peter's great Pentecost sermon (Acts 2:14-41), Peter made it clear that it is God's will that we should repent, be baptized for the forgiveness of sins, and believe the gospel. Yes, and it is the power of the Holy Spirit working in that gospel message that moves people to repent and trust in the Savior's work for their salvation. What a miracle! Peter didn't mince any words: "You killed the Son of God, the Lord of life!" Who could help but despair when faced with his own guilt over such a monstrous crime? But, Peter declared, "God used your utter wickedness to accomplish his purpose and now wants to forgive you and claim you for his own dear children." What power there was in the gospel he preached! Who would dare to hope for such a thing or believe such a message? The message itself, the Holy Spirit working through it, had to overcome the guilty and utterly rational despair of those who tortured and murdered God's own Son! And so it did. The gospel message accomplished God's will and purpose as thousands repented, believed the gospel, and were baptized. God's will was done! God saw to it! God caused it!

Paul too tells us that it is God's will to create faith through the Word (Romans 10:17) and that apart from the Holy Spirit's working through that Word, no one will believe it (1 Corinthians 12:3). The same holds true of the sacraments. It is God's will that Baptism forgives sins and creates faith and so it does, as Paul declares in Romans 6:1-14. Yes, Paul tells us (Ephesians 5:25,26) that it is God's will that the Sacrament of Baptism works for the perfect and perpetual cleansing of the church from all sin. That's what Peter had proclaimed already in his Pentecost sermon when he urged that the people repent and be baptized for the forgiveness of their sins. And that's what he tells us as well in his first letter (1 Peter 3:21). It is God's will that Baptism be a saving means of grace, and so it is. The same holds for the Sacrament of the Altar. It is God's will that by the power of his Word, Christ is really and truly present with the elements of bread and wine. And that substantial and, therefore, powerful presence of Christ in the Sacrament is mighty and effective to forgive sins, and thus, to give life and salvation. It is so because God wills it, because God promises it, because God through his Word in the Sacrament brings it to pass.

Let those who wish that God still performed miracles listen to the gospel in Word and sacraments. What mighty miracles the eyes of faith will there behold! Forgiveness, life, and salvation are there by the power of words. Forgiveness, life, and salvation are hidden there in the water with the Word! Forgiveness, life, and salvation flow there from the food made sacred by the presence of Christ in his Word. And it is all so plain and clear to the eyes of faith opened by that same Word.

God's effective and effecting will and working through the gospel in Word and sacraments, however, is not merely a mechanical, mindless, or automatic thing. It is not like a rule of nature that works without any interest in the individuals affected by it. The law of gravity, for example, applies to the apple falling from the tree and no less to the little boy jumping from its branches without caring about either one. Not so with God's will and work through the gospel! Just the opposite is the case. When the gospel creates and preserves faith, it is because God chooses not to be separated from it and its effect. It is because God is intimately and personally concerned with each individual who hears it and who, because of the gospel's power, believes it. It is mind-boggling to us that such is the case. We are, after all, but dust and ashes. How much attention do you pay to dust? How much care do you exercise over each ash in the hearth? But God, the Almighty, who is sublimely independent, who needs nothing and no one, nevertheless is mightily exercised over each of us. He was so in eternity; he is so now; he will be so forever.

We need to ponder this matter of how in the gospel God is concerned with each individual and accomplishes his good and gracious will on and in us personally. The Bible clearly teaches in so many passages that, to be sure, Christ died for all. St. John the Baptist said it so simply and clearly: "Look, the Lamb of God, who takes away the sin of the world" (John 1:29). Paul likewise makes it clear that God wills, God wants, all people to receive the saving benefit of Jesus' redemptive work for the world. He tells us that "[God] wants all men to be saved and to come to a knowledge of the truth" (1 Timothy 2:4). Peter says the same thing: "[The Lord] is patient with you, not wanting anyone to perish, but everyone to come to repentance" (2 Peter 3:9). But beyond that, God also declares in his Word that each and every one who believes the gospel message has God's personal choice to thank for it—it was no coincidence, and there was nothing automatic or mechanical about it. The faith of the individual and perseverance in faith to the end are the result of God's will and God's work in the gospel message proclaimed to that individual.

Of the many places where the Bible speaks of this concern of God and the effectiveness of his will in the faith of the individual, we will note just a few of the most striking ones. St. Paul sings the praises of God's will in effectively choosing each one who believes:

Praise be to the God and Father of our Lord Jesus Christ, who has blessed us in the heavenly realms with every spiritual blessing in Christ. For he chose us in him before the creation of the world to be holy and blameless in his sight. In love he predestined us to be adopted as his sons through Jesus Christ, in accordance with his pleasure and will—*to the praise of his glorious grace, which he has freely given us in the One he loves.* (Ephesians 1:3-6)

Could the point be made more emphatically, more powerfully? God knew each one who would believe and persevere in faith to the end. And why would they believe? Why would they persevere? It is because God chose each one of them already before the world began, in eternity! Each one who believes and perseveres was in God's mind and heart before he or she ever came to be, before he or she ever had done anything to merit God's attention or choice.

Paul underscores the great truth that the choice of God was entirely his free choice, a choice made in grace according to his purpose and pleasure. God owed his choice to no one, not to the believer's future faith and not to any future merit that the believer might have. It had nothing to do with anything in the one chosen. The believer's faith and subsequent good works have God's choice as their cause, not the other way around. There is one exclamation point after another under the truth that God's will was done, that it was carried out and accomplished for the praise of his own name—not the praise of the one chosen—and that the choice is entirely tied up with the saving work of Jesus. Paul makes and underscores the same point in Romans 1–11. Over and over again he says it in all of his epistles: Our salvation is the result of Christ's work alone; our faith is the result of God's choice made personal in the proclamation of the gospel to each one who believes individually. Again, God's choice is an entirely free choice, an entirely gracious choice.

St. Luke tells us the same thing in Acts 13:48: "All who were appointed for eternal life believed." They believed because they were chosen—not they were chosen because they believed. Likewise, St. James declares, "[God] chose to give us birth through the word of truth, that we might be a kind of firstfruits of all he created" (James 1:18). The analogy is perfect: No one chooses to be born; physical birth is the result of choices made by others. Just so our birth as children of God. It is the result of God's will. He becomes our Father, and the church, so to speak, becomes our mother through the proclamation of the gospel. These and so many other passages that say the same thing bid us to apply Jesus' words to the disciples also to ourselves individually, personally: "I have called you friends, for everything that I learned from my Father I have made known to you. You did not choose me, but I chose you and appointed you to go and bear fruit—fruit that will last" (John 15:15,16).

It is simply impossible to exhaust the comfort for each penitent sinner that comes from this truth. Am I good enough for God to choose me? Is my faith strong enough for God to elect me? Away with all such questions! They have nothing to do with God's choice. Your faith is neither your own work nor the result of your own merit nor the consequence of a coincidental birth in a Christian family or near a Christian church. No, it is all God's arrangement. It is all the result of his will in eternity, worked out in time, reaching its blessed fruition in you in the here and now. Have you been baptized? God arranged all of history so that you would be baptized. Do you at least in your mind's eye fall down before the altar of God in church on Sunday to confess that you deserve nothing but wrath and punishment? It is God's effective ruling over history that you hear in the voice of the pastor, Jesus' own voice: "Be of good cheer! Your sins are forgiven! The one who comes to me, I will never cast out!" And it is the result of God's will that this precious, life-giving gospel proclamation creates faith in your heart; that faith sighs with joy and relief that God has not lied; that just for you, even for you, Christ died and rose again.

So then, God wanted to redeem the world and to do it by the sacrificial and substitutionary death of his virgin-born Son. And that happened because God willed it and caused it to happen.

God willed to create and preserve the church through the proclamation of the gospel and the administration of the sacraments. And that happened and happens still because God wills it and causes it to happen.

And no less, God willed that those who believe the gospel and die in faith would believe the gospel and die in faith. It happens thus with each individual who ends up in heaven because God willed it and caused it to happen. Listen to the hymns of the angels and the saints in heaven in Revelation 7:9-12 and 19:1-9; all praise goes to God and to the Lamb; there is not a hint or a word of, "Well, at least I had the sense to decide to believe and the virtue to obey!"[2]

Things that God wills and causes to happen that are not directly connected to the gospel

Are there other things in history that happen as they do because God willed them and caused them to happen just as they did? Our knowledge here is much less complete because God does not give us a complete answer to that question. In the Old Testament, we do have instances of specific events in history that God arranged. They are always events that have some bearing on his will for the church. Thus, for example, God raised up enemies of Israel to chasten his people when they fell into idolatry. He raised up the kingdoms of Assyria and Babylon to destroy the obstinate and apostate kingdoms of Israel and Judah. And then he raised up the Medes and the Persians to end the Babylonian Captivity of Judah. He did it all just as he had promised and just in the amount of time that he had promised. It all happened as a result of his will and of his rule over history and, most important, as part of salvation history. It all happened with the gospel goal that his people should recognize their sins, repent, and flee to his grace and mercy in the promised Messiah for forgiveness. It all happened so that the promise that the Savior would come through the family of Abraham and the house of David would not be lost.

But did God will that Napoleon invade Russia and that his empire perish in the snows of Moscow? Was it his unalterable will that caused The French Revolution or the American Revolution? Did his will force the rise of other kingdoms and nations and ultimately author their success or failure? That he rules over all of history for the benefit of the church and so that those he has cho-

---

[2] We will return to the theme of God's election again in chapter 8, where we will consider the middle between God's election on the one hand and the Great Commission on the other hand.

sen will in history hear the gospel and believe it is certain. But could so many of the things that happened in history have happened differently? Did they have to occur just as they did? The answer is hidden in the mind of God, and he has not chosen to tell us how much of history had to happen just the way it did and how much of it could have happened other than it did. He tells us only that nothing in history can destroy the church or prevent those whom he has chosen from hearing the gospel, from believing it, and from finally entering into eternal glory. He tells us only that his ultimate goal must be reached, but not necessarily the details of the road taken on the way to that goal.

To put it most simply, we rejoice in the certainty that he controls and directs what he wants to for the preservation of the church and for the gathering of those he has chosen. He bids us focus on that blessed truth because that's the one he has made clear in his Word.

What role is there for man's will, and what does man control or cause?

As clear as it is that God rules and controls all things for his own purposes and for our salvation, it is just as clear that there is much in history that happens contrary to his will, in spite of the fact that he is almighty. Human beings are not robots or puppets moving on the ends of strings, irresistibly moving at the impulses of the divine puppet master. Already at creation he implanted in Adam and Eve a capacity to frustrate and hinder his will. Is that not an amazing thing?

We can even be so bold as to put it this way: God had such respect for humanity that from the very beginning he did not choose to force us to carry out his will. God wanted Adam and Eve and their descendents to live in the Garden of Eden in blissful communion with him. But that didn't happen. Adam and Eve used their capacity to frustrate the will of God, and God did not prevent it. They exchanged freedom for slavery to sin. They threw away peace in exchange for fear; love from and for God in exchange for hatred of God, contempt for one another, and the hostility of nature. They gave away the freedom to live and then to live forever in exchange for death. None of that was the will of God. None of that was caused by God. For all the misery that they brought on themselves and that ever since all mankind brings on itself, mankind has only itself to blame. In spite of the fact that we should know from experience that sin never gives what we think it will, we nevertheless fall for the blandishments of the world and the seductive voice of the tempter again and again, day by day, all the way to the cemetery. None of that is the will of God. None of it is caused by God.

So perverse is mankind that even the very concept and the word *freedom* have been woefully corrupted. Ask anyone what the word *freedom* means. The answer you get will be this: The ability to do whatever you want, be it good or evil or somewhere in-between. But that wasn't God's definition of freedom when he created man, and it isn't his definition of freedom now either. God's definition of freedom is quite different. God's gift of freedom to Adam and Eve was the ability to choose to do what God wanted them to do, to choose to continue in the perfection that he gave them at their creation. When they threw it all away, they lost freedom and became slaves. They no longer could choose even to return to fellowship with God; their freedom was gone! And once lost, they had no capacity—no freedom—in themselves to regain it.

To be sure, Adam and Eve had and their descendents now have a certain amount of what we might label "wiggle room" in their slavery. They may choose to commit this sin rather than that. They may even choose to lead what on the outside appears to be virtuous lives. But that alters not in the least their fundamental condition of slavery. The master over the cotton fields might have told the slave, "Choose for yourself whether you want to work in this field today or in that one." But would you say that the slave must, therefore, be free? Hardly! He is still a slave. And so it is with us. It is so, not because God willed it or caused it but because Adam and Eve exchanged freedom for slavery when they sinned in the garden quite contrary to God's will. And it is so to this day in each of us as we are by nature.

Indeed, man daily confirms his loss of freedom and his bondage whenever he sins. That's what Jesus said in his own great discourse on freedom in John 8:34: "Everyone who sins is a slave to sin." That's what Paul says too in Romans 6 and 7 where he speaks of the difference between freedom and slavery. The slavery was not and is not God's will, and God does not cause it.

God's will is for us again to be free. But that will of God can only be caused and brought about by God. And it is caused by him when he liberates us from our slavery by forgiving us and creating faith in the gospel message by means of the gospel message. In Romans 6 and 7, Paul speaks of the freedom that only those have who have been rescued from slavery by the redeeming work of Christ, by the washing of Baptism, and by faith in the gospel message. Jesus too tells us in John 8 that only when he has made us free are we really free. And that freedom is a freedom given and then exercised in the ongoing fellowship with God through the gospel. Or do you want to call it freedom when you choose to continue in unbelief? That freedom, again as Paul says so forcefully in Romans 6 and 7, is the freedom to be ashamed, the freedom to die. Some freedom! Let all those ponder that point who insist, "I'm free to do what I want! Neither you nor even God has the right to limit my freedom!"

But let us return to the question of whether everything that has happened in history had to happen the way it did or could it have happened differently. Let us consider how that question is connected to the will of man and his ability to frustrate the will of God. The best that we can say is this: Just as the individual has what we called a certain amount of wiggle room in his condition of slavery without any natural ability to become free, so in history in general there is all kinds of wiggle room for people to act according to their own fallen wills. This ruler could have done other than he did; this people could have followed that path instead of the one they followed.[3] There is nothing in the Bible that says they were all puppets on a string. But this much they were not "free" to do: They could not destroy the church; they could not prevent the gospel from being proclaimed and believed by those whom God had chosen for himself already in eternity.

That's a lot of wiggle room for people, a lot of wiggle room in history. People can and do choose things that are not the will of God, and they can frustrate the will of God by their choices. It is

---

[3] Among those who most famously—and unsuccessfully—wrestled with this problem of contingency in history, the question of whether things in history could have happened other than they did, was Tolstoy in his essay on history at the end of his novel *War and Peace*.

clear in many places in the Bible that when people frustrate the will of God, God is not the cause. The blame, the cause of the evil, is always laid squarely at the door of the one who does evil. That is true also and especially of those who heard the gospel but, in spite of God's desire to create faith in them, perished under the wrath of God and in unbelief. Consider for example the Bible's description of the destruction of the Northern Kingdom of Israel in 2 Kings 17:7-18. Then read of the fall of Jerusalem in 2 Chronicles 36:11-19. Listen in on the prayer of Daniel in Daniel 9:4-19. What is the recurring theme? It is this: Yes, God brought about the destruction of Israel and Judah, but it was caused by the sins of the people, sins they chose to live in, sins altogether against the will and Word of God. God had caused their earlier prosperity; they caused their own ruin.

Jesus makes the same point in that dread chapter, Matthew 23, when he pronounces woe over those who had his Word but rejected it. He wept over Jerusalem in anticipation of its destruction. And why? Because he wanted people to despise his Word and Jerusalem to slay the prophets? Certainly not! The people did it in spite of God's will and in spite of his desire to rescue and to save. He would keep his Word and destroy. But the blame would be entirely theirs, not his. That's the same point that St. Stephen makes in his great sermon before his martyrdom (Acts 7:51-53). Thus, the church will always survive and the gospel will always be preached and the elect will always be brought in. That's God's will, and he will certainly bring it to pass. But he gives no guarantee that the church will always prosper in this place, or even in this church body. It lies within the wiggle room of fallen men to reject the gospel, to drive the church underground, to make it all but disappear. God will preserve a remnant of his church to manifest his power and his grace in preserving her and calling even those who have rejected him back again. We see that in Palestine, in Turkey, in Europe. In short, we see that everywhere where the gospel was once so successful but now is all but absent.

So then we have this paradox: When one believes the gospel and perseveres in faith to the end, that one has God's choice to thank for it, God's grace to thank for it, God's power in the gospel to thank for it, Christ's work in the redemption of the world to thank for it. Such a one deserves not the least, not one shred of

111

personal credit for it. He cannot even congratulate himself that at least he had the good sense to believe. No, his faith was entirely God's gift in the gospel, the result of God's choice in eternity.

On the other hand, when one sins, he has only his own evil nature and will to blame for it. And when one rejects the gospel message, he does so of himself; it was not God's will. He exercised his—can we put it that way?—negative capacity to frustrate and hinder the will of God.

Enter Dame Reason with her objections!

As shy as Dame Reason may have been at the beginning of our look into this pool, she has never been shy about contradicting the answers from God's Word here given to the question of why some believe and not others. She wants to insist that if only those believe whom God has chosen, then God must not have wanted the rest to believe and must have predestined them to damnation. Indeed, with her objection she insists that she is merely defending God's honor, his attribute of omnipotence. She will argue that since God is almighty, his will cannot be resisted. Therefore, if he willed that someone believe, they *must* believe, and the rest *cannot* believe because God didn't want them to believe and, therefore, prevented them from coming to faith. But as we have noted previously, that's not what the Scriptures teach. In every instance the cause of, the fault for, unbelief is laid squarely at the door of the unbeliever. Or do we want to accuse Jesus of crying "crocodile" tears over Jerusalem? May such a thing never be!

At other times Dame Reason has argued that God must have chosen the ones going to heaven because they were somehow worthy or more worthy than those not chosen. God, she argues, knew in eternity that they would believe, or they would want to believe, or they would act virtuously once they did believe. Therefore, he chose them. Or this: God presented fallen man with a choice, to believe or not to believe. Those who decided to believe, he chose. But as we have seen, that is not what the Scriptures say. In point of fact, these arguments confuse and reverse cause and effect. The scriptural truth is this: People believe the gospel because God chose them, not the other way around. Indeed, if God chose people because he foresaw that they would believe, then he chose nothing. His choice would be meaningless and without effect. But finally, God does not ask us to answer Dame Reason with anything other than beating her over the head with the mop that she is using in order to muddy the water in the pool. We merely note some of the objections that reason raises to demonstrate the point that often her reasonable-sounding arguments are not only contrary to the Scriptures but contrary to sound reason as well.

But what should I do if I am worried about God's choice? The Formula of Concord in Article XI beautifully sums up the answer of the Scriptures: search for your election in Christ! Focus not on your own feelings and fears, not on past sins and falls, not on still present weaknesses and temptations. Focus rather on what Christ has done and on the will of God revealed in his Word. It is in Christ's wounds and in his Word that you will see how he earnestly desires your salvation; you will see how he has accomplished everything in his grace and with his powerful Word to bring you to faith and preserve you in faith. Do not fall into despair because of your admitted unworthiness and ever present weakness and temptation. Likewise, do not plunge into that arrogance which concludes that since Christ died for all my sins, now I can sin without repentance and with reckless abandon, as though I have been saved *for* my sins rather than *from* them. (We considered this point at some length in chapter 3.)

What about the will of God and the will of the Christian?

Again, it is a wondrous thing to note that God has such respect, if we can put it that way, for humans that he has given them the capacity to frustrate and hinder even God's own good and gracious will. It is a wondrous thing to note that natural man in his lost freedom nevertheless has a lot of wiggle room for doing his own will in opposition to the will of God. It is a wondrous thing to note that even with all that wiggle room, God nevertheless remains in control of history to this extent that his church is preserved and those he has chosen are called to faith, come to faith, and persevere in faith until the end. What awe and wonder these clear truths at the bottom of the muddy pool should provoke in us!

But is there still more at which to wonder? Does the Christian, once he has come to faith and is striving to live his faith, also have wiggle room? Or are all his actions preordained and predestined so that whatever he does or does not do is outside of the realm of choice? Is the Christian a puppet?

It would seem strange indeed to assert that once God has restored the freedom we lost because of sin by forgiving it, that then there would be no wiggle room, no choices for the Christian to make. But that is nevertheless what some assert. In fact, they allow for no wiggle room in anyone, Christian or not. They even quote some passages from the Bible to try and prove their point. They especially like Proverbs 16:1,9,33. There the holy writer under the inspiration of the Holy Spirit says, "To man belong the plans of the heart, but from the LORD comes the reply of the tongue." And, "In his heart a man plans his course, but the LORD determines his steps." And, "The lot is cast into the lap, but its every decision is from the LORD." They cite as well the words of Jeremiah: "I know, O LORD, that a man's life is not his own; it is not for man to direct his steps" (Jeremiah 10:23).

The question is, however, do these passages speak of a total lack of choice, whether that be choices in slavery for the unbeliever or choices in freedom for the Christian? Or do they speak of God's ultimate control over history for the ultimate accomplishment of his purposes? It should be clear from what follows that the answer is that these passages refer to God's ultimate control over history for the accomplishment of his purposes. To find that answer and to clear the mud from the pool, we need to look at *all* that the Scriptures say about man's will and his ability to accomplish it. We need to see if there are places in the Bible where God clearly gives people a choice. We have already noted that it is the unbeliever's own choice when he rejects the gospel and acts wickedly counter to God's Word and will. But what about Christians? Do the passages just mentioned deprive them of any wiggle room, any kind of freedom when they act *after* the gospel has brought them to faith?

The whole of what God says about our lives in Christ and with Christ in faith demonstrates that the Christian has countless opportunities to exercise the restored freedom that he has in Christ. While the Christian's faith is entirely God's work through the gospel in Word and sacraments, the Christian's life is a cooperative work between himself and the Savior. On his side, God gives the Christian abundant gifts and blessings. Then he gives countless opportunities, more than we can ever take full advantage of, for using those gifts and blessings to his glory and in the service of one another. He especially implants in the Christian the earnest desire to live in accordance with God's Word and his will as expressed in that Word. And with all of that he gives us a blessed freedom to make choices every day and choices beyond counting. We see it already in Adam before the fall, in Genesis 2:19,20. God brought the animals to Adam for him to name. He gave Adam wisdom to choose a name appropriate to each; God did not pick the names himself. While in the garden, God told Adam and Eve to tend it; but he did not give a detailed set of instructions of how they were to do that and when each task should be done. That was for them to figure out.

After the fall, to be sure, the choices that even Christians make in their restored freedom are bound to be stained and flawed. We are still sinners, and what we do is always stained by that fundamental fact of our existence. Nevertheless, the freedom we have in Christ, the wiggle room, the choices we can make, are real. We are not puppets on a string. God chooses to respect the relationship that he has established with us. God chooses to give us choices that show his respect for the freedom he has given us. Should I be a pastor or a teacher, a carpenter or a plumber, a farmer or a tradesman? God has not decided that for us. He has left it to our choice. He has given such and such gifts for our use and bids us use those gifts to his glory and for the service of our neighbors. So I examine as best I can his gifts. Then I determine, and that perhaps with the advice of others, how best to use them. But the choice of how I will offer back to God the gifts he has given for service to a considerable extent remains mine.[4]

In that choice the Christian offers up to God his service in whatever arena he has chosen to serve. If someone becomes a pastor or a teacher, it should never be because he thought that God would be angry or disappointed with him if he did not. No, such service is a gift from the pastor or teacher to God, a gift

---

[4] We are not here considering the divine call of Christ through the church for pastors and teachers of the church. The point here is just that those who serve the church have on their part chosen to do so, that is, to prepare for such service and to continue in such service after Christ has called them through the voice of the church.

for which God gave the ability, the desire, and then the opportunity. It is not something extorted from the servant of the church against his will. So too the factory worker, the manager, the carpenter, the plumber, the farmer, the doctor, the nurse, the secretary—all of them have gifts that God has given and opportunities to use them for service. Often they have gifts enough that they could choose other than they did. God lets them use the gifts he has given as they choose to use them. They exercise freedom in his service. Paul encourages us to think thus in 1 Corinthians 12,13 and in Ephesians 4.

So we will not look into our imaginations, our feelings uninformed by the Scriptures, our reason, or even our prayers (as we noted in the last chapter) to find out the will of God. He has revealed his will in the Scriptures. If we want to know what God thinks, we should go where he has clearly spoken, to his own verbally inspired and infallible Word. We follow this rule: *We can know nothing with certainty about the will of God apart from the Scriptures.* To do as so many do these days, to consult our own hearts and wills for the will of God, can lead to devilish delusions that easily end up contrary to the revealed and sure Word of God: "Well, I just really feel that God won't send anybody to hell." Or, "But we love each other, and so I can't imagine that God should have any problem with . . ."

Thus, in so many things we are free to choose between this and that and need not torment ourselves with trying to guess what God has chosen for us. God lets us choose, for example, to be married or single, and if married, whom to select for a spouse. Paul says of himself that he chose to remain single because of his particular circumstances in his apostolic service (1 Corinthians 9:5). He urges others to make the choice to be married or single likewise on the basis of God's gifts and their circumstances in life (1 Corinthians 7). He bids us to examine what God says about marriage and the family in his Word. But then he leaves it to us to apply that to our specific situations in life. Often the advice of others and, yes, the choices that others make will play a part. And certainly we will pray for God's blessing on our choices and as we make those choices. But the point is that the choices we make are real choices. God neither asks nor expects us to climb up into his mind in an attempt to figure out which choice he wants us to make. Again, he gives us a good deal of wiggle room, of freedom to serve now in this way, now in that, and to delight in both the freedom and the service.

And so on and on it goes. How much time should I spend in prayer, and how much in reading the Bible? How much time should I spend in work and how much with the family and how much in rest? He tells us to do all these things. But he leaves it to us to balance all of the things he has given us to do. Some days there will be more of one, and then another day, more of the other. Should I buy this house or that or no house at all? Should I take this job or that or find another line of work altogether? Should we have chicken or a roast for Sunday dinner? Should I join in another worthwhile activity at church, or do I need to spend more time with my family right now? All these things are matters of choice that God gives the Christian freedom to make.

At the same time, as the Christian recognizes and gives thanks for his freedom to make choices in response to God's gifts and to God-given opportunities, he also thanks God for the results of those choices. We do that almost automatically. We thank God for our meals in our table prayers: God gave every bite we eat. But we do not suppose that God picked the chicken over the roast. We thank God for our spouses. But we need not imagine that God picked this one over that one. We thank God for our work and for rest. But we need not think that God determined this job over that one or that he has decreed what time we should go to bed.

In it all we listen to the Word of God, as, for example, St. Paul expressed so simply yet so comprehensively: "Whatever you do, whether in word or deed, do it all in the name of the Lord Jesus, giving thanks to God the Father through him" (Colossians 3:17). Paul then goes on to give the general rules of thumb for each of us in our varied walks of life for how we ought to conduct ourselves. Luther's Small Catechism does much the same in the Table of Duties at the end of the Catechism.

In 1 Corinthians 10, especially in verses 31-33, Paul takes it as a given that the Christian is free to make many choices among things that are neither commanded nor forbidden in God's Word. And then he tells us how to use our freedom in making those choices: always to the glory of God for the benefit of those around us. In 1 Corinthians 12, he describes the rich generosity of God in

117

giving Christians so very many gifts with which to serve. In it all, he says, let each use those gifts for service.

In Ephesians 2:8-10, the apostle gives us the always blessed and needed reminder that our salvation and our faith are entirely the gift of God. And then he concludes by telling us the result of that gift: "We are God's workmanship, created in Christ Jesus to do good works, which God prepared in advance for us to do." Just what are those works? They are all those works that God commands in the law, in the Ten Commandments. And how are they prepared in advance for us to do? God so rules over history in things both great and small that he places in our paths each day opportunities to serve him, yes, so many opportunities that we cannot possibly take advantage of all of them. And then he is pleased with our service to him through our service to one another, service that we render in freedom.

We cannot help but remember the words that Jesus tells us he will speak on the Last Day (Matthew 25:31-46). When he was hungry, we fed him; when he was thirsty, we gave him something to drink. When he was sick and in prison, we visited him. He will praise the elect for the choices they made in serving him by serving one another. Notice that he does not say, "At least you figured out exactly what I wanted in a moment in time and had the good sense to do it." Notice as well that the saints do not say in response to his praise of their works, "Well, what else could we do? You preordained it all!" No, the response rather is the response of believers who looked for opportunities to serve and found that God gave such opportunities in abundance. The response is to use the gifts God gave, not least the gift of a desire to serve, in gratitude to God for all God's grace and mercy.

To put it another way, the way that the Lutheran Confessions most often put it,[5] we have a free will to choose "in those things that are subject to reason." That is, we can decide for ourselves all of those day-to-day things that belong to our lives in this world, those things just discussed. God does not force us into this occupation or that, to outwardly avoid this vice and nurture

---

[5] Cf., for example, the Apology: Article XVIII, 4,7 and the Formula of Concord: Solid Declaration, IV, 80.

that virtue, to read this and eat that. All these things, for believers and unbelievers alike, are subject to reason. Thomas Edison figured out how to harness electricity. Henry Ford devised a way for mass-producing automobiles. Aristotle searched for definitions of virtue and vice in common life. Mendel figured out rules of genetics by experimenting with peas. Jefferson and John Adams devised a constitution for a nation. All these things were subject to reason. The Christian participates in many of them and then adds his own exercise of his renewed and restored free will in carrying out much of his Christian life. He figures out how much to contribute to his parish and to missions. He decides how best to raise his children in accordance with the Word of God. He devises a family budget that reflects his appreciation for God's gifts to him for the support of his family, to help the poor, and to prosper the work of the church. He decides when to pray, when to read his Bible, whether to go to church this Sunday, whether to attend Bible class. Again, all these outward acts are subject to reason.

In the chief matters of the First Commandment, however, whether to come to faith and persevere in faith, free will has no role to play. To be sure, we can decide whether or not to go to church, but we have no natural ability to decide to believe what is heard there. The outward act of going to church or even reading the Bible is subject to reason. But the inward obedience of faith is not. As we have noted previously, everything that has to do with trusting Jesus as our only Savior is a gift of God in the gospel. God overcomes our fallen will with the gospel and apart from our will gives us faith and, yes, in the Scriptures the content of faith as well. Once he has created in us another and new will by the gospel, that is, once he has created faith, our new will, our faith, delights in his gift of grace. It wants to persevere. It wants to remain with Christ for time and for eternity. To paraphrase St. Augustine: In the matter of coming to faith, God comes to the unwilling (for that is what we are by nature), makes us willing (by the gospel), and then dwells in the willing.

To be sure, with all of the wiggle room that God has given to believers and unbelievers alike in those things subject to reason, we can sometimes make a terrible mess of things. We see that already immediately after the fall in the Garden of Eden. Adam and Eve used their reason in a matter subject to reason. They wanted to make clothes so that they could hide from God. What a mess they made of it; they put leaves together for clothes. Apart from the fact that they were altogether foolish in reasoning that they could hide from God, they were not very clever in their choice of materials for clothing. When God expelled them from the garden, he showed his mercy by making clothes for them that would protect them from the elements and hide their shame from one another. Yes, and if they thought about it, the clothes God made could even remind them of the dread consequences of sin: their clothes were made from the skins of dead animals, a death in which they would share. Then he left them their reason to function as best it could in their new state as fallen but redeemed children of God.

Just so, God leaves us free to make choices in those things that are subject to reason. But often (though not always) in our lives and in history in general, he will intervene to limit the damage that we do in our exercise of the wiggle room we have. So, for example, the violent and the wicked persecute the church. But God limits their ability to do her harm and intervenes to prevent the destruction of the church. It is an observation made often in many languages that *Man denkt, Gott lenkt* ("Man proposes, but God disposes").

So, to cap it all off, God in his might and in his wisdom so rules over time and eternity that it all turns out for our best (Romans 8:28). Could we have decided many things differently than we did? Yes. But still God took all of our decisions into account and so ruled over them all that all things ended up in our best interest. What an absolutely amazing thing! To sum it up most briefly: *God stays God*—in ultimate and absolute control, a control that he exercises in grace for our benefit—and *man stays man*— a creature with wiggle room when he is a slave and freedom to exercise his sanctified will when he is a child of God by faith in Christ Jesus. Yes, an amazing thing indeed! How well the psalmist put it in his words already noted: "How precious to me are your thoughts, O God! How vast is the sum of them! Were I to count them, they would outnumber the grains of sand. When I awake, I am still with you" (Psalm 139:17,18).

Make sure that Dame Reason stays behind the mop pail!

We noted at the beginning of our visit to the pool that even Dame Reason does not venture answers to the difficult questions we have considered in this chapter. She does not venture answers, that is, until God's Word has given the answers; the answers in his Word clear up the muddy water as much as it can be cleared up, given our limited ability to fully grasp the mind of God. After God has spoken, Dame Reason is, however, quick to reemerge and to presume to criticize God's answers, or at least to suggest "improvements" on his answers. So, as we bring our stay beside the pool to a close and get ready to resume our journey along the narrow middle road, we want to be sure that reason is used only in service as a handmaid and not allowed to take the role of queen. We want to be assured that as best we can we follow the example of St. Paul. He demonstrates the right use of reason and makes it clear that reason is servant, Christ is Lord. Therefore he, and we along with him, want to "take captive every thought to make it obedient to Christ" (2 Corinthians 10:5).

Some of the greatest of the church fathers followed this dictum of the inspired apostle when they wrestled with the matter of God's will and man's will. Using reason as a handmaid, not as queen, they made some useful distinctions that are in harmony with the Word of God. We will note them briefly and in summary in the hope that their thoughts will contribute to the clearing away of the mud in the water.

The fathers, for example, in defending both God's control and man's humanity—man's God-given wiggle room—distinguished between the *antecedent will of God* and the *consequent will of God*. The antecedent will of God is his will that comes *before (ante-)* man does or wills anything at all. It is that will in God that takes no note of any causes in man, a will that acts altogether in freedom. It is his will that has causes only in God himself. We summed up much of this antecedent will of God earlier when we said that it can be summed up by one word: *gospel*. The causes of our salvation all rest in the gospel, all rest in this antecedent will of God. His grace alone prompted our salvation. The sacrifice of his Son alone merited our salvation. The power implanted in the means of grace, in the gospel in Word and sacraments, alone is his power; it effectively creates faith when and where God wills it because that is what God wills and what he brings to pass.

Dame Reason might want to stick her mop into the pool to muddy the waters by pointing out that without sin there would be no salvation; thus, she might want to conclude that sin too is a cause of salvation. In this argument reason is again unreasonable. To say that sin is a cause of our salvation is like saying that sickness is the cause of healing; after all, without sickness there wouldn't be any healing. Who would be so foolish as to raise such an argument? No, sickness does not cause healing; it shows the need for healing. So too, sin does not cause salvation; it shows the need, a desperate need to be sure, for salvation. Just as sickness too cannot bring about healing, so sin and the man it infects cannot bring about salvation. The healing for sin must come from outside of sin's cause, sin's victim. Sin did not in any way force God to save us. Rather, it was in God's own grace and mercy that Jesus became man and paid for our sin by his life and his sacrifice for us on the cross. That plan and its execution has God's own will, his *antecedent* will, as the cause.

But does man, and does sin, cause nothing in God? The church fathers answered with a consideration of the *consequent* will of God: when man willfully rejects the will of God for his salvation, then God in his justice damns such a wicked contempt for all of God's grace and Christ's suffering. God's justice, to be sure, was satisfied when Christ paid the penalty of the whole world's sin on the cross. That's how his grace and mercy were satisfied too. Grace and justice met on the cross. But should man through his own perverse will reject that perfect resolution of grace and justice, there is no other way in which that man can be saved. Jesus said that in John 3:16, in Mark 16:16, and in so many other places. And St. Peter said it too in Acts 4:12, "Salvation is found in no one else, for there is no other name under heaven given to men by which we must be saved," and in Acts 3:23, "Anyone who does not listen to him will be completely cut off from among his people." Notice how absolute is the distinction between God's antecedent will and his consequent will: those saved have only God to thank for it; those damned have only themselves to blame for it. So again the formula: The ultimate salvation of any man is the result of God's antecedent will; the ultimate damnation of anyone comes from the man himself as a consequence of his own unbelief, a consequence that God wills for those who despise his grace and goodness in Christ.

Closely connected to this matter of the antecedent will and the consequent will of God is the matter of God's *foreknowledge* and God's *eternal election.* This latter distinction is to a certain extent just another way of considering the same thing. It boils down to this: God knows everything before it happens. But that doesn't mean that God wills everything that happens. The Formula of Concord makes the distinction very simply and very clearly in Article XI. It declares:

> [The] foreknowledge extends equally over godly people and evil people, but it is not a cause of evil. It is not the cause of sins, when people act wrongly (sin proceeds originally from the devil and the wicked, perverted human will), nor of human corruption, for which people are responsible themselves. Instead, God's foreknowledge provides order in the midst of evil and sets limits to it. It determines how long evil can continue and determines also that everything, even if it is evil in itself, serves the welfare of God's elect.

> [Predestination] however, or God's eternal election, extends only to the righteous, God-pleasing children of God. It is a cause of their salvation, which God brings about. He has arranged everything that belongs to it. Our salvation is so firmly grounded on it [cf. John 10:26-29] that "the gates of hell will not prevail against it" [Matt. 16:18].[6]

So God limits and even uses the wickedness of men, as he did most notably in our redemption when wicked men crucified the Lord of glory. But he is not the cause of evil, and he did not will it. Our redemption he did will; the election of those who finally end up in heaven he willed and brought also to pass in his grace and mercy and through the work of Christ for our salvation and

---

[6] Formula of Concord, Epitome, Article XI, 3-4, Kolb-Wengert, p. 517.

the work of the Holy Spirit bringing us to faith through the gospel in Word and sacraments.

But Dame Reason is not yet through with her objections. Still one more objection she raises up to keep the waters muddy. She asks this: Did then God, because he is gracious, have to save man? Did grace mean that he was not free to damn the whole human race forever already in the Garden of Eden? The Fathers answered: nothing could force God to save us. He did it because he chose to do it in his grace. He did it because he determined that "it was not fitting" to allow creatures (the devil and the will of man) to ruin his creation and thus to appear more mighty than he is. By his determination to rescue us, he showed both the exceeding riches of his grace and the excellence of his power that he used it not to annihilate what he had made but to save it.[7]

That's essentially the argument which Moses used in Exodus 32. He pleaded and prayed for the people who had fallen so soon into idolatry. God was ready to destroy them in his justice. But Moses made a two-pronged—and rational—argument in his prayer.

1. God's honor would be destroyed among the heathen if he destroyed the people he had saved from slavery in Egypt.

2. Then, and most important, he appealed to God's own free and gracious promise to give the land to the descendents of Abraham, Isaac, and Jacob.

---

[7] Anyone interested in a further and more complete consideration of these questions should refer especially to the Formula of Concord, Articles I, II, and XI. This last problem, the problem of whether God had to redeem the world, the question of the necessity of the work of redemption, is probably considered nowhere as thoroughly as it is in the works of St. Anselm, chiefly in *Cur Deus Homo*. Someone interested in a further exploration of the subject of human freedom will also find St. Anselm interesting in his *De Concordia*. While we might not agree with all of St. Anselm's conclusions, he is nevertheless among the most interesting of the fathers for those who want to see an example of someone who strove to use reason in subjection to the Word of God; one of Anselm's guiding principles was this: *We do not seek to understand so that we may believe; we believe so that we may understand;* his point: Reason must be subject to faith formed by the Word; the only real value that it has in theological argumentation is in apologetics, in showing the scoffer that the truths of God's Word are not really at variance with reason rightly used.

By extension, St. Anselm and others of the church fathers put the emphasis on the first of these when considering the question of the necessity of salvation. The necessity is not one imposed on God from outside of himself. It is the necessity only of "what is fitting" for the God who is in his essence not only just but also gracious. The great miracle is, again, that both his justice and his grace are satisfied and can only be satisfied on the cross of his only begotten Son.

But we have lingered long enough at the pool. Muddy as its waters are apart from the Word of God, we will not deny that even with the Word of God the pool is deep indeed. And why should we expect it to be otherwise? We have been searching the holy, the all-wise mind of our Creator. The wonder is not that his mind is so deep that we never get to the bottom of it. The wonder is that we can fathom the depths of his mind and heart at all. Again, we are but dust and ashes. So great, however, is God's love for us, so ardent his desire for fellowship with us, that he comes out from behind the mask that hides his might and his wisdom; he delights to show himself to us in his Word. That's what Jesus said so shortly before he died: "I no longer call you servants, because a servant does not know his master's business. Instead, I have called you friends, for everything that I learned from my Father I have made known to you" (John 15:15).

Let us then rejoice in his revelation of himself to us. Let us never tire of that Word by which he shows himself and brings us into such blessed communion with him by faith that our fellowship will last for all eternity. The closer we draw to that Word, the closer he draws to us in it. The greater our delight in what he has to say, the greater will be his delight in revealing ever more of his grace and goodness in that Word (a point, by the way, that St. Anselm never tires of making). We will never exhaust all that is in his Word or finish in our joy in learning of him through it!

But it's time to get back to the road.

6

The Narrow Lutheran Middle Between *Good* Good Works and *Bad* Good Works

We noted earlier that Aristotle in the *Ethics* was looking for the middle road in the search for the virtuous life. In his search for the virtuous life, he noted that if a virtue is overemphasized, it can turn into a vice. Thus, for example, truthfulness is a virtue. But one's claim to being truthful can be exaggerated or minimized; in either case, the virtue has become a fault, a vice. The one who is too confident of his own truthfulness is a boaster, even if he is truthful. The one, on the other hand, who understates or undervalues the truth displays a mock modesty or a false humility. The real virtue of truthfulness lies somewhere in the middle between boastfulness and mock modesty. In behavior, he says that the person who has a ready wit needs to avoid the two opposite extremes of a ready wit: he needs to avoid excess that makes him a buffoon; and on the opposite side, he needs to avoid falling short of a ready wit lest he be a boor and a bore. Courage is the middle between cowardice and rashness. Liberality is the middle between stinginess and wasteful extravagance. Proper modesty is the middle between shamelessness and bashfulness. Friendliness is the middle between empty flattery and surly quarrelsomeness. So, to put it another way, a vice is often an exaggeration or an underestimation of a virtue.

Aristotle was a very wise man. He took reason about as far as it can go without the bright light of the Word of God. Without that Word, as wise as Aristotle was and as good as his counsel may be, he fell far short of the wisdom hidden in the mind of God and revealed in God's own Word. The middle road to which Jesus points us in his Word is one that leads us to a God-pleasing life here and to heaven hereafter. Aristotle never found that road. The best he could do is show us a road that is personally satisfying for the one on it and perhaps useful for the society of this world that ends in death. For the unbeliever, that is sadly enough. But not for us.

It is perhaps on this next stretch of the narrow middle road that Aristotle would be most offended, even shocked, were we to tell him of it. On this stretch of the road, we seek not so much the middle as we seek a loathing and a fear of one side of the road and an eager holding close to the opposite side. There is a steep cliff on the wrong side, and it is as easy to fall over it as it is steep. What makes this stretch of the road so perilous is the simple fact that outwardly the two sides of the road appear to be identical. It takes a sharp eye, an eye of faith formed by the Word of God alone, to see the fence that would keep us from falling over the cliff on the wrong side of the road. It takes a sharp eye and a steady foot to keep to the one side and to dread and avoid the other.

On this stretch of the road, the one side has on it *bad* good works and the other side has *good* good works. But they look so much alike. On both sides we see honesty and decency. We see charity and kindness. On both sides of the road are generosity and help for the needy, tenderness to the weak and the frail, food offered to the hungry and clothes for the naked, patience in suffering, cheerful words of comfort for the depressed, a forgiving spirit even for the depraved, companionship for the lonely, a shoulder for the weeping, a strong arm of protection for the helpless and the fearful. We see on both sides a disciplined life adorned with many of the virtues that Aristotle praised and that the Word of God urges. It is exactly the similarity in outward appearance that makes this stretch of the road so perilous to the incautious. Yes, immediately when we enter on this stretch of the road, we need to pay attention to a sign that marks the path:

Warning!

The warning sign reads: *Watch Out! Danger Ahead! Dame Reason with her cousin, Unbridled Emotion, threaten!* On no stretch of the road is Dame Reason's voice louder than on this one. And she takes to herself her friend and cousin, Unbridled Emotion. Together the two of them will push and shove and shout to get us off of the road and over the cliff. So take warning! We will need to give careful attention to the Word of God and exercise discipline over both Dame Reason and Unbridled Emotion if we are to stay safe and secure in Christ and his Word. In his Word, God has erected a fence to keep us from falling over the cliff on the wrong side of the road. With his Word we can see through the fence well enough to distinguish between the two sides and to see how perilous the wrong side of the road really is. Sadly, many who want to be Christians in both faith and life fail to take the warning seriously. They climb to the top of the fence with a ladder provided by Dame Reason, and then with a push from Unbridled Emotion, over the fence they go. They fall over the cliff and get stuck in the muck and mire below to the ruin of their faith.

Having heard the warning, let us consider first:

Bad good works

When we consider *bad* good works, it is first of all of utmost importance that we remember that we are considering those works from *God's* standpoint, not our own. We are looking for the answer to this question: What works are bad and good *in the eyes of God?* If we can just get that straight in our minds, much of the difficulty will be removed. It should even be obvious to reason that for the answer to that question, we must ask God. It is not up to us to decide what is pleasing in his eyes. That is up to God alone. And he isn't the least interested in our advice on the subject.

What then does God have to say about those works which are good and bad in his sight? That blatant sins against the Ten Commandments are bad in his sight needs little proof. Reason even agrees that stealing and murder, adultery, even disrespect to parents are bad. But what about their opposites? What about lives that are adorned with all of Aristotle's virtues? What about lives of hard work and honesty, chastity and reverence towards parents and the like? What about lives that even have the Word of God and prayer as important parts of the mind and the life?

All of these seemingly good works are bad, are vile sins in the eyes of God, when they are done apart from Christ! That's the long and short of it. Jesus said it completely and simply in John 15:4-6:

> Remain in me, and I will remain in you. No branch can bear fruit by itself; it must remain in the vine. Neither can you bear fruit unless you remain in me. I am the vine; you are the branches. If a man remains in me and I in him, he will bear much fruit; *apart from me you can do nothing*. If anyone does not remain in me, he is like a branch that is thrown away and withers; such branches are picked up, thrown into the fire and burned.

Thus, for a work to be good or bad in God's eyes, the connection to Christ is the decisive factor. The one who is not connected to Christ cannot do a single thing, bring forth a single work, that will be pleasing in the eyes of God. No matter what the individual's intentions were; no matter how sincere he may be; no matter how good the work looked on the outside; yes, no matter how useful and beneficial the work may have been to family, friends, or society; if it was not done in connection to Christ, it was all vile, all a sin, in the eyes of God. Both the work and the one doing it are, as Jesus himself plainly said, fit for nothing but the fire.

As we have noted elsewhere and repeatedly, our connection to Christ is a connection that God offers and gives, creates and preserves in the gospel. Those are connected to Christ as branches on a vine in whom Christ lives by faith in his work as our only and all-sufficient Savior. Apart from such a connection it is impossible to please God—again, no matter how glistening we with our works may appear on the outside.

Dame Reason is offended. Unbridled Emotion is shocked. They say: "People give to the poor. They help the needy. They have good and noble intentions when they strive to live decent and honorable lives. Some even pray, even read the Bible, even go to church. How dare you say that their works are an abomination to the Lord?"

But that is in fact the Lord's own verdict, and he is unmoved by any contradiction on our side. In a certain sense, even reason should be able to understand that. After all, God did not spare his only begotten Son but gave him up for our redemption. His Son suffered the humiliation of taking on the form of a servant and then of suffering the agony of crucifixion. He endured the whole wrath of God against the sin of the world for us and for our salvation. He purchased our redemption from sin, death, the devil, and the torments of hell. But someone says: "Well, that's all fine and good, but I want to contribute to my own salvation or earn it myself; his sacrifice just doesn't do it for me! I really feel that I'm good enough to get to heaven on my own, or at least with only some help from Jesus. That's why I do good things, lead a decent and honorable life. That's why I read the Bible, go to church, and pray. And I expect God to take note and reward me according to my will, my work, my intentions."

What should even reason conclude of such a person? What else but that such a one is guilty not only of contradicting the heart and core of the Word of God but is guilty of the most horrible ingratitude? Such a one dares to insult the Son of God and belittle the Savior's work. Such a one dares to put his own puny and imperfect works on par with those of the crucified. Such a mindset tramples underfoot the amazing grace and mercy of God by which God yearns to receive each sinner by grace alone, through faith alone. God even gives, works, and preserves that faith with his gospel in Word and sacraments. But that isn't good enough? But that someone rejects in favor of his own paltry efforts, his own opinions about them, and that, again, in flat contradiction of God's Word? Such a person calls God a liar and Christ's work inadequate! How could even reason imagine or dare to argue that such a one could please God? Such a person is more wicked than the foolish child: her mother told her to wash the dishes and that she would be happy if the child did so, but the wicked child said, "No, I prefer to smash the dishes and expect you to be happy about it when I do."

Such a person, even if he says that he believes in God, even if he goes to church and prays, is not in Christ the vine. Such a person has rejected the whole reason Christ came and lived among us and died for us and is, therefore, nothing but a dried-up branch fit only for the fire.

Jesus demonstrated the point a number of times in the gospels. We want to look at a few of the more striking examples of this point that works are bad in the eyes of God when done apart from faith in Christ's redeeming work, no matter how good they look on the outside. Think, for example, of the two men who went up into the temple to pray (Luke 18:9-14). Luke tells us that Jesus addressed the parable particularly to those "who were confident of their own righteousness." Such neither yearned for grace nor longed for forgiveness. But they led noble and outwardly virtuous lives. They went to church. They prayed. In their daily lives, they did what the law required and even more than was required; and they worked hard at it. But what does Jesus say of the Pharisee who stood and thanked God that he was righteous in his own works? Jesus declared that he did not go down to his house justified. That is, he was not declared forgiven before God's judgment seat but remained with his sin and guilt. His virtue, his works, including those that were in accord with the law of God, were nothing but sin and vice and abominations in God's eyes.

Or consider the rich young man who came to Jesus (Matthew 19:16-22). He really wanted to obey God. He was earnest and sincere in seeking after the truth. What parent would not be proud to have such a son? He could honestly say that he had kept the commandments from his youth. No doubt he did so with considerable effort. After all, the works he did do not come easily or naturally, especially when we are young. But what was the end of it all? He went away from Jesus sad. Jesus told him to do something that he just would not do. Jesus told him to give up his wealth and come and follow after the Lord. The young man's unwillingness to do such a thing, something that Jesus never asked of anyone else, should have shown the young man his real need: for all the good works that he had done, he had not kept the First Commandment; he put his wealth before God, treasuring it more than he treasured Jesus. That in turn should have brought him to see that he was in desperate need of a Savior, of grace, of forgiveness. All of the good works in the world cannot make up for idolatry. Sadly, the young man came to no such conclusion. Going away from Jesus! What could be worse than that? The young man's works could never atone for such a crime, no matter how good they were on the outside. All his works, his whole life—all was bad in the eyes of God because it was all done apart from Christ.

Then we have the parable of the workers sent out into the vineyard (Matthew 20:1-16). Jesus tells us that the kingdom of heaven is like this: God sends workers into his vineyard—some early in life, some later, some even at the last hour. But at the end, the workers called at the beginning, who worked longer and harder than the others, are rejected when he tells them to go their way. Why? Not because they didn't work and work hard. They are rejected because they did not see their works as a result and fruit of their connection to Christ. They are rejected because they thought their works merited God's favor and eternal reward. Thus, all of their good works, works done at the call and command of God himself, are deemed *bad.* The parable ends with these words: "Friend,[1] I am not being unfair to you. Didn't you agree to work for a denarius? Take your pay and go" (20:13,14). They had their reward in the time they spent in the vineyard. But that's it! They go! None of what they had done counts as an entry price into the kingdom of heaven. It all ends up, as far as getting into heaven is concerned, as good works gone bad.

These warnings of Jesus to guard against *bad* good works are especially striking when he issues them to those who serve in the church. It is possible that someone who has been called to serve in the public ministry could end up with all his works declared to be *bad.* It is possible for those who preached and taught altogether in accord with the Word of God to end up cast out into outer darkness. What a dreadful thought! How it makes those of us called by Christ to serve as his ambassadors shudder! How it

---

[1] Greek scholars will want to note that the word which Jesus uses here for "friend" is not *philos.* It is *etaire,* the word used by Jesus in the parable of the wedding (Matthew 22:12) and again in addressing Judas in the Garden of Gethsemane (Matthew 26:50). The word always connotes someone who has been befriended most generously and graciously but who has betrayed the grace and goodness of his benefactor by acting unfaithfully, ungratefully, and altogether counter to the intention of his benefactor.

should cause us to heed with greatest care and earnestness the exhortation of St. Paul to Timothy: "Watch your life and doctrine closely. Persevere in them, because if you do, you will save both yourself and your hearers" (1 Timothy 4:16). St. Paul is, as the context certainly makes clear, not telling Timothy to earn his own salvation by his faithfulness. But he is warning against unfaithfulness by which salvation can be lost both in the preacher and in some of those who hear him. That's what Jesus said as well at the conclusion of his great Sermon on the Mount:

> Not everyone who says to me, "Lord, Lord," will enter the kingdom of heaven, but only he who does the will of my Father who is in heaven. Many will say to me on that day, "Lord, Lord, did we not prophesy in your name, and in your name drive out demons and perform many miracles?" Then I will tell them plainly, "I never knew you. Away from me, you evildoers!" (Matthew 7:21-23)

Oh, what a horrible prospect! All of the good work done in his name may well have done much good in the world and in the church. The work could have served to bring many into the kingdom of heaven as the Holy Spirit worked through the Word preached and the sacraments administered by such people. But in the end, as far as the one preaching and teaching is concerned, the good works were *bad* good works. They were done with what was ultimately an unbelieving attitude. Some were hypocrites and lived lives that were a denial of what they preached and taught. Some were just in it because the work afforded them a good living. Some tragically did what they did to earn their way into heaven, perhaps to atone—at least in their own minds—for sins of the past. Whatever the reason, no matter how powerful or even sincere, no matter how effective the work on the souls of others, such people hear for all eternity that most dreadful verdict: "I never knew you. Away from me, you evildoers!"

With such a possibility and prospect in mind, the greatest of the apostles says of himself: "I do not run like a man running aimlessly; I do not fight like a man beating the air. No, I beat my body and make it my slave so that after I have preached to others, I myself will not be disqualified for the prize" (1 Corinthians 9:26,27).

Again, a work that to all outward appearances seems good, even very good, is a *bad* good work *in the eyes of God* if done apart from Christ; it is a *bad* good work if it is separated from trust in him as the only and all-sufficient Savior of sinners always in desperate need of grace and forgiveness.

Paul knew and understood this point so well that he never tired of driving it home. In Philippians 3:7-9, for example, he speaks of all the good works that he had done before the Savior brought him to faith. They were works in accord with the law. He had been zealous and eager in his keeping of the law and could boast that he exceeded most in his life of obedience to the law. But what was his conclusion of his entire life apart from Christ the vine? He declared, "I consider [all of it] rubbish, that I may gain Christ and be found in him, not having a righteousness of my own that comes from the law, but that which is through faith in Christ— the righteousness that comes from God and is by faith."

Read the epistle to the Galatians. It begins with the strongest possible condemnation of all the apparent good works that the Galatians had adopted from the law in order to contribute thereby to their own salvation. In words inspired by God himself, he has this to say of those who taught them and moved them to such *bad* good works: "If anybody is preaching to you a gospel other than what you accepted, let him be eternally condemned!" (Galatians 1:9). And lest anyone was dozing when he said it the first time, he repeats it!

Indeed, as Jesus also makes very clear, the worst of all of the *bad* good works are those taught and done in the name of God but apart from trust in God alone for mercy and grace. Jesus quotes from the prophet Isaiah when he warns: "You hypocrites! Isaiah was right when he prophesied about you: 'These people honor me with their lips, but their hearts are far from me. They worship me in vain; their teachings are but rules taught by men'" (Matthew 15:7-9).

Lumped together with those who were hypocrites even when they taught the truth are those who may not have been hypocrites but who taught false doctrine. Against all such, Jesus also gives warning, as do almost all of the writers of both the Old and New Testaments. Jesus puts it most succinctly: "Watch out for false prophets. They come to you in sheep's clothing, but inwardly they are ferocious wolves" (Matthew 7:15). The sincerity of the wolf is not at issue; there is no doubt that the wolf is sincere when the wolf does what a wolf does. But what is the result for those caught by the sincere and hardworking wolf? The result of his false teaching is the point: teaching contrary to the Word of God always harms the connection of the branch to the vine, always damages, and may ultimately destroy faith. The work of the wolf may not always reach the goal the devil has in mind when he works through the false teaching of the wolf; but that doesn't alter his goal, nor does it do away with the damage, even when the goal is not fully reached. Therefore, Jesus warns, "Watch out!" One would be a fool indeed who would answer, "But the wolf is a beautiful animal; and he doesn't always kill, so I'll take my chances!"

Thus, whether the teaching is true but done by hypocrites or whether the teaching is false but done in the name of God by heretics, it is all *bad*. The hypocrite, even if he is teaching correctly, loses his own soul; the false teacher damages and may ultimately also ruin his own soul and the souls of others. Therefore, in the church of God, let the teacher ever be on guard over his own soul lest in the end he be found wanting because, as good as the work appeared, he did it apart from Christ the vine. And let both teacher and learner ever be on guard that their teaching and works are always in accord with the Word of God, not a mishmash of God's Word and their own.

It is when this discussion of *bad* good works gets applied in the here and now that people get upset. Our forefathers in the Lutheran Confessions and Luther repeatedly in his writings condemned the works of the whole of the Roman papacy as works of the antichrist prophesied by Paul in 2 Thessalonians 2:1-12. Luther and the Lutheran Confessions declared the Mass to be an abomination together with the whole of monasticism and the enforced celibacy of the clergy. And why? Because all those in a monastery or convent were insincere? Because all who claimed to be celibate were liars? No, that wasn't it. Whether some in monasteries and convents were hypocrites or not, the real and fundamental objection was this: The whole work of the Mass and the whole and declared intention of monasticism and priestly celibacy was that by such works one can at least in part merit his own salvation; a person can even do works greater than those commanded in God's law and credit them to the accounts of others, since he doesn't need all of them for himself!

Such teaching and all such works are monstrous in the eyes of God! They rob Christ of his glory as the only and all-sufficient Savior. They are works that are either condemned in the Scriptures or that in any case God never asked for. They give fallen human beings credit for work that only Christ can do. Yes, and they either make people self-righteous and proud when they do such works or drive people to despair of God's mercy when they fail. That should certainly be sufficient reason to condemn such works as *bad* good works—no matter how sincerely done, no matter how glistening and holy they appear on the outside.

The same verdict falls on all of the teachings and works of those who teach and work apart from Christ in whatever religion they may be. Christ's words stand: "Apart from me, you can do nothing!" (John 15:5).

Oh, but now Dame Reason protests and, together with Unbridled Emotion, gets angry. "But don't people in other religions do many fine things? Don't they help a lot of people when they teach and when they build hospitals and when they serve the poor? And don't we all basically worship the same God? Why do we always have to criticize as though we are the only ones who have the truth? Doesn't even Jesus say, 'Don't judge'?"

Jesus does indeed say, "Do not judge, or you too will be judged" (Matthew 7:1). But did you notice that he said it in the same chapter in which he warned so sternly against false teaching and false teachers? When he tells us not to judge, he is warning against all self-righteousness; he is warning us not to sit on our proverbial high horses as though *we* of ourselves and with our own merit were free to look down our noses at others or, indeed, to concoct our own doctrines apart from him and from his Word. But as he himself makes very clear in the rest of the chapter and in all of his Word, we are to judge on the basis of his Word, with a spirit of humble trust in his Word and work and in dread of ever departing from either what he has said in his Word or what he has done for us on the cross! Such judging is in point of fact not ours but his.

Indeed, those who refuse to judge have missed the whole point of the Scriptures. God gave them to teach us *the* way—not just *a* way, one among many—of salvation and thereby the difference between truth and error. St. Peter and St. Paul tell us that when they speak of the goal of the Scriptures in 2 Peter 1:12-21 and in 2 Timothy 3:15,16. Paul urges us to give heed to the words of the apostles and prophets so that we will know the difference between truth and error and "no longer be infants, tossed back and forth by the waves, and blown here and there by every wind of teaching and by the cunning and craftiness of men in their deceitful scheming" (cf. Ephesians 4:11-16). All of these and so many other passages require us to judge and to make sure that the judging is on the basis of God's own Word, not on the basis of unaided reason or unbridled emotion.

Yes, let those who follow Dame Reason and Unbridled Emotion practice what they preach. Let them try to conduct their lives without ever judging. They will have to raise their children without any instruction at all. Truth and error to such must all be the same thing. So such passionate non-judgers should let their children hang out with thugs and drug dealers—you don't want to judge. Let them eat what they want and go to bed when they will—perish the thought that you should judge. Let them do just as they please and utter not a word of rebuke when they turn out and live like rabid beasts—after all, we shouldn't judge. Oh, but if you don't want to live like that or raise your children for this life like that, why then should you object when God's Word and his servants warn against all that would damage us in the eyes of God and hinder our entrance into life eternal?

Again, we want to keep this in mind: We are talking about works that are bad *in the eyes of God,* particularly as those works are related to faith and eternal salvation. All those works that are done apart from Christ, no matter how good they may appear on the outside, even such as are done in all sincerity, are *bad* good works. They are done without trust in Christ as the only and all-sufficient Savior. Or they are works that are done without and contrary to the Word of God.

As a final note in our consideration of *bad* good works, we should observe how God deals with such works *in this life.* It is a mark of God's special grace and mercy that he does not immediately reveal his anger against all those works that are done apart from Christ and are, therefore, in his eyes *bad* good works. Were he to rain down his wrath and punishment on all such works, the world would have perished long ago. The time will come, of course, when all *bad* good works will be seen as such and judged as such. But that time is not yet. It awaits the return of Christ on the Last Day.

Until the Last Day, very many *bad* good works are in fact outwardly rewarded. That may seem at first blush a terrible contradiction. If God is going to judge and condemn all *bad* good works on the Last Day, why would he *outwardly* reward many of them in the here and now? There are so many reasons, and all of them point to his grace and goodness and mercy:

1. He tolerates and even rewards outwardly many *bad* good works for the sake of the church. The Bible gives us one particular example of this point. St. Paul urges us in 1 Timothy 2:1-6 to pray for governments and rulers. Why? Because governments are Christian and rulers are godly? Hardly! They certainly were not in Paul's day. Almost without exception, the rulers were vile and depraved, even persecutors of the church. Why then should we pray for them? Because governments perform a most useful service for the church and for believers, even when the rulers are wicked, even when on their best days their works are *bad* good works. To the extent that they maintain law and order, they make it possible for Christians to lead, as Paul says, "peaceful and quiet lives in all godliness and holiness." Will such rulers on the Last Day escape God's wrath? Certainly not! For such good as they did for believers was not done in Christ the vine. Moreover, most often the rulers did the works with not the least intention of benefiting the church. But God in his wise providence, in his goodness to us, used them nevertheless and often contrary to their own will for our benefit. That benefit, whether intended by rulers or not, is evident when we look at countries that have no government; it is almost impossible in such places for anyone to lead a peaceful, quiet, or godly and honest life.

2. In the same passage, the apostle gives us another reason why God would not punish immediately the works of

those who labor outside of Christ the vine. He says that we should pray for government and for rulers: "This is good, and pleases God our Savior, who wants all men to be saved and to come to a knowledge of the truth. For there is one God and one mediator between God and men, the man Christ Jesus, who gave himself as a ransom for all men." Good order in the state and rulers who maintain it serve the mission of the church. That is so regardless of their own personal agenda or intention. Where there is no order in society, in the state, it is very difficult and sometimes impossible for the church to proclaim the saving gospel. So in his love for us and so that we may have the blessed privilege of sharing the gospel with those who still need to hear the gospel, God outwardly blesses the works of even the most corrupt of rulers.

3. He does not immediately judge works that he himself counts as sins because his patience with the unbelieving world is so great. Some of those with whom we share the gospel by its power will come to believe it just as we do. We don't know who will believe it and who will not; only God knows that. But as evidence of his patience with the fallen world, he gives it time. Consider Noah: He preached for 120 years before the flood finally came and swept away the godless of his day.

4. In his patience with us too, God does not immediately pour out his anger on all evil and on *bad* good works. Who among us will dare to claim that all of his works were done in Christ, out of love for him, and trusting in him alone as God and Savior? Who among us has not had times, perhaps many of them in a lifetime, when he followed the example of the rich young ruler? For whatever reason, we went away from God's Word and will because we did not fear, love, and trust in God above all things. St. Peter, as we remember such times, comforts us with the patience of God also with us: "The Lord is not slow in keeping his promise [of judgment], as some understand slowness. He is patient with you, not wanting anyone to perish, but everyone to come to repentance" (2 Peter 3:9).

5. Perhaps most surprising to us, even inside of the church God does not immediately pour out his anger on the works of hypocrites and teachers of false doctrine. The day will come when those who harm the faith of others will be judged, as Jesus tells us a number of times (e.g., Matthew 11:20-24; Luke 17:1,2). But for now, out of patience with the hypocrite and the false teacher, he endures their works. Also, in order to test and thereby to strengthen the faith of believers, he puts up with it for the present. Paul, in pointing out the difference between false doctrine and true, between genuine teachers and self-appointed ones, urged the Corinthians: "Examine yourselves to see whether you are in the faith; test yourselves. Do you not realize that Christ Jesus is in you— unless, of course, you fail the test?" (2 Corinthians 13:5). In the same vein, he calls to mind how so many in the Old Testament perished in their hypocrisy and idolatry and then warns us, "So, if you think you are standing firm, be careful that you don't fall" (1 Corinthians 10:12).

Thus, while God is patient and tolerates for the present *bad* good works, and that even for our sake, his patience toward evil is not a pattern for us to follow in our own lives. That is, his patience is not an excuse for us to be lazy and indifferent toward our own *bad* good works. Nor is it an excuse for the toleration of false doctrine and false teachers in the church. They are tolerated for the present by him for our warning and so that we may prove our faithfulness. We prove our faithfulness by following him and his Word, by clinging to it all the more as we see the day of judgment approaching. That's exactly the point of St. Paul's warning in citing the example of Israel in 1 Corinthians 10. And that is the point of St. Peter's warning as well in 2 Peter 3 when he reminds us: "The day of the Lord will come like a thief. The heavens will disappear with a roar; the elements will be destroyed by fire, and the earth and everything in it will be laid bare. Since everything will be destroyed in this way, what kind of people ought you to be? You ought to live holy and godly lives as you look forward to the day of God" (2 Peter 3:10-12). Jesus tells us that an important element in a holy and godly life is, as noted earlier, that we watch out for false prophets (Matthew 7:15). St. Paul tells us too that we should avoid and have nothing to do with them (Romans 16:17,18).

So then, and to sum it all up, *bad* good works are all those works that are done apart from Christ the vine. They may look good on the outside. They may be works that are outwardly obedient to the Word of God. But if they are done with the notion that they somehow merit heaven or help in some way towards our salvation, then they are by definition *bad* good works. Then the worker places himself and his works alongside of Christ as a reason for his hope of heaven. That robs Christ of his glory as the only Savior. That places such a person in the shoes of the self-righteous Pharisees who rejected God's grace and Christ's merit. By their self-righteousness they lost the forgiveness and eternal life that Christ came to win for them. No matter how good their works appeared on the outside, whether they were hypocrites or heretics or both, the bottom line was this: Their works were apart from Christ. May God preserve us from the deadly end of *bad* good works!

Good good works

Perhaps there is no doctrine of the Bible more misunderstood than the Bible's teaching about genuine good works. We Lutherans in particular are accused by many outside of the Lutheran church of teaching that good works are unnecessary. Luther was accused of teaching that too; and the rumor was that Lutherans all lived like beasts, with no government, no discipline, no marriage even. Emperor Charles V in the Edict of Worms condemned Luther as a heretic and an outlaw, charging Luther with teaching such things. St. Paul was accused of the same thing and, ultimately, so was Christ.

The accusation arises from our drumbeat urging of the basic truth of the Bible, the truth that no good works can save us or contribute in the least to our salvation. It arises from the never-too-often-repeated cry of Lutherans in private prayers and in the Sunday morning liturgy: "God, be merciful to me, a sinner." That is what I am from the hairs on my head to the soles of my feet, from the moment of my conception to my dying breath.

The emphasis in orthodox Lutheranism on salvation by grace alone, through faith alone, because of Christ alone, is *almost* impossible to overstate. We know well the pride that lurks just beneath the surface of every human heart. We know how easy it is for us to boast in the presence of God as though we merited something from him on account of our own goodness. And so we rehearse it endlessly in our minds: "I know that nothing good lives in me, that is, in my sinful nature" (Romans 7:18). And there echoes in our souls the reminder that Jesus also gives us on our best days: "So you also, when you have done everything you were told to do, should say, 'We are unworthy servants; we have only done our duty'" (Luke 17:10).

Yes, it is *almost* impossible to overemphasize the fundamental truth of the Scriptures and of our Lutheran faith that salvation is free, entirely the work of Christ for us. It is *almost* impossible to overemphasize the truth that salvation is given entirely and alone through faith created and preserved by the Holy Spirit in the gospel message of the Word and the sacraments. But this blessed and most comforting truth is overemphasized and perverted when the careless and the lazy proudly declare: "I'm a Lutheran; we don't believe in good works. Since we are saved by grace through faith, it doesn't matter what we do or if we do nothing at all." That is certainly not what the Bible says! And that's not what our Lutheran Confessions say either. St. Paul summed it up best:

> The grace of God that brings salvation has appeared to all men. It teaches us to say "No" to ungodliness and worldly passions, and to live self-controlled, upright and godly lives in this present age, while we wait for the blessed hope—the glorious appearing of our great God and Savior, Jesus Christ, who gave himself for us to redeem us from all wickedness and to purify for himself a people that are his very own, eager to do what is good. (Titus 2:11-14)

So there is such a thing as *good* good works. They are works done, as St. Paul here tells us, not to earn our salvation but as a result of our salvation. They are works that are done in accord with the law of God summed up in the Ten Commandments. They are works done eagerly by those whose whole goal in life is to please the God who loves us and gave himself for us.

To be sure, there is no such thing as a perfect good work. Even the best of our works are stained by the imperfection of the sin that remains in us. But the imperfection in our works drives us all the more to trust in the Savior's work for our salvation and not to trust in our own efforts for any part of that salvation. If we trust that God has forgiven our obvious sins that had not a shred of good in them, why should we not trust as well that he forgives those sins that stain our good works? Forgiveness for the stains on our good works is certainly included when St. Paul assures us that for those who live in Christ by faith, there is no condemnation (Romans 8:1). Trusting in that forgiveness, so gracious, so full, so free, we strive to heed the exhortation of Jesus: "Let your light shine before men, that they may see your good deeds and praise your Father in heaven" (Matthew 5:16). In our guilt we look to Jesus alone for rescue. In our good works we still look to Jesus alone for their acceptance and God's good pleasure in them.

Notice that Jesus does not say "that [people] may praise you for your good works" but "that they may . . . praise your Father in heaven." Our good works bring praise to our Father in heaven in much the same way that a child's useful, good, and decent life brings credit to his family on earth. The world is drowning in the chaos that comes from lives which reflect only lust and greed and obsession with self and pleasure. What a witness to the gospel is the life that outwardly is the opposite! How many have come to hear the gospel because of the peace and the order, the decency and the usefulness to others that they saw in the life of a humble and pious Christian? Such a life certainly brought praise to the Father on those occasions—however rare they may be—when someone was first drawn to hear the gospel by the light of Christ radiating from the life of a Christian!

We should not imagine that such works, the *good* good works of a Christian, are a matter of indifference to God. Perhaps an analogy here will be useful. A father is teaching his little boy to ride a bicycle. He holds his son and the bicycle so that the boy does not fall off. He runs alongside for a time, even after he has let go of his son and his bike. The little boy squeals with delight when he has gone a way on his own. He looks back with a broad smile at his father, expecting his father to be proud and to share in his joy at his accomplishment.

What a wretched father he would be if he were to say this to his son: "I don't know what you're so pleased about. After all, I bought the bike. I ran alongside you and held you up. You could have accomplished nothing were it not for me." What a grouch! That's not at all the way a good father would act. Though it is all true, that the whole business would be nothing at all were it not for the father's efforts, nevertheless, the father will behave as though his son has done the greatest thing in the world. He will be pleased and proud. He will even praise his son, as though his son did it all on his own! A mother acts the same way; she takes the mindless scribblings of her little child and puts them up on the refrigerator door. She treats them as though they were more precious than the *Mona Lisa*. It doesn't occur to her to say, "Well, it's really just silly scribbles, all accomplished with *my* paper, *my* paints and chalk, and *my* cleaning up the mess afterward!" No, in each case the work is viewed with delight because it came from a heart eager to please the watchful eye of a loving parent.

And that's to a large extent the way God is with our good works. He knows, and so do we, that he gave us whatever ability we have to do good works. He knows, and so do we, that the desire to do them comes from him, from the desire implanted in us to respond to the gospel with a life of thankful obedience. He knows, and so do we, that he has in his providence provided us with just such opportunities to serve him as match the abilities that he has given us. But knowing all of that, he beams with pleasure and satisfaction when in our own faltering ways we love and serve him.

That's what the psalmist says: "The LORD delights in those who fear him, who put their hope in his unfailing love" (Psalm 147:11). All of that fear which dreads displeasing God and all that hope which trusts in his unfailing love is one hundred percent God's gift in the Word. But, nevertheless, he accepts it and more; he is delighted with it as he sees it take root in us. Is that not an amazing thing? Is that not a wondrous incentive to these preeminent good works of receiving his gifts with thanksgiving? Ultimately, that is the best of all good works, to dread offending him and to delight in receiving his grace heaped upon grace.

We see that same delight from God in the gospels when Jesus praises faith, whether the faith of the woman who touched the edge of his cloak (Matthew 9:22) or of the centurion (Matthew

145

8:10), to mention just two of the many such examples. In each case the faith was entirely Jesus' gift through the message that these people had heard of or from him. In each case they had applied what they knew from that message to their particular situation; and then with their God-given trust in him, they came to him and received his help. But Jesus never says something like, "Well, at least you had the good sense to believe." No, he praises his gift in them and their subsequent use of it.

And if God is delighted with those preeminent good works that are so completely his gift, how could we doubt that he is delighted as well with such other works as flow from his gifts of penitent fear and confident hope in his mercy? We are not left to guess that such is the case. Indeed, the least little thing, something noted by few and looked down on by those who did note it, receives from Jesus the highest praise. Consider the widow who placed her fraction of a penny in the offering box in the temple. With what extravagant words Jesus praises her! "[She] has put more into the treasury than all the others" (Mark 12:43). Or think of the woman who anointed Jesus in Mark 14:3-9. His praise of her goes way beyond what that woman could have possibly thought of the work she had done—that's how generous he is in his acceptance of what we do in love for him! He says of her: "She poured perfume on my body beforehand to prepare for my burial. I tell you the truth, wherever the gospel is preached throughout the world, what she has done will also be told, in memory of her." Then there is the example of Mary and Martha in Luke 10:38-42. Jesus praises Mary, and for what? For listening! She had chosen to do the best of works. That didn't mean that what Martha was doing was all wrong and bad; it just wasn't, as Jesus himself put it, "what is better" and the "only one thing [that is] needed" (better translation: "necessary").

Again, it boggles the mind: Jesus receives and is pleased with what we do for him and is most pleased of all when we are happy to receive from him what he has to give in his gospel. And that is so without in the least diminishing his pleasure and God's delight in those things that we do for the church and in service to one another simply because we love Jesus and want to please him.

In obedience to his command, we pray for peace and order in the state; and he shows his delight by preserving the world to this

very moment so that it will be easier for us in our weakness to
serve him. We listen to his Word and strive to live our lives
according to it; and he shows his good pleasure by not allowing us
to be tempted beyond our ability and then even still forgiving us
when we do not avail ourselves of the help he offers us in the
hour of temptation. We support the work of the church, and he
blesses such support by preserving his Word and sacraments in
our midst. We play the part of the boy who shared his few rolls
and pieces of fish with Jesus so that Jesus could feed the thousands with it (John 6:9-13). We go with the Magi to worship the
Christ Child, little realizing the use he will make of our gifts to
him or the blessing he will bestow on others from our humble act
of worship. We clothe the poor and thus put a blanket around the
shivering Christ who lives in them. We feed the hungry and
thereby nourish the Savior who feeds us all. We give a drink of
water to the thirsty and so quench the thirst of him who is the
Water of Life.

Do you not notice it, especially in Jesus' words to us about the
last judgment, how he treasures the littlest things? He saves
them up. He counts them. He is eager to bring all those little
things out to show the whole world on the Last Day.

> I was hungry and you gave me something to eat, I was
> thirsty and you gave me something to drink, I was a
> stranger and you invited me in, I needed clothes and you
> clothed me, I was sick and you looked after me, I was in
> prison and you came to visit me. . . . I tell you the truth,
> whatever you did for one of the least of these brothers of
> mine, you did for me. (Matthew 25:35,36,40)

See! The devil didn't destroy goodness and virtue. See! The
gospel did produce fruit appropriate to the vine. See! God is
pleased! What more incentive do we need than to strive after a life
in the vine, a life that reflects that we have been with Jesus?

The works praised in the gospels are not splashy and highly
regarded by the world. They are simple reflections of Christ's love
for us in our loving service to him in our service to one another.
Certainly some will be able to do great works because of the
greater gifts that God has given them. But in their own eyes, the

147

works are on the same level as the works of the lowliest of Christians doing what he is able to do with the different gifts that God gave him. The gifted and faithful teacher or preacher brings thousands to Christ with the gospel and his God-given understanding of it. The mother teaches her children about Jesus and how to pray with the gift that God has given to her to do with her children what no one else could. Both do works great, high, and holy in the eyes of God. The little old lady who is a shut-in or the shy old gentleman in the hospital invites the pastor in and listens with gratitude to the pastor's simple devotion. Little does he or she know what a great work was done just by a kind smile and a "Thank you for coming, Pastor!"—so different, so encouraging for the pastor compared to the reception he gets on many a discipline call or when the door is slammed in his face on an evangelism call!

In sum, as St. Paul reminds us, whatever we do, we should strive to do it to the glory of God (1 Corinthians 10:31). He mentions the most common works of all: eating and drinking. How can those be works done to the glory of God and, therefore, works in which God delights? We give thanks to God for food and drink; we use the strength he gives from nourishment to carry out our duties in life in accord with his Word. That praises him; that pleases him. Those simple works begin in a heart devoted to God and his Word, as Jesus shows us in the Beatitudes (Matthew 5:1-11). They are works possible for the great and the small and works treasured by Jesus as fruits of faith in all who exercise themselves in them. They are works that he blesses and rewards beyond all possible merit, and that because he himself is ultimately their source. Thus, not one of them escapes his notice, his pleasure, his corresponding blessing (Mark 10:28-30[2]). Yes, we cannot out-give or out-serve him. He always gives back more so that he will never be in

---

[2] This passage is especially interesting because it lists persecution as one of the blessings that comes as a reward for putting Christ and his kingdom first! Persecution confirms for the Christian that he was right in putting Christ and his kingdom first, since everything else is always at risk, can easily be lost, or can be taken away. But when Christ and his kingdom come first, the losses are put into perspective: they weren't all really that bad or that much of a loss; for as good as the things lost were, they were never what really mattered—and that no one can take away. See also in this connection Matthew 6:25-34 as an excellent commentary on this verse.

our debt and we will always be delighted to serve him still more (Malachi 3:8-14; Luke 6:38).

So the little girl helps her mother. The little boy helps his sister and imitates his father. The mother cares for her children and her husband. The husband looks for ways to please his wife and works with a mindset of providing for the needs of his family. The pastor prepares his sermons, and the teacher prepares the lessons for the day. The policeman stands guard. The ruler and the judge govern honestly and in the fear of God. The old set a good example and pray for the young. The young show reverence for the old and patience when they are slow. And on and on it goes. All things great and small done in accord with the Word of God, done out of love for Christ and to serve those around us, are *good* good works. They are remembered by God. They are taken out like precious jewels for God to show off to the world of saints and angels and to spite the devil on the Last Day. They are done in the humility of those who are confident and trust not in their works but in God's mercy, his grace, his generosity, his faithfulness to his Word.

And did you notice in Jesus' great parable of the sheep and the goats, in Matthew 25:31-46, that many of those works were done almost by reflex? The saints do not answer Jesus' praise of their works by saying, "Of course! That's why we did them, so that you would notice and finally praise us for them." Rather, their answer is one of humble instinct, something like this: "Oh, I wasn't even thinking of that when I did those things. Besides that, I didn't do them perfectly or often enough." Jesus' words of praise are for us even when we were, as it were, on "automatic pilot." How more than kind of him! And did you notice too that he never mentions the facts that the works were not perfect and were not done as often as they could have been? And why doesn't he mention that? It is because all of our sins—including those that stained even our best works—have been washed away. There is no further need to mention them!

If we have a mountain of sins that need forgiveness, and we do, then let us strive to build a mountain of good works that thank and praise him for the forgiveness he won for us at so great a price. We build that mountain when we hear his Word and delight to receive his grace heaped upon grace. We build it when we worship and pray in response to his Word. We build it when we look to our stations in life (Luther's Table of Duties in the Catechism) and serve one another in our stations in life. We do it when in love to him and to one another we forgive one another and help one another grow in faith, in doctrine, in life. We build it when as much as possible we seek only his honor and not our own, only the service of another and not the service and praise of self.

So let no one say, "I'm a Lutheran, and we don't believe in good works!" Both the Bible and the Lutheran Confessions show no patience for that kind of an attitude. Instead, both urge on us the patient and persistent encouragement of the Savior himself that we abound in good works as branches in the vine. If you doubt it, read the Sermon on the Mount (Matthew 5–7). Read Romans 12; Ephesians 5,6; Galatians 5,6; 1 John; James—in short, any book of the Bible. Read the summary refutation of such a perversion of the truth in Article IV of the Formula of Concord, a refutation repeated often also elsewhere in the Confessions. You will find in the Bible and in the Confessions one urging after another to abound in good works. You will find them urging us to do good works not to contribute to our salvation but because of the love of Christ and the needs of those all around us. And yes, they will urge us to good works also because of our own great and very personal need to show our love and gratitude to him who loved us first and gave himself for us. If that doesn't move us to strive after *good* good works, then we can only conclude that we are dead branches already broken off from the vine and fit for nothing but the fire, just as Jesus said.

We do well to note yet another benefit that each one of us can derive from our own good works. One almost hesitates to mention it, lest it be misunderstood. But there is this benefit: that our own good works, when they are *good* good works, are evidences of Christ's life and the Spirit's work within us. Our real certainty of Christ's presence and the Spirit's work, of course, comes from the testimony and promise of Christ in the Word and sacraments. But it is also true that whenever we do something out of love for Christ, in accord with his Word and for the benefit of someone else, we have a proof and an evidence of faith, of Christ's life in us as well as his life for us. Where did the desire come from? Where did the impulse come from? Where did the ability to carry out the desire and the impulse as an act of service and obedience come from? It was all from Christ the vine. It was all from the Spirit alive in us by the power of the gospel.

Perhaps we so seldom consider this other benefit because of our justified fear that we might fall into work-righteousness. We know how easy it is for us to slip into the idolatrous notion that somehow our works may contribute to our salvation. To escape that danger, we may too easily disparage the good works that flow from faith and their benefit even to faith. But keeping the warning in mind, there is nevertheless a great benefit to our own souls in these evidences of God's effective working in us. The evidence of his work in us can be a comfort to us especially when our consciences are ready to damn us and drive us to despair because of our sins. We can be so thoroughly aware of our inclination to evil and of the rot within us that we might start to think that we have no good works at all.

Oh, but we do have good works. We deplore our sin and shame. And Psalm 51 says that God does not despise the broken heart and the contrite sigh, that they are sacrifices which please him (51:17). We cry to God day and night for help; that's a good work; that's what he wants us to do (Psalm 91:15). We do strive, however imperfectly, to serve our neighbor out of love and not from compulsion; God is the one who planted that impulse in us—he is always pleased with his own work within us (Philippians 2:13). We do listen to the Word of the Lord and find in it all our health and help; that's why he gave us his Word, and he is delighted that we listen to his voice in it (Psalm 91).

Those are all good works. And where did they come from? From Jesus! From the Holy Spirit! St. Paul reminds us that no one can confess that Jesus is Lord except by the work of the Holy Spirit (1 Corinthians 12:3). As already noted, even the desire to do works that are pleasing to God is a gift and work of God in us (Philippians 2:13). Jesus says the same thing from a slightly different perspective when he reminds us that without him we can do nothing good, that the good we do comes from him; he gives the desire, the ability, the opportunity, the strength (John 15:1-6).

What a comfort! How is it that I confess Christ, that I pray, that I hear his Word with gladness? How is it that I want to do what he wants me to do? How is it that, however imperfectly, I actually love and serve, seeking no reward save that of knowing that it is what he wants? How is it that, however weakly, I do struggle against temptation out of love for God and gratitude to Christ? It all happens and comes about as a result of his life in me through the power of his gospel in me in the Word and sacraments.

How then can I despair? Why then should I look only at the fault and the sin, which have in any case been forgiven? Far better that I should look sometimes at the works; I look at them not as proofs that I am better than someone else, nor as my contributions to my own salvation. No, rather, I see Christ in them; I see that he really does live in me. I see the Holy Spirit in them; I see that he really does provide the impulse, the desire, the longing to serve God out of love for his perfect gift of full salvation. So then, God has not abandoned me. He has kept his promise to be with me. See, his Word promised it. See, the works are evidence that he has kept his Word and promise. Is there always room for growth and for improvement and always reason for confession that I have not done as much as I could or should? Of course that's true. But that is not a reason to ignore, much less to despise, such evidence as there is of Christ's life in me. Again, it's a matter of balance, a matter of striking the narrow middle way.

Luther, who more clearly than most saw the danger of relying on works for salvation, saw also this point with equal clarity. One of his recurring themes in condemning the scholastic theology that did so much damage to souls in his day was this: The scholastics taught that a person could do good works, works that were pleasing to God, without the assistance or the gracious presence of God. No, Luther declared, and that on the basis of texts we have already considered! No, works truly pleasing to God cannot be done without the presence and assistance of God himself (e.g., Smalcald Articles, III, I, 7; cf. also Apology, Article IV; Formula of Concord, Solid Declaration, Article IV, par. 38). In fact, that's what makes good works good: Christ is in them; he motivates them; he gives opportunity for them, desire to do them, strength to do them. And then, in and with him, we do them.

How good and gracious God is! Even in our works he points us to Christ and forgiveness. Even in our stumbling, feeble, faltering works he wants to remind us that we are his and he is ours. Even in our struggle with despair he points us to the evidence that we are trees with good fruits, branches grafted onto him, the vine. What a beautiful thing that will be on the Last Day when before all the saints and angels he points to these fruits of his in us; what a beautiful thing it will be when he points to each one of us and says in effect, "See, I was alive in him and in her; see, this is the evidence of it; look what he did, what she did, just for me!" (Matthew 25:40). So the primary truth of the gospel is *Christ FOR us!* But we rejoice also in the consequence of that truth: *Christ IN us.*

As we rejoice in these two truths, it is a great relief for us to know that our works do not contribute to our salvation. Think what torment it should be for us if they were a part of our salvation. We would or should then constantly be in fear that we had not done enough or done it well enough to accomplish the goal of our salvation. We would at the hour of death remember all the failures and only the failures. With only reason as our guide, we would die in despair.

But thanks be to God! We are free from such torment. Our works are those of children made heirs of salvation by grace alone through faith alone! We are not trying to earn God's favor; as children we already have that. We are not trying to earn our salvation; as those forgiven we already have that. We are not trying to set aside God's wrath at our failures and imperfections, our weaknesses and temptations, our stumbling and our stupidity; Jesus set aside God's wrath fully on the cross. Our works then are done freely, gladly. They are done as the works of children eager to please a kind and loving Father. They are done as the works of the already redeemed whose lives are hidden in the Redeemer as branches in the vine. They are done as the beloved of God in love to God. He is pleased to count it as service to him when we serve those around us, those he loves as much as he loves us.

God's reward for *good* good works

As if God could not find enough ways to bless us, he blesses us and rewards us already in this life for those works we did out of love for him, in obedience to his commandments, and in service to one another. Jesus says it so simply, "I tell you the truth, anyone who gives you a cup of water in my name because you belong to

Christ will certainly not lose his reward" (Mark 9:41, cf. also Matthew 10:40-42). St. Paul reminds us of the promise of long life attached by God to the Fourth Commandment. And then he adds additional promises of reward from God to all those who serve as Christians, who do their duty (Ephesians 6:1-9). As we noted earlier, the blessing is out of all proportion to the merit of the work. That's the way God is—always so generous, always giving more than can ever be deserved, lest he ever be considered in someone's debt!

Sometimes the blessings that reward good works may in a certain sense be considered *natural*. Thus, for example, the one who leads an outwardly moral and decent life has the reward of a good reputation. Such a one is spared the shame and disgrace of the outwardly immoral and indecent. We see the good and bad of that in the parable of the prodigal son—really of the two prodigal sons (Luke 15:11-31). The first son suffered well-deserved misery because of his sins; the second son, as a blessing of his obedience, enjoyed all that his father had while he was with him. The sad element in the parable is that the second son did not grasp that the blessings he had from his father outweighed his own faithfulness. Instead, the second son imagined that he deserved all that he had, that in fact his father owed him for his works. But the point remains that there are abundant blessings which flow from faithfulness and obedience; the blessings are always out of all proportion to the merit of such works. And the Lord rules over history in such a way that we receive those blessings.

Some of the rewards that God promises to our good works are *super*natural. The greatest of these are reserved for heaven. And that's a good thing. If we received in the here and now all that God intends to give us, we would probably become puffed-up even more than the second of the two sons was in Luke 15. Paul understood that when he spoke of his thorn in the flesh; it was sent and designed as a gift of God to keep Paul humble in the face of so many blessings that God had given him for his work as an apostle.

Nevertheless, one day we will be dazzled by how much God treasured our responses to his gospel by obedience to his law. He promised that to Daniel in a most striking image that has comforted and encouraged pastors in particular during dark and difficult days: "Those who are wise will shine like the brightness of the heavens, and those who lead many to righteousness, like the stars for ever and ever" (Daniel 12:3). Yes, it is true: God only knows how to bless his own, bless them in such abundance that none will ever say that God was left owing anyone anything. Those blessings we experience in part in this life, and that more than we ever fully realize. His blessings and gracious reward will come in fullest measure in eternity. That's what he has promised us (Mark 10:29-31), and he would never lie to us or deceive us.

And now: an *almost* unLutheran thought

We rightly concentrate most of our thinking on what God has done for us in Christ. We rightly loathe any thought of contributing to our own salvation by our good works. We rightly give thanks chiefly for the work of Christ for us on the cross.

But sometimes it is worth giving thanks also for Christ's work *through* us. We can—and we Lutherans tend to go in this direction—become so anxious that we not be proud or self-righteous that we end up denying that God ever accomplishes anything good through us. We end up all but denying that he has given us any gifts by which we might be his instruments for good in the family, the church, the world. We almost want to be humble to such an extent that we become proud of being lazy; because our works are never good enough, never perfect, never a reason to boast, why even bother trying? But that's not the example which the Scriptures set for us. They bid us to appreciate not only God's gifts *to* us but also God's gifts and blessings *through* us.

In the Old Testament, we have a couple of especially striking examples of people who appreciated the blessing that God gave them, the blessing of being a blessing. In a passage that some at first find shocking, if not offensive, Nehemiah prayed, "Remember me for this, O my God, and do not blot out what I have so faithfully done for the house of my God and its services" (Nehemiah 13:14). But it was a worthy prayer! He was not claiming merit for himself or salvation as a reward for his work. He was giving thanks to God for the great gift that God gave him and for the ability to use that gift so successfully for the benefit of God's people. Confident of God's mercy, he called on God to remember the work and so prosper it that the work might remain for the benefit of God's people. We have another such example in the book of Esther. When the Jewish exiles were threatened with destruction, Esther was the favored queen in the palace. With her blessings, she alone could become a blessing by interceding for her people with the king. Mordecai reminded her of that: "Who knows but that you have come to royal position for such a time as this?" (Esther 4:14). God blessed her and blessed his people through her.

We have similar examples in the New Testament, examples of people who understood that they were a blessing. For the sake of (as our church fathers so often put it) useful brevity, we will mention just two of them. There is the example of Cornelius in Acts 10. He was a Roman centurion who believed in the God of Israel and waited for the message of salvation through the promised Messiah. Even before he heard from Peter the message that the Savior had indeed come and accomplished the work of salvation, Cornelius used his position to encourage faithfulness and obedience to the Word of God. God blessed richly his special use of his gifts by giving him the incomparably greater gift of the full message of salvation from Peter. Cornelius understood that he had been a blessing; he understood as well that in response God gave him still greater blessings in the gospel so that Cornelius could become, on his part again, a still greater blessing.

Then, of course, there is the example of St. Paul. He knew very well the gifts of God to him, and he understood just as well the blessings of God *through* him. How perfectly he explains it to us in 2 Corinthians 10–12. He understood that all the gifts God had given him were designed with this in mind: that Paul should be a blessing. All of the weaknesses and problems that God did not take away were likewise designed so that Paul should be a blessing. After his lengthy defense of his service, actually of his life of being a blessing, he nicely summed it all up for us: "We are weak in him, yet by God's power we will live with him to serve you" (2 Corinthians 13:4).

So the grapes in Christ the vine soak up all of the life that the vine has to offer. They drink in richly the sweetness of the gospel and the fragrance of God's grace and mercy for time and for eternity. And then the grapes are plucked and squeezed out to give what they have received, to become and be the blessings that Christ has made them in the gospel. May God grant us grace that we recognize and understand it; God has created and redeemed us so that we may both receive his grace and then reflect it in lives of *good* good works (Ephesians 2:8-10), through which he blesses the world, the church, and those around us.

The mother may lament that someone else would have been a better mother for her children. But someone else is not their mother. That's the blessing God gave her in order to be a blessing. The father may feel bad that he is not a better father to his children than he is. But that's not an excuse to be a poorer father than he can be. God gave him his station as husband and father so that he could be a blessing to his wife and children. The pastor may look over his service and say, "Oh, but so and so could have done it so much better." But it's not the call that God gave to so and so; he gave it to this one to be a blessing with both his obvious gifts and perhaps his obvious limitations as well, so that in all things Christ might be glorified.

Indeed, Jesus himself expects us to be blessings. Since that is so, why should we work so hard to deny that we are or imagine that we need not be? He says, "Let your light shine before men, that they may see your good deeds and praise your Father in heaven" (Matthew 5:16). The good deeds of which he speaks are of benefit even to those outside of the church. Were it otherwise, they would neither see them nor think to be drawn to the praise of God for them. Clearly then the one who does good deeds has been a blessing. And that is all by Christ's design; Christ gives us gifts in order that we might be gifts. Or, as he puts it, he gives us light and is the Light for us so that we may be lights. It is false modesty and a thin veil for laziness and ingratitude when we, to continue with Christ's analogy, hide our Christ-given light under a bushel basket.

Without boasting, without self-righteousness, it is possible, and should be done more often, that we look into the face of God and say: "O Lord, I can never thank you enough for your abundant blessings to me in Word and sacraments, in the gift of the Savior who comes to live for me and in me by that precious gospel. But I want to thank you also for this gift: that you have permitted me to be a blessing to those around me in family, church, and state. What an honor! What a delight to grow in grace and then to grow in the art of being one who is blessed so that I can be still more of a blessing!"

So it's not such a bad thing to examine our own lives from time to time and to look for the ways that God has made us blessings to our families, our churches, our society. Such an examination can help cure us of the depression that Satan sends to those who say that life is pointless and their own lives in particular are of no value. Yes, and it can spur us on to continue to be and to grow in being blessings from God to those around us.

St. Paul has a final piece of advice for us as we do that: "Carry each other's burdens, and in this way you will fulfill the law of Christ. If anyone thinks he is something when he is nothing, he deceives himself. Each one should test his own actions. Then he can take pride in himself, without comparing himself to somebody else, for each one should carry his own load" (Galatians 6:2-5).

Excellent advice! We look as honestly and realistically as we can at the gifts that God has given us *for service*. It is ungrateful to fake modesty and deny that we have gifts. Then, with the emphasis on serving more than on self-congratulation, we quietly and within our own souls give thanks for the honor that God has given us. By his generosity, we carry our loads and are useful to others in helping them to carry theirs. We need not bother letting others know how useful we are. Just be useful and give thanks that you have the honor of being a blessing. On those perhaps too rare occasions when another expresses gratitude for our service, we need not foolishly and ungratefully protest that the service was nothing. Nor is it necessary every time to make a long speech about how it was all God's doing; said too often, that may well come across as false modesty, a vice that is only a thin veil used to cover arrogance. It is enough to just answer, "Thank you! I was glad I could help/be useful." Then to God you can say, "How kind of you to make of me, even of me, a blessing!" That's the narrow Lutheran middle between boastfulness and false modesty.

So much for our *almost* unLutheran thought.

But it's time to move along to another stretch of the narrow middle road.

7

The Narrow Lutheran Middle Between an Idolatrous Love of the World and an Ungrateful Contempt for the World

Perhaps by now we are getting the hang of it. Finding and keeping to the narrow middle road requires eyes that are fixed on Christ, minds that are bent on submission to his Word, and hearts that want nothing more than to draw ever closer to him who loves us and gave himself for us. The middle road despises neither reason nor emotion. Rather, it keeps them in their places. We give thanks for them and use them. At the same time, we recognize that they can push us off the narrow middle road. That's what happens when we take our eyes off of Christ and let our minds wander from his Word. Then they seize control and push aside both the cross and the Word, and that to the peril of our faith and life in Christ.

In this chapter, with the same goal of sticking to the narrow middle road, we want to travel along a stretch of the road with ditches that should be very obvious to each of us. But as obvious as they should be and as easy to avoid, there are still many who plunge headlong into one or the other of them.

It is easier to travel this section of the narrow middle road in theory than it is in practice. The Bible has uncounted references to the material world as a blessed gift of God. To despise it or treat it with contempt is a sin of ingratitude. It often betrays a false spirituality that imagines God is somehow pleased by a renunciation of the beautiful gift of his creation. But on the other hand, the Bible also contains countless warnings against the idolatrous love of this world. That kind of love has been the downfall of many who once were on the narrow middle road.

On the idolatrous love of the world

That his world and all that it contains is a great blessing from God is already evident in the creation account in Genesis 1,2. God made it. God declared it to be good. God gave it into the hands of Adam and Eve, that they should act as his regents and as stewards of his beautiful creation. Certainly it was his intent from the very beginning that they should enjoy his creation as well as manage it. It was their sin and our resultant sinfulness that has made the middle between an idolatrous love of the world and an ungrateful contempt for it such a problem for so many. Using our fallen nature as a launching pad, the devil together with the now-corrupted world itself tempt us to turn the material world into a god instead of receiving it with thanksgiving and using it as a precious gift of God.

It was sin that brought down a curse on the material world, a curse whose effects will continue until the end of time. Now creation resists our rule over it and frustrates it. Now the sweat of the brow often makes work drudgery for many, instead of a blessed means of serving God and one another. Yes, and it is the sinfulness that inheres in all of us from the moment of our conception which ends up turning our hearts and minds to the worship of this perishing world even though it resists our control at every turn.

So how shall we sort it all out and find a middle between worshiping a beautiful and useful creation of God and having contempt for it because of its resistance and our own weakness? We can begin by remembering that God designed the world and gave

it to us as a *means* to an end. It should serve as a means that
points us to the power and the goodness of God. God's generosity
to us should move us to see ourselves as stewards of his goods
and goodness. A steward does not consider what he has to be his
own but to be his to use according to the direction of his master—
again, the world and what it contains are not ends but means.
Our sinful nature, however, wants to turn the world and what it
contains into *ends;* that is, it wants to make things the reason for
living and the acquiring of things the goal of life. And therein lies
the problem. St. John puts the matter into perspective for us
when he tell us:

> Do not love the world or anything in the world. If anyone
> loves the world, the love of the Father is not in him. For
> everything in the world—the cravings of sinful man, the
> lust of his eyes and the boasting of what he has and
> does—comes not from the Father but from the world. The
> world and its desires pass away, but the man who does
> the will of God lives forever. (1 John 2:15-17)

Did you notice that St. John does not tell us to despise the world
in an absolute sense? He warns us against a love of the world that
takes precedence over and is in opposition to a love for God. With
such a love of the world, the heart longs for the things in the world
as ends themselves: how much of what I see do I crave, and how
much of it can I get? In striving with all my might to get what my
heart craves, the world and what it contains becomes the be all
and end all of life—that is, it becomes my god.[1]

Yes, and that craving of the heart extends to more than just
the material things in the world. It extends to all those "things"
that we crave, things that become more important to us than
Christ and his Word, more important to us than serving him and
those around us. We think here of nonmaterial things. There is,
for example, the lust to be respected or famous for mental or
physical ability. There is the accompanying pleasure in looking
down on those less gifted. There is the desire to pull down those
more gifted. There is the ambition to rule more than serve, to get

---

[1] Cf. Luther's comments in his Large Catechism under the First Commandment.

my own way rather than yield in loving service to another. There is the addiction to popularity, to the praise of the world that causes me to keep silent in the face of evil or to deny the truth of the Word of God. All these nonmaterial things come easily under the heading of the *"cravings of sinful man, the lust of his eyes and the boasting of what he has and does."*

To be sure, some of what the heart craves may or may not be evil in itself. Someone desires to make a decent living so that he can support himself and not be a burden to society. He works so that he will have enough to provide for his family, to help the poor, and to support the work of the church. There need be nothing wrong with that, and there is a good deal that is right with it.

Indeed, the Bible tells us that we should work. St. Paul reminded the Thessalonian Christians, "Even when we were with you, we gave you this rule: 'If a man will not work, he shall not eat.' We hear that some among you are idle. They are not busy; they are busybodies. Such people we command and urge in the Lord Jesus Christ to settle down and earn the bread they eat" (2 Thessalonians 3:10-12). And in his first letter to young Pastor Timothy, the apostle urged him to remind his members, "If anyone does not provide for his relatives, and especially for his immediate family, he has denied the faith and is worse than an unbeliever" (1 Timothy 5:8). To the thief who craved the things of the world so much that he didn't care how he got what he craved, Paul said, "He who has been stealing must steal no longer, but must work, doing something useful with his own hands, that he may have something to share with those in need" (Ephesians 4:28). St. John likewise exhorts, "If anyone has material possessions and sees his brother in need but has no pity on him, how can the love of God be in him? Dear children, let us not love with words or tongue but with actions and in truth" (1 John 3:17,18). So it is not work or even the desire to work hard and be rewarded for it that is evil in itself.

And certainly a desire to have a good reputation in the world is not wrong in itself. We should strive for a good reputation, not least because a bad reputation harms not just us but those who will sneer at the gospel because of what they see in us. How many children turn their backs on the church prompted at least in part by the bad example of their parents, who did not even bother to have a good reputation with their own children? And so Jesus exhorts us in the Sermon on the Mount, "Let your light shine before men, that they may see your good deeds and praise your Father in heaven" (Matthew 5:16).

Even to be aware of the gifts that God has given to us individually, be they gifts of a good appearance or of physical or mental ability that rises above the average, need not be evil. To acknowledge such gifts and to receive them with thanksgiving can be a good thing. To deny that we have them would be a mark of ingratitude to the God who gave them. St. Paul was not unaware of the gifts that God gave him. He was grateful that they could be put to good use in the service of Christ the giver and of Christ's flock (1 Corinthians 15:9-11). We considered this point in the last chapter.

But at the same time that we recognize the good in work, in reputation and honor, in God's particular gifts to us as individuals, we are quick to recognize something else as well. There is nothing in the world that may be good and a gift of God that cannot be easily corrupted by us with our fallen nature. Is there anything that cannot be used by the devil to push us into a ditch? Even family and other loved ones can become for us the ultimate reason for living and thus be turned into gods enticing us into a ditch. Jesus in a most dramatic way warns us against that possibility; he says, "If anyone comes to me and does not hate his father and mother, his wife and children, his brothers and sisters—yes, even his own life—he cannot be my disciple" (Luke 14:26). And this from the God who in so many other places tells us that the essence of obedience to the commandments is love to God *and* love for one another! How could he possibly mean what he says in that passage? He explains it when he says, "Anyone who loves his father or mother more than me is not worthy of me; anyone who loves his son or daughter more than me is not worthy of me" (Matthew 10:37).

Jesus' point is clear. Though other people, family, and other loved ones are among his greatest gifts to us, we fall into the ditch when we no longer see them as means to provoke us to thanksgiving and service. We fall into the ditch when for their sakes we are willing to turn our eyes away from the Giver and his Word. We fall into the ditch when we make them the ultimate

163

reason for living. And how often and easily that happens. The child does what he knows is wrong in order to be popular with the friends God gave him. The friends God gave become more important than the God who gave them. The couple is willing to sacrifice obedience to the Sixth Commandment in order to please the beloved. Either personal pleasure or that of the beloved replaced the God who "sets the lonely in families" (Psalm 68:6). The spouse gives up on personal or public worship to keep peace with an unbelieving partner. Parents abandon expectations of decent behavior from children lest the children "hate" them. In these and in so many similar situations, beautiful gifts of God have become ends rather than means.

Even life itself can become a god, a *thing* that we love more than the God who gave it. Jesus said in Luke 14:26 that unless we hate our own life, i.e., unless we love him more than life itself, we cannot be his disciple. How often do we hear and maybe even use the cliché "As long as you have your health, you have everything?" It's not true. As precious as life is, as much to be cherished and nurtured as it is, life is not the goal of life! The goal of life is the hearing of the gospel and the receiving of its life-giving promises in faith. The goal of life is grateful obedience and service to him who lived and died for us and for our salvation. The goal of life is heaven. The one who is jogging and doing sit-ups on Sunday morning instead of giving attention to the Word of Life has doubtless missed that point. The one who is terrified of death as though it were the worst thing that could ever happen to him has not taken to heart the glorious promises of eternal life.

So it is not work in itself, nor what we gain by work, that is evil. Nor is the desire for an honorable and good reputation wrong in itself. Nor is the effort that it takes to have a good name evil in itself. And certainly, the desire for a happy family life and good friends and good health is not evil in itself. Rather, it is the attitude with which we pursue and use all these things that can become the problem. What if lurking beneath the desire for a good reputation is simply a craving for the praises of men? What if supporting family and helping the poor and giving to the work of the church has become a bother to us? What if our effort to stay healthy has behind it chiefly a fear of death or only the desire to enjoy ourselves rather than the desire to serve? Then it is clear that we love the world in the way that John warns against in the passage cited previously. Then the world and what it contains have become ends in themselves rather than means to an end. Then we have fallen off of the narrow middle road, even though the work and earnings from our labor, a good reputation, a happy family, good friends, and a healthy lifestyle were not sinful in themselves.

It isn't the "how much" that matters but the attitude toward the "how much"

In all of these "things," how much of them we have is not the issue. Whether we have many friends, really good health, a good income, or the reverse is not of itself the problem. It isn't even a matter, for example, of how much of this world's goods we receive as the fruit of our labors. The Bible shows us any number of people who were rich, who had large and often happy families and many good friends; they were not condemned for it. The patriarchs of the Old Testament were wealthy men. Solomon was perhaps the richest man who ever lived. Job was wealthy and healthy and had a large and happy family before God tested him; and after the test, he was again blessed with wealth and family even more than he had been before. St. Paul wrote an entire epistle to a wealthy man, his letter to Philemon. Nowhere are any of these individuals told to divest themselves of all their worldly wealth and live as beggars or as hermits in a cave. They are not even told to give away most of what they had and to keep only so much as was absolutely necessary for them to get by.

Only once in the Bible do we have an example of someone told to give everything away. That's the example of the rich young man (Matthew 19:16-26). The story of Jesus' encounter with this young man is instructive on so many levels.[2] But for our purposes here, it is enough to say that Jesus' primary intent was to show the young man that he desperately needed a Savior. All of the obedience of the young man to the law of God was nothing compared to his great sin: he loved his wealth more than God and more than his

---

[2] For a more complete consideration of the account of Jesus with this young man, see chapter 3, pp. 43,44.

neighbor; thus, he had broken the First Commandment and was an idolater. Only by telling him to give it all away could Jesus bring that sin and, more important, the young man's great need to light. In spite of the fact that the young man wanted very much to be on the narrow middle road, he had fallen deeply into the ditch of love for the world. At least on the occasion of this encounter with Jesus, the man was not moved to cry out for help and rescue from the idolatry into which he had fallen. But otherwise, Jesus never made poverty a condition for following him.

To be sure, the apostles left their earthly occupations when Jesus called them to follow him full time. But there was in that call no requirement that they should forever be destitute and beggars. St. Paul tells us that those who serve God's people full time as pastors and teachers should be supported by those they serve (1 Corinthians 9:1-14). He does not suggest that the level of that support should leave the worker on the brink of financial ruin or with just enough to get by. In 1 Corinthians 9 Paul even points to the example of the priesthood of the Old Testament. The priests were supported by the gifts of the people; they were never required to take a vow of poverty; Jesus never required that of anyone either.

Some might want to point to the example of the early church in Acts 2:42-47. There we note that people sold their possessions and gave to the poor among them as they had need. But the text doesn't say that they sold everything they had. Nor are we told that that was a requirement for fellowship in the church. Indeed, the account of Ananias and Sapphira (Acts 5) makes the point that such was never a requirement. The crime of Ananias and Sapphira was not that they refused to give all they had for the support of the poor; their crime was that they deliberately lied about what they had given. Acts 6 and the calling of the serving deacons likewise indicates that as generous as the members of the congregation were, they did not live a totally communal life. The deacons were needed not to divide up food for the whole community but only for the needy widows. The rest provided for themselves and in the process gave what was needed for the support of those in need.

In point of fact, those who imagine that taking a vow of poverty somehow makes them more worthy in the eyes of God make of their poverty a god just as much as those who worship their wealth. Whatever we make the goal of life, and that which gives it meaning either here or hereafter, is our god. The one who imagines that his self-chosen works (any works for that matter) will contribute to his own salvation robs Christ of the glory he has and wants as our only and all-sufficient Savior. Luther had a great deal to say about the imagined holiness of those who lived off of the labor of others in idle contemplation and prayer; nothing of what he had to say about such a lifestyle is complimentary. His conclusion too was that many of those who have fallen into the ditch of contempt for the world are idolaters just as much as those who have an excessive love for the world.

So neither poverty nor wealth can save us. Indeed, those who are poor for whatever reason are just as capable of greed as the rich if their lives are ruled by the desire for wealth or by envy toward those who have it. That's what St. Paul warns against in 1 Timothy 6:9,10: "People who want to get rich fall into temptation and a trap and into many foolish and harmful desires that plunge men into ruin and destruction. For the love of money [note: not money itself!] is a root of all kinds of evil. Some people, eager for money, have wandered from the faith and pierced themselves with many griefs."

Jesus too warns us more than once against the dangers of wealth, of how treacherous it can be and how easy it is for this world's goods to seduce us into idolatry. He does that in the passage noted previously (Matthew 19:16-26), in which he tells the disciples how difficult it is for those with wealth to be saved. It is so very easy to fix one's heart on the desire to have and then always to have more that the slope into idolatry is a slippery one indeed. Jesus makes the same point when he speaks of the deceitfulness of riches—whether we have wealth or have wealth as our goal—in the parable of the sower and the seed (Mark 4:18,19). In the story of the rich man and poor Lazarus, Jesus highlights the problem: the rich man was not condemned because he was rich but because he had no compassion. He thereby showed plainly that he loved his wealth more than God and more than he loved his poor neighbor. God gave him such a neighbor so that the rich man could show his love for God and man by generous service to the one in need (Luke 16:19-31). Notice that even in that story the rich man's greatest crime was that he did not listen to Moses and the prophets. He was too busy acquiring and enjoying his wealth to be bothered with either poor Lazarus or with the Word of God. So whether it is wealth itself or work to acquire wealth or the enjoyment of wealth, when these become the goals of life, we have fallen into the wide ditch of idolatry (Mark 8:36,37; Luke 12:13-21). The same point can be made with respect to anything else in the world—to family, to friends, to health, and to life itself.

But is it not an amazing thing, a remarkable testimony to the goodness, the kindness, the generosity of God? He could have put us into a dreary gray world without any beauty, without things that make life easier and more enjoyable. He could have set us in as solitary a society as that of some animals in the forest, without family and friends. He could have made us without the vigor that health affords and the pleasure of being alive. Had he done that, we would have none of the temptations to turn his gifts into gods. Had he done that, our only temptation would have been to a sullen grumpiness and an ever-complaining spirit. But he didn't want that for us. And so he gives and then gives more. He heaps on us one blessing after another of things, of people, of health, and of life itself. He does that even though he knows full well that in our fallen nature, we can easily make any or all of these things substitutes for him. He does it knowing that we can turn our love from the Giver to the gifts. Yes, is that not an amazing thing? His kindness in contrast to our perversity is a thing of endless wonder— and a reason for unending praise and grateful adoration.

Consider the example of the leper in Mark 1:40-45. In his need, the leper was willing to submit everything to the will of Jesus. But once he was cleansed of his leprosy, he thought he knew better than Jesus what was best. Jesus sternly warned him not to publish the miracle; but the leper in understandable excitement over his healing, pushed aside the warning of Jesus and did exactly what Jesus told him not to do. But didn't Jesus know that that would happen? Of course he knew. Nevertheless, in his kindness, in his grace and goodness, he healed the man. Jesus' eagerness to help and serve that man overcame his own understanding of the damage the man would do after Jesus helped and healed him! What a remarkable thing! Whose life doesn't resemble that of the leper? We cry for help in time of need. We plead for mercy in our days of affliction. And God, knowing how easily we turn his gifts into substitute gods, hears our cries for mercy. He delivers us today and wards off threatening peril tomorrow. And merrily we go along, unmindful of today's blessing and tomorrow's promise. Could the contrast between God's goodness and our perversity be sharper? Only the utterly perverse notion that God forgives us so that we can sin all we want is worse.

Contempt for the world is not the answer

And that point brings us to at least a brief consideration of the opposite ditch, that of ungrateful contempt for God's blessings. God does not tell us to despise his gifts of material things, of family and friends, of health and life itself. Those who treat all these things with contempt are ungrateful for the bounty that God bestows. It is a sorry spectacle indeed when someone imagines that all laughter and pleasure, the joys of marriage and children, the vigor of a healthy body and a sound mind are evil. In point of fact, St. Paul warns against an ungrateful contempt for the world in the same book in which he warns against a worship of the world. He tells us:

> The Spirit clearly says that in later times some will abandon the faith and follow deceiving spirits and things taught by demons. Such teachings come through hypocritical liars, whose consciences have been seared as with a hot iron. They forbid people to marry and order them to abstain from certain foods, which God created to be received with thanksgiving by those who believe and who know the truth. For everything God created is good, and nothing is to be rejected if it is received with thanksgiving, because it is consecrated by the word of God and prayer. (1 Timothy 4:1-5)

Pride in poverty or celibacy or the hermit's life does not make us somehow more worthy of God's favor than we would be otherwise. That some against nature impose on themselves and others such unnecessary misery and then imagine that for it they deserve heaven, at least in part, is a tragedy indeed. As wealth and marriage, family, friends, and health cannot save us, so too

169

their renunciation will in no way contribute to our salvation. Even when one undertakes a solitary life or a life of poverty willingly, the ditch is inviting. Such a one may fall into a self-centered idleness. He may yield to the temptation of contempt for "the common herd" of mankind who are living a different life than the one he has chosen. It is after all just as easy to be proud of what one has given up as it is to be proud of what one has and enjoys.

The ditch of contempt for the world may be a less appealing one than that ditch on the opposite side of the road, but it is a ditch nevertheless. Choosing to fall into it does not reflect the grateful joy of the psalmist who sings his praise and thanks to God for all that God has given, as for example in Psalm 103. It misses the good in the gratitude of the psalmist who calls children a special gift and blessing of God (Psalm 127:3-5). And it takes no notice of the fact that from the beginning of the world God commends marriage as a mark of his kindness (Genesis 2:18-24).

St. James sums it all up for us when he reminds us that all we are and have we should see as good and perfect gifts of God, gifts that begin with the gift of faith but certainly do not end there (James 1:17,18). It is interesting to note that such a reminder comes in a book which contains also the sharpest warnings against the ditch on the other side of the road, the ditch of an idolatrous love of the world.

The middle between the two ditches

How then shall we find and stay on the narrow middle road? How shall we avoid the ditch of ungrateful contempt and the doubtless wider ditch of an idolatrous love of the world? Of all that the Bible has to say by way of warning and encouragement to travel the narrow middle road, we will consider just a few of the passages that well serve as road markers along the narrow middle way.

The first of these is in Luke 12:22-34, where Jesus gives us his perfect instruction on the whole matter of the proper attitude towards wealth and what it can buy. In his instruction he wants to ward off the very beginnings of a false attitude toward wealth. The false attitude begins not with wealth itself. It begins with worry that we don't have enough or might not have enough in the

future. He urges us to avoid worry and the ditch of idolatry over
against wealth by telling us what our real, our primary, our only
concern should be.

Read the verses carefully! Jesus does not say that we should
sit down and wait for manna to fall from heaven. He is not sug-
gesting either that food and clothes or house and home are useless and of no value. In point of fact, he recognizes that they are
important. It's just that they should not be what we set our
hearts on, should not be the goals, the be-alls and end-alls, the
definitions of our existence. What then should be? The kingdom of
God. Jesus says that we should seek first and foremost his rule in
our hearts and lives and trust him to give us what we need of
these other things. He will give these other things in such a measure as we need and as suits us as we go about earning our daily
bread with thanksgiving to its ultimate source.

Whether he gives much or little, we shall not be disturbed if
our real need and goal in life has already been accomplished. And
it has been. He won the kingdom for us on the cross. And he
plants that kingdom in our hearts through the gospel in Word
and sacraments. He tells us plainly, "Your Father knows that you
need them [i.e., food and clothes and the like]. But seek his kingdom, and these things will be given to you as well" (12:30,31).
Then he goes on to urge us to generosity with "these things" that
God gives us in the course of our earthly lives through work or by
other honest means: "Sell your possessions and give to the poor.
Provide purses for yourselves that will not wear out, a treasure in
heaven that will not be exhausted, where no thief comes near and
no moth destroys. For where your treasure is, there your heart
will be also" (12:33,34).

What a master teacher he is! He makes much the same point
and expands on the thought in Luke 16:9-15. It's not a question of
wealth or possessions. Nor by extension is it a matter of health
and reputation in and of themselves. It's all a matter of the heart.
It's a matter of priorities. It's a matter of the use to which we put
all these "things" in response to the gospel of the kingdom won by
him for us and given freely to us in the gospel. It's a matter of
knowing the difference between means and ends.

Clearly these words of Jesus will often strike a guilty note in
our hearts. Who is there among us that has not worried more

about his bank account, his popularity, his health, than about the condition of his soul? Who is there who does not fret at least from time to time about whether he has enough or how much more he can get? Who is there who is never stirred by envy or greed or by resentment at the seeming prosperity of another? Even the psalmist recognized this problem in himself when he was grieved at the prosperity of the wicked (Psalm 73). Who is not sometimes troubled, as the psalmist was, by the gifts of God to another—gifts of talent, wealth, or beauty? If we nurse such thoughts, we come soon to bitterness, even to resenting God for not giving us what he has given to another. Yes, we become no different than the pagans of whom Jesus speaks in these verses. On rare occasions we may even run to the opposite ditch and declare ourselves more worthy than these others because we have less.

All such thoughts should quickly remind us of how perverse the human heart is. They should move us anew to recognize how desperately we need the fact that the kingdom of God is entirely God's gift on account of Christ's work and not our own. If we had to merit it even in the least small part, we would have long ago lost any hope for it by our slips on the edges of these ditches. Yes, and the very reminder of the richness of God's grace and mercy should move us again to desire that kingdom first and foremost. What do all the riches of the world have to offer by comparison? Nothing but things to lose!

And that's how Jesus gives us the desire to see ourselves as stewards, managers, of his treasures. He gives us things so that we may, to be sure, enjoy them. He gives us things so that we may use them gratefully and in service to those around us. Yes, he gives us so often so much more than we need so that we can give it away. We get some idea of how close we may be getting to Jesus' intended attitude adjustment when we have learned to love being generous. Someone has well said that the last part of the Christian to be converted is his wallet. But when we finally come to see our treasures—be they of money and goods or of time and talents—as having this value that we can use them for the benefit of others, then we have started to get the point. Then, when we love being generous just out of love and gratitude to our Savior, we are storing up treasures in heaven.

How richly those treasures given away will pay dividends Jesus indicates in Matthew 25:34-36. As we have already noted several times, on the Last Day he will call it all to mind and praise us before all the saints and angels. That's how much he treasures our use of his treasures of time and talent and the fruits of our labor. His praise will not be that we have merited heaven thereby; that is entirely his gift. He will praise us for showing that we understood how rich we were in being those "blessed by my Father" (verse 34). We were so rich that we could easily afford to be generous in service to him by serving those around us. As St. Paul says when he is encouraging such generosity, "God loves a cheerful giver" (2 Corinthians 9:7).

The prophet Joel in the Old Testament shows us the right attitude in a most interesting way. He was writing at a time of famine in the land, at a time when God visited his people with one pestilence after another in response to their idolatrous love of the world. When God through Joel urged his people to repent and to pray for an end to pestilence and famine, listen to how he framed the issue:

> "Even now," declares the LORD, "return to me with all your heart, with fasting and weeping and mourning." Rend your heart and not your garments. Return to the LORD your God, for he is gracious and compassionate, slow to anger and abounding in love, and he relents from sending calamity. Who knows? He may turn and have pity *and leave behind a blessing—grain offerings and drink offerings for the LORD your God.* (Joel 2:12-14).

Isn't that interesting? The goal of restored prosperity was not prosperity itself. He doesn't even say, "O Lord, bless us so that we won't go hungry and starve to death." Rather, the goal was that there would be enough so that the people could give it back to the Lord who gave it all. Giving back came first. How often do we think that way? How often do we hope for prosperity, for a raise in salary or other income primarily so that we will have a greater ability to give? Isn't it rather more often our hope that with an increased income we can get more and more things, not just things we really need but things we just want? That is not to say

173

that we should shun an increased income or that every getting of things we want is bad. It's just a question of where generosity and the opportunity to serve fit into the equation that needs some more thought from most of us most of the time.

Another of the many passages in the Bible that merits our consideration in making sure that we are on the narrow middle road is in 1 Timothy 6. We have already noted part of the chapter that warns us against greed. Now we listen to the apostle's inspired pointing to the positive, to the narrow middle road. Paul tells us:

> Godliness with contentment is great gain. For we brought nothing into the world, and we can take nothing out of it. But if we have food and clothing, we will be content with that. But you, man of God, flee from all this [i.e., the love of money, greed], and pursue righteousness, godliness, faith, love, endurance and gentleness. (1 Timothy 6:6-8,11)

"Contentment!" That is a noble goal in and of itself—even to reason, even for Aristotle. But it is much more than that for the Christian. Paul said it all so well in the epistle to the Galatians: "I have been crucified with Christ and I no longer live, but Christ lives in me. The life I live in the body, I live by faith in the Son of God, who loved me and gave himself for me" (2:20). To be content with God's gifts comes from a recognition that our goal in life, the meaning of life itself, is all wrapped up in Christ, in the gospel, in the pursuit, and yes, in the enjoyment of the kingdom of God. That is followed to be sure by the work that is necessary to support ourselves and our family. But the pursuit of a living should be accompanied by contentment with what God gives in the process. We recognize that this world will perish, but while we wait for that to happen, God through our labors gives what we need to survive and sometimes much more. And when we recognize as well that he promises to provide for us also in the future, then we are on the way to contentment.

Paul gives us something of a commentary on or a definition of this contentment in 1 Corinthians 12,13. There he urges us to remember that God has been generous to all of us. To each and every one of us he has given gifts. To some he gives the ability to teach. It might be the gift to parents who teach their children when they read a devotion or a portion of the Bible at the dinner table. It might be the ability of grandparents who teach their adult children to be patient and wait for the Lord's help when their adult children are in distress or fearful of the future. It might be the ability of another to serve as a pastor or a teacher.

To another he gives the ability to heal. The gift of healing might be that of those who performed miracles in Bible times. Their number was always small, and miraculous healing was never promised as the normal way that God would deal with us. There are other healing gifts besides those very rare ones. There is the gift of healing that God gives to doctors and nurses and other healthcare workers. They should see their professions as more than just jobs. Theirs is an ability that God has given to be used to his glory for the benefit of others, even while it provides a living to the healer. But others heal or help heal in other ways. There is the healing that comes from patient listening to the woes and cares of another. There is the healing that comes from a cheerful word or kind counsel to one in need of advice that is grounded in the Word of God. There is the healing that comes from the simple, "Here, let me help you with that!" The one helped is raised up from the burdens and cares of the moment and has the balm of a Christian's care and concern.

Another has gifts of money more than of time. Another has more time than money. Another has a voice to sing, another an ear to hear, another a mouth to speak the wisdom and the glory of God. Another has the physical strength to shovel the walk at church or of the neighbor next door. Another has a garden that gives more tomatoes and potatoes than the family needs. What a good witness to the neighborhood when one sees the tables outside of a church weighed down by produce from family gardens; they were brought to church for those without gardens to take home whatever they might need.

Obviously making a list here of all possible gifts and how they can be used to the glory of God and the benefit of others is impossible. But it is not a waste of time for each Christian to spend some time considering the gifts that God has given; once we have counted up such gifts, it is further a good use of time both to give God thanks for his generosity and then to look for opportunities to use them. God is way too generous with us to ever leave any of us without more gifts and more opportunities than we can count for using them to his glory and the benefit of those around us. If someone doesn't see the gifts, that one should ask another what they might be; often others know us and God's blessings to us better than we know them ourselves. The narrow middle avoids loving things in themselves as well as ungrateful contempt for the things that God has given us. Again, it's all a matter of attitude. The narrow middle is a grateful heart that seeks to serve with God's bounty while at the same time enjoying it.

In sum, Paul bids us in 1 Corinthians 12,13 to remember that we all have gifts. He invites us to consider the gifts that God has given to each of us and to look for ways to use them in love to him and for the benefit of one another. We are Jesus' hands and feet and mouth during this time of grace before he comes again. He served us and gave his all to redeem us for himself. So we live to move and act in his name and for the benefit of the rest of his mystical body on earth. That is a high honor indeed, to serve him in serving his mystical body for the short time that we have here. Looking at life that way is a mark of having found the middle road between excessive love for the world and ungrateful contempt for it. With such an attitude, we do not imagine that the goal of life is just to get more for my own indulgence; nor do we look at life with sour and grumpy ingratitude for God's blessings to us in the world and the good reasons he has for being so generous to us.

Jesus puts this all in context for us when he encourages us to be ambitious. Ambition is not the opposite of contentment in the way that Jesus uses the word. The opposite of contentment is selfish striving or lazy indifference to anyone but myself or those who can somehow benefit me. Jesus sets the tone of a good ambition that accompanies contentment when he dealt with the disciples and their wrong ambition in Mark 9:33-37. It is a lesson Jesus had to teach more than once—and a lesson we too no doubt need to keep relearning! The disciples were ambitious; each wanted to be more important than his fellows. Each wanted to be on top and to rule. And what did Jesus say to their ambition? Did he tell them to deny any and all ability and quietly sit with heads down in the dark? Not at all! He encouraged an ambition that would match contentment with God's gifts and the opportunities he gave to use them. Their ambition should be directed toward taking advantage of even the lowliest of opportunities to serve, to be useful. How beautifully he put it:

> Sitting down, Jesus called the Twelve and said, "If anyone wants to be first, he must be the very last, and the servant of all." He took a little child and had him stand among them. Taking him in his arms, he said to them, "Whoever welcomes one of these little children in my name welcomes me; and whoever welcomes me does not welcome me but the one who sent me." (Mark 9:35-37)

What a joy he gives us! To the greatest and to the least he gives the honor of receiving him by receiving and serving those he puts around us, be they great or seemingly insignificant. When we understand that, we will not need to spend a lot of time arguing about how much we should give of time or treasure. When we understand that, the love of Christ for us will move us more and more to ask a different question: how much more can I do? We will search the New Testament in vain for a law that dictates or limits "how much."

In the Old Testament there was, of course, the law of the tithe. Ten percent of income or produce was to be law for giving. But in the New Testament, there is no set percentage or limit. One with the responsibility of raising and supporting a family may have less to give of time or treasure outside of the family than the one who is single or whose children are out on their own. Circumstances are different, and circumstances change.

Each needs to look at the blessings God has given and at the responsibilities and at the opportunities that God gives as well. Then each should determine in his own heart what he gives of time and treasure for the support of himself and his family and what he gives for the work of the church and to help those in need. Clearly we want to give more than just the leftovers. We look for balance. We look for the middle road. We want to shun the lifestyle that is never satisfied until it has all the latest and all the best. But there is no requirement that we go around looking like refugees from the ragpickers' ball either. Most will probably try to find a percentage that they want to give either of time or of treasure or of both—again depending very much on individual circumstances.

In sum, an obsession with "how much" can best be avoided by considering all of God's blessings and our consequent fervent desire to serve him in love with those blessings. That's also Paul's inspired advice to the Corinthians in 2 Corinthians 8,9. Paul's encouragement to generosity should be coupled with Jesus' promise that he will bless us as we give away what he has given to us. Jesus says, "Give, and it will be given to you. A good measure, pressed down, shaken together and running over, will be poured into your lap. For with the measure you use, it will be measured to you" (Luke 6:38). He would not lie to us! So we have Jesus' generosity on the cross always at the front of heart and mind. Then we have close at hand his assurance of his never-ending generosity to us in our daily lives as he answers the Fourth Petition of the Lord's Prayer. And notice in that petition that he bids us to pray, "Give us this day *our daily bread,*" and he promises to hear and answer that prayer. He does not invite us to pray for the satisfaction of every want that the advertising world plants in our heads, nor to give us so much today that we will never need to ask him again for his generosity tomorrow. He wants us to see ourselves as in constant need of his grace and goodness. Then, by satisfying that need day-to-day, he inspires in us both a deeper sense of dependency on him and a gratitude to him for his unfailing goodness.

With all the evidences of his never-failing grace and goodness, we can do battle against what someone has called donor fatigue, i.e., weariness in the face of never-ending needs and requests for help. And at the same time, we may even grow in the grace of a generosity that sometimes puts the *needs* of the poor and of the church ahead of our own *wants*. It's a good thing at times to say to oneself, "This is what I want and can really afford, but I think I'll forego it or at least put it off for a while so that I can help out a bit more in relieving that need."

Certainly there may be times in our lives when we ourselves are in need. There may be times when unemployment or ill health or other circumstances beyond our control make it impossible to be very generous. We may have to rely on the generosity of others. At such times, the middle road is still contentment! At such times, with all the fears and uncertainties that may plague us, we still look to the hand of God for help and rescue. When that help comes from others, we will strive to receive such help with thanks both to them and to the God who moved them to help. Yes, and we will look forward to the day when, calling to mind the previously cited prayer of Joel, we too may once more be generous. Indeed, our time of need may serve to help make us all the more generous when that again is possible.

On the other hand, many people, even Christians, are drowning in debt because of an undisciplined, not to say greedy, satisfying of *wants*. Clearly they will find it impossible to be generous. If we find ourselves in their number, that would be a good indicator that we have probably fallen off the narrow middle road. We may be deep in the ditch of an idolatrous love of the world. The time then has come for a cry for mercy from the Savior, for rescue in the gospel of forgiveness, for restoration to the middle road of contentment and generosity. Such a restoration may indeed take some time as we reorder our priorities. But the goal, not just of a renewed financial sanity but of the ability to be generous again, will certainly be a God-pleasing one.

Yes, and then, to say it once more, we will have found the middle road between excessive love for the world and ungrateful contempt of the world. We will have found godliness with contentment wedded to an ambition to receive and use his gifts with thanksgiving. And as he gives us opportunities to serve, to be useful, we will not grumble that others and their needs are an inconvenience and a burden. The opportunities to serve are gifts as much as the gifts he gives for service.

8

Finding the Middle in the Work of the Church

In this chapter we want to find the middle road with respect to three areas of concern in the life of the church. Each of the three sections of the road is relatively short. Nevertheless, people have found problems in each of these three short sections, problems that are ditches on the sides of the road.

The universal priesthood of all believers and the holy office of the ministry

In the history of the church, these two doctrines have often been pitted against each other. Damage has been done to the church when one of the two has been emphasized at the expense or to the exclusion of the other.

The universal priesthood of all believers

The doctrine of the universal priesthood of all believers is most beautifully expressed in the New Testament. St. Peter is addressing every Christian when he tells us, "You are a chosen people, a royal priesthood, a holy nation, a people belonging to God, that you may declare the praises of him who called you out of darkness into his wonderful light" (1 Peter 2:9).

Notice how all-inclusive Peter's words are. Is there any dignity that God has withheld from some Christians in order to give it to some other Christians? No, not one!

Each and every Christian is a Christian because he has been *chosen* by God. Not one can claim that his status before God was of his own choosing. His status with God is always and alone the status of one chosen. And that choice for the greatest saint as for the lowliest and the least was by grace alone; it had nothing at all to do with the merit of the chosen. In point of fact, all of our dignity and merit and worth are donated; they are the gifts of the One choosing, gifts purchased at so great a price on his cross.

And the results of that choosing on God's part could not be richer than they are. Each and every Christian is part of a *royal priesthood*. What a concept! In the Old Testament, the office of king and priest were under normal circumstances kept separate and, in any case, reserved for a privileged few. But now, because of our status as the chosen, we are all kings and also priests. We are kings in the sense that Christ the King rules over all of history for our benefit (Ephesians 1). He rules over it so that his choosing will be brought to pass. He rules over it so that all things in life will ultimately be for our good (Romans 8). It is no accident that we were baptized. It is not a coincidence that we have subsequently continued to hear his Word and believe it. No, all of that is the result of his rule over time and tide; it is all his work to bring into effect his choosing. Now we are, therefore, kings in a richer sense than any mere earthly king. Earthly kings come and go; today one succeeds and another fails, and tomorrow it is the reverse. At their best, not a one of them can know whether he will succeed or fail, be an ornament to history or a disgrace. But that's not the way it is with us! We are assured of victory and ultimate glory because Christ has won them for us by his death and resurrection. And Christ has promised them to us in his always true and faithful Word. Nothing could be more certain! The kingdom of God is a kingdom of kings. There are no slaves in it. There is not one who is the water carrier for another.

And all these kings have no greater joy in heaven than casting down their crowns before the One who chose them and made them kings by his choosing and by his cross.

Yes, and we are priests too! It was the work of the Old Testament priest to offer sacrifices to God according to God's command in the ceremonial law. But now those sacrifices have been set aside. Christ's sacrifice on the cross fulfilled and completed what they pictured and foretold. The entire epistle to the Hebrews describes how Christ's sacrifice brought all the Old Testament sacrifices to an end. Likewise, the Old Testament priesthood that was limited to males from the tribe of Levi has been set aside. Now each Christian, young or old, male or female, is a priest before God. Each and every one offers up sacrifices of prayer and thanksgiving and obedience to God. The sacrifice is that of a Christian life; it is a life in which we strive to walk by faith and in obedience to the Word of God (Romans 12). Again, what an honor! Royal priests live lives of sacrifice to God. Christian priests pray. They serve. They obey. And they do all of it with the certainty that their priestly sacrifice made in obedience to the Word of God is pleasing and acceptable to God. It is offered up in union with the Great High Priest, made perfect by his sacrifice, and washed in the water of Baptism (Ephesians 5:1,25-27).

As kings we live in joyful confidence—no matter what the circumstances of the moment—that we will ultimately be victorious over sin, death, and hell. As priests we see our whole lives as devoted first and foremost to him who has loved us and gave himself for us. With all of that in mind, Peter exhorts each of us to live as a royal priest so that "you may declare the praises of him who called you out of darkness into his wonderful light." You may be husband or wife, father or mother, parent or child. You may be carpenter, farmer, factory worker, office worker, employer, or employee. You may be brilliant or dull, rich or poor, or somewhere in-between. Whatever your station in life, as part of the royal priesthood of all believers, you have this one overarching goal in life. By your life and your position in life, you declare the praises of God.

How do we declare his praises? Jesus tells us, "Let your light shine before men, that they may see your good deeds and praise your Father in heaven" (Matthew 5:16). And St. Peter says the same thing: "Live such good lives among the pagans that, though they accuse you of doing wrong, they may see your good deeds and glorify God on the day he visits us" (1 Peter 2:12); from there he goes on to describe just what those good deeds are. In each description, Peter sees royal priests who occupy different stations in life. But regardless of their stations, royal priests want those around them to see from the way they live that they are children of God, brothers and sisters in Christ. They want to imitate the humble life of obedience and service that they see in Christ (Philippians 2).

Yes, and as priests they want especially to share the forgiveness won for us all by the high priestly sacrifice of Christ. Husbands and wives, parents and children, act as priests when they forgive one another. A Christian neighbor or coworker acts as a priest when he seeks and finds opportunities to share the gospel with those around him. That sharing may come when someone asks him something like this: "What makes you tick, anyway? You seem different." The sharing may come when tragedy strikes a neighbor and the opportunity presents itself to comfort that neighbor with the message of the Savior's rule over all things in grace. It may come through a member of the evangelism committee in the local parish. It may come the way that it came to Philip, whose first missionary effort consisted of the simple invitation to a skeptical Nathanael: "Come and see" (John 1:43-46). Too often Christians fail to share the gospel with those who do not know it because they are afraid that they might say the wrong thing. But any and all can imitate Philip, at least at the beginning. Any and all can say, "Come with me to church." Or, "Why don't you just visit a Bible class with me?"

Yes, to "declare the praises of him who called you out of darkness into his wonderful light" is what the life of royal priests is all about. They declare his praises by the way they live in their families, in their neighborhoods, at work, at pleasure. They see as the cardinal mission of life the carrying out of Jesus' commission shortly before his ascension. That mission (Matthew 28:18-20) is to do all they can individually and in union with their fellow royal priests to carry the message of redemption and salvation into all the world.

The message is Jesus' message, all of it! His message is our mission. In the process, we want always to be faithful to all he has taught in the law and to give all that he gives in the gospel. Royal priests do not pick apart his Word. They do not consider themselves free to leave out things from his Word that some may object to or find offensive. Even if in their weakness Christians imagine that some parts of God's Word keep people away from the gospel rather than draw them to it, it is not a Christian's business to act on that weakness in their faith. Rather, it is our business to strive for a life of obedience that begins with submission to all of his Word and then extends outward to the rest of life. We do not declare God's praises by presuming to correct him or tell him what he should have said and what would have been better left unsaid. That's not the behavior of a royal priest; it's the behavior of a rebel, of a pagan priest.

The keys of the kingdom of heaven are in the hands of each and every royal priest. The key to heaven's gates is exactly that message of forgiveness on account of the grace of God and the merit of Christ. It is the message of forgiveness that unlocks heaven for the penitent and slams shut the gates of hell. The praise of God that is the Christian life is always aimed at that, at drawing men and women, young and old, to the gates of heaven. It is focused on sharing all that he has taught, the center of which is the gospel message that forgives sins, that creates and preserves faith (Matthew 18:15-20; John 20:19-22).

The holy office of the ministry

Well then, if each and every believer is a royal priest, what purpose do pastors and teachers serve? Why do we even need them? After all, God teaches us himself through his Word. He gives to each and every believer the keys of the kingdom of heaven and the privilege, yes, the duty, to forgive one another. What then is the holy office of the ministry? How does it differ from the universal priesthood of all believers?

In the history of the church, there has been a tendency either to overestimate or to underestimate the holy office of the ministry. In the Roman papacy at the time of the Reformation, the office of the ministry was so exalted that the church was pictured as a ship on which were only priests and nuns and bishops with the pope as the ship's captain and pilot. In the swirling sea, the common people floundered and struggled. Their only hope was to catch hold of a staff extended by a priest from the ship of the church. The doctrine of the universal priesthood of all believers had disappeared.

To this day, Roman Catholicism teaches that it is not faith in Christ as the only and all-sufficient Savior that assures us of our peace with God and eternal salvation. Instead, Catholicism teaches that it is fellowship with the church headed by the pope that gives peace and ultimately the certainty of salvation. To be outside of fellowship with the pope is to be outside of the true church. That the pope contradicts the Word of God and demands obedience to himself instead of to the clear Word of God is supposed to make no difference to his members. So the pope dedicates himself and his church in devotion to the saints and especially to the virgin Mary. He and his priests offer masses to rescue people from a mythical purgatory. He and they sell masses in his cloisters, monasteries, and parish churches in order to obtain the favor of God for this or that intention. It is all idolatry, and it is all at bottom a gross exaggeration of the holy office of the ministry. Yes, it is exactly what St. Paul describes as the great falling away in 2 Thessalonians 2:1-12.

This most horrible of all exaggerations of the office of the ministry ends up turning the eyes of faith away from Christ and his work, from God and his grace, from the clear Word of God. It gives to the priests and their papal head a right that belongs only to God: God alone can establish doctrine, and he has done that in his own unerring and verbally inspired Word.

Additionally, that exaggeration robs Christians of their distinction as royal priests. Christ earned that distinction and the work of royal priests for them; and he promised and gave these to them already at their baptisms. Any teaching about the holy office of the ministry that turns pastors into a special caste on which others must depend for their salvation is contrary to the Word of God. It is a contradiction of the doctrine of the universal priesthood of all believers. Even more important, it is a contradiction of the doctrine of salvation by grace alone through faith alone on account of Christ alone.

But there is another tendency that is also contrary to the Word of God, a tendency to underestimate the holy office of the ministry. One sees this tendency in much of Protestantism and in some

Lutheran circles as well. Many think that pastors and teachers of the church are really not much more than hired hands. Their thinking goes something like this: We hire and contract with them to do for us what we as individuals cannot do. Most members don't have the ability or the training or the inclination to conduct worship services. Most, because of the press of other responsibilities, don't have the time to be missionaries, even in their own communities. Most aren't skilled enough to teach children and adults, to comfort the sick and the dying, to counsel the troubled and the fallen. So, we hire somebody to do that in our stead, in our name. We tell them what we want them to preach or teach, and we expect them to follow our instructions. As long as we are in agreement, they will stay in our employ. If, for whatever reason, we or they decide that it's just not working out, well, then we can fire them or they can quit and we can hire someone else.

But that's not the picture which we have of the holy office of the ministry in the New Testament. To be sure, those called to be the pastors and teachers of the church are in their persons no different than any other Christian. They are by nature sinners, frail and fallen. And even in the exercise of their offices they recognize that in their persons they are nothing: Christ and his Word is everything. That was the attitude of St. John the Baptist, who wanted nothing else than to exalt Christ. John was just the voice in the wilderness (Mark 1:1-8; John 1:6-36).

St. Paul speaks of himself and of his coworkers that way too. Among the most striking metaphors that he uses when speaking of his ministry, and by implication the ministry of all called pastors and teachers, is the one in 2 Corinthians 4:7. There he tells us, "We have this treasure in jars of clay to show that this all-surpassing power [i.e., the power of the gospel to save] is from God and not from us." People in Paul's day would hide and bury treasures in clay jars; it was the business of the jar to conceal and to protect the treasure. The pastors and teachers of the church, even the greatest of the apostles, are but fragile containers for the treasure. The treasure is hidden in the jar so that it may be taken out and shown to the world. Furthermore, the jar does not protect the treasure but the treasure protects the jar!

Both the description of St. John and that of St. Paul put the office of called workers in the church into perspective. St. John was just a voice; the message is what is important. St. Paul was just a clay jar, nothing beautiful or impressive in itself. It is the treasure of the gospel that is beautiful and God himself working through it that is powerful and glorious. That is the lowliness of the gospel ministry.

At the same time, that lowliness is the greatest joy and highest glory of the ministry. St. John was just a voice. But what a voice! It was a voice that God was pleased to use to exalt his Son and to point to his Son as the saving and sacrificial Lamb who took away the sin of the world. St. Paul was just a clay jar. But where would the treasure be and how would it have come to us were it not for that lowly clay jar that carried it? Read the rest of what Paul has to say about the office of the ministry in 2 Corinthians, especially in chapters 1–6. There you will find this constantly recurring double theme: No one is more lowly than the minister of Christ; he is the servant of all, with no glory of his own but only the glory of Christ and his message of salvation. And at the same time, no one has a more glorious office; and that for exactly the same reason: the minister of Christ is the ambassador sent from God to proclaim salvation to a doomed, a damned, a dying world. Glorious indeed is the office with that message—the message that brings life to the dying, rescue for the damned, freedom and salvation for the doomed.

And so, in the New Testament, the office of a called servant of the gospel is most highly praised. St. Paul reminds the members of the church in Ephesus that apostles and pastors and teachers are God's gifts to them. God gave them for this high and holy work of serving the servants of God. He gave them to build up his kings and priests through the teaching and preaching not of their own word but of his Word. Again, notice both the dignity and the lowliness of the office: it is high and holy because of its purpose; it is humble and lowly because it is all directed to service of another. The office is devoted first of all to the service of Christ himself and then to the service of his people (Ephesians 4:7-16).

Because of the nobility of the work and the nobility of the One who sends pastors and teachers, we honor them and hold them in high regard. When Jesus sent out the 72 to preach and teach, he commissioned them with promises and warnings for those to whom they were sent. Those sent would bring Jesus' peace to those who heard Jesus' words through them. But the wrath of God would fall on those who would reject the message and the messengers God sent: "He who listens to you listens to me; he who rejects you rejects me; but he who rejects me rejects him who sent me" (Luke 10:16). Because they bring Christ and his saving message, they should enjoy the respect owed to the One who sent them.

So the messenger is not a hired hand. He is Christ's ambassador. He is the servant of Christ in the midst of the people of God (1 Corinthians 4:1). Because of his work, an ambassador deserves respect, just as his message deserves obedience when it is the message that Christ has given in his Word. That's Paul's instruction too in 1 Thessalonians 5:12,13: "Now we ask you, brothers, to respect those who work hard among you, who are over you in the Lord and who admonish you. Hold them in the highest regard in love because of their work. Live in peace with each other." What a terrible witness it is to our children and to the community when pastors and teachers are treated with disrespect by their own members. Should anyone be surprised that the next generation does not listen to the message and the community isn't much interested in it either? After all, if the ambassador is held in contempt, what attention do we expect people to give to the message?

On the other hand, what a blessing it is in the family when the office of the ministry is honored. What an incentive for children to listen to those their parents hold in such high regard and for whom they pray. Yes, and in the community as well: when the pastors and teachers of the church are so obviously honored by their members, those outside of the church may well ask what it is that makes these people so respected. The answer of course will be this: *the message!* The epistle to the Hebrews sums it up so well: "Remember your leaders, who spoke the word of God to you. Consider the outcome of their way of life and imitate their faith" (13:7). That's a worthy work for hearers.

It is a noble goal for pastors and teachers that their lives as well as their doctrine should be worthy of such respect and imitation. Pastors and teachers need always to remember that it is not because they in their own persons are so great that they are

189

respected and honored. It is all about the message. It is all about the One who sent them. Their words are his words. Their lives should match their words and be an imitation of his life as the Good Shepherd, who laid down his life for the sheep. St. Paul exhorted the pastors of Ephesus to pay strict attention to both their doctrine and their lives. They had been called and sent by Christ to feed his flock. The flock is so dear to him that he purchased it with his blood (Acts 20:28). St. Peter urges the same thing. He reminds the pastors and teachers of the church both of their own lowliness and of their high office as those sent to serve (1 Peter 5:2-4).

So the office of the holy ministry is a special gift of God to the church. God himself considered it important enough to have three of the epistles addressed especially to pastors: 1 and 2 Timothy and Titus.

But someone at this point might say, "Wait a minute: the work of the apostles and, by extension, the work of the called pastors and teachers of the church doesn't sound like it is any different than the assignment that Christ has given to all of his royal priests. So, we still haven't discovered why God sends and gives them if their work is no different than that of all his royal priests." In essence, the observation is correct that the pastor does what all Christians are to do. His message of forgiveness is no different. But while the essence of the message is the same, the manner of its presentation is different; and that is by God's own design and arrangement. Let us say, for the sake of analogy, that a prisoner hears on the radio that all the prisoners are to be released. He eagerly shares what he has heard with his fellow prisoners who did not hear the message. The message shared would certainly excite and thrill the rest of the prisoners, and they would eagerly look for the unlocking of their cell doors. Then in comes the warden. And he declares, "You are all free to go! See, here I have the pardon from the governor in my hand!"

The message is no different in its essence. Merely the form that it takes, merely the position of the messenger, is different. So the neighbor, the husband, the wife, the parent, the child says, "Christ died for you; your sins are forgiven." Then on Sunday morning I hear it from the called representative of Christ: "By virtue of my office as a called servant of the Word, I forgive you all your sins, in the name of the Father and of the Son and of the Holy Spirit." Again, there is no difference in the essence of the message. It is the same—and yet it is different. And that is by God's own design and arrangement.

But why would God entrust the same message to all his royal priests and then to called servants of the church? Because it is God's way to be generous! That's the way he always is. He gives the gospel message so beautifully and clearly in the words of the Bible. Then he gives us the same powerful and faith-creating message in the Sacrament of Baptism. Then he assures us of the same so wondrously in the Sacrament of the Altar. In the Bible he speaks to us individually and to the world and to the church collectively. In the sacraments he says the same thing, but he says it to each of us, one at a time. He is so generous that he has his gospel touch the ears and the heart with words. Then he comes to us with water and the Word and with his own real presence with the forms of bread and wine. So, he appeals and comes to the ears, to sight and sound, to touch and taste. It's all the same message—only different.

That generosity is pictured already in creation. He gives colors, not just black and white or grey. He gives variety in geography and weather, not just flat plains or stagnant water. He gives abundance of tastes and sights and sounds. That's just the way he is: generous.

And so he gives the message to be shared by all his royal priests. And then he gives his message to be proclaimed by his called representatives. They are not in their office by their own choice but by his. He has called them. He does it not with an inner whisper. He does it through the church to which he sends them. In the gospels, he called his apostles directly. Now he calls indirectly, through the church. But the call remains his. They are his servants. They carry his message. They proclaim his Word. They belong to him wholly and entirely. That's why we don't speak of hiring and firing pastors and teachers of the church. We call them. Technically we don't even speak of paying them a salary. We support them. They are our servants, but servants given to us by Christ, whose servants they still remain; they belong to Christ first. They live to serve us; but their service to us

191

is real service only when it is with the message Christ gives in his Word and sacraments.

Yes, and before we call them, we train them. It is certainly true and obvious to anyone who thinks about it: not all of God's royal priests are able to preach and teach, to counsel and console, to have a thorough knowledge of the difference between true and false doctrine and to know why that difference matters. Indeed, as errors have multiplied over the ages, as the demands and distractions of modern life have multiplied as well, the careful and thorough training of our pastors and teachers has become all the more important. It is a tragedy that in so many churches the urgent need for pastors and missionaries has put thorough training on a cold back burner. Thorough training costs money; it limits the number willing or able to undergo such training either because of its cost or because of the time and effort required to finish the course of study. So, some cut back the requirements to a bare minimum just to get more workers out more quickly—and at less expense. The result is that the message of the church may come from more and more but be always less and less of the "all things" that Jesus commanded us to teach. To put it another way, the careful training of the ambassadors of Christ and the sharing of the message of Christ belong together: if all the energy is devoted to training and none to sharing, then the role of ambassador has largely disappeared. But if all the energy is devoted to sharing and less and less to a thorough knowledge of the message to be shared, then too the role of ambassador disappears. It's another one of those many narrow middle roads that we need to seek and find. We look for the middle with zeal to be faithful royal priests—faithful to the commission to go, faithful to the commission to teach all things.

From all that has been said, it should be clear that the universal priesthood of all believers and the holy office of the ministry are intimately connected to each other. The royal priests are anxious that their pastors and teachers be as well-trained as possible for their all-important work. They extend to their pastors and teachers the call of Christ to serve with his Word and sacraments. Then those called live for Christ and for us. They fulfill an important role in calling others to be royal priests. They strengthen with the Word and the sacraments those who are already royal priests and help them carry out their roles as royal priests. It is all a beautiful circle of mutual dependence and support. Each needs the other; each supports and sustains the other. And it is all according to God's most kind and generous design. And in the middle, at the center of it all, is Christ!

The middle road that connects the two can best be illustrated with the last words of Jesus to the congregations of Asia Minor in the book of Revelation. Notice in 1:20 how the relationship between Jesus and his pastors is described; notice how the relationship between Jesus and the churches is described. Jesus holds the pastors as stars in his right hand; they are close to him and dear to his heart. The pastors as stars shine in the church with light from him. At the same time, he calls the churches lampstands; they too shine with his light into the dark world. Again, the stars and the lampstands have the same function: they shine and radiate the light of Christ, the Light of the world. They are the same—only different. To despise either is to despise their Light, their Lord. For the stars to shine on the lampstands is their great honor. For the lampstands to hold in high esteem the stars that Christ holds in his right hand is to honor Christ, who treasures them and sends them.

We have found the narrow middle road when pastors and teachers of the church cherish and prize both their office and those they serve in that office. We have found the narrow middle road when we honor Christ by honoring those he has sent to serve us with his pure Word and sacraments. The flock was not created to trample the shepherd. The shepherd was not sent to devour the flock. Both exist for the glory of the Shepherd, who gave his life for the sheep and is Lord of both the flock and the shepherds he sends to guard and feed his flock.

The narrow middle between the doctrine of election and the Great Commission

On another short stretch of the narrow middle road, we note two doctrines that are rich with application, each in its own way. A problem can occur, however, when one of them is emphasized without thinking about the other. We will look at each and then consider the middle road that connects them.

The doctrine of election

The doctrine of election is a beautiful and most comforting doctrine. It will not be our purpose here to deal with all of the controversies that have arisen over this doctrine. We wish here merely to summarize what the Bible tells us about election and then in due course to make the connection between this doctrine and the Great Commission.

The Bible tells us that already in eternity God knew and chose those whom he would bring to faith and ultimately to heaven. Of the many places in the Bible that deal with this doctrine, we will consider one of the most beautiful. Read Ephesians 1:3-23. How beautifully Paul portrays the doctrine of election! God's choice was not based on anything good or meritorious in the elect. It was based alone and altogether on his own grace and on the merit of Christ.

God was not idle in bringing his choice into effect. He so ruled and governed all of history that those he had chosen would hear his Word, believe it, and die trusting in his grace and in Christ's merits alone for their salvation. In heaven the elect will sing forever the praises of God's grace that caused their election. They will worship and adore forever the Lamb of God who earned their salvation. They will give thanks for all eternity to God for his Word of the gospel that created their faith and preserved faith in them at the hour of death.

Again, read Ephesians 1:3-23. If we pay attention to all that Paul says there, we will avoid the temptation to misuse this beautiful doctrine. The words of the apostle begin and end with praise and thanks to God for his grace and for the comfort that this doctrine affords. There is not a word of speculation about why God chose some and not others. Paul is very clear about it: those chosen have only God to thank for it; those who perish have only themselves to blame for it. In the same chapter Paul makes it equally clear that this doctrine is not revealed so that we can wallow comfortably in our sins. Some people come to this conclusion: "Since I'm one of the elect, I can never fall, and therefore, it doesn't matter if I sin or not; it doesn't matter if I pray or not; it doesn't even matter if I listen anymore to God's Word or receive his sacraments." What an abuse of God's grace that would be! What a horrible mark of unbelieving ingratitude for the price of our salvation that would be!

Rather than wallowing in sin, the so gracious and expensive choice of God moves us to an adoration that does not end with words. Our adoration is one of a life of thanksgiving, thanksgiving lived out in the obedience of royal priests to their King of grace and the Lord of their salvation.

The doctrine of election is meant for our comfort and encouragement. Let the Christian whose memory of past sin and present weakness drives him to fear that he could not possibly be good enough to enter heaven think on this doctrine: God's choice is one of grace alone, not at all of our merit—past, present, or future. Let the one whose life is weighed down with problems that make him fear that God is punishing him for his sins consider this doctrine: In the midst of all of life's tragedies and torments, this truth is forever sure: Christ died and Christ rose; Christ reigns to bring us through joys and sorrows, through death itself to himself in glory. He will not allow anything in history to prevent his chosen from reaching the goal of heaven. Instead, he will use all of history to further his gracious choice and purpose. It's not so important that we see or fully grasp and understand how that works in any given moment. He sees it. He fully grasps and understands it. He is in control, and that's what matters. He will not fail in carrying out his rule for our benefit and the ultimate fulfillment of his choice.

Those who stick to the presentation of this doctrine in Ephesians 1 and elsewhere in the Bible will find rich comfort and encouragement in this doctrine. Those, of course, who depart from the Scriptures and try to satisfy curiosity and fallen reason will find themselves entangled and ensnared in one doubt and difficulty after another. Therefore, let us here, as on every stretch of the narrow middle road, look straight ahead to Christ and to his Word lest we go astray and miss the comfort and encouragement he wants to give us also with this doctrine.

That's the way our Confessions also present the doctrine of election (cf. especially Article XI of the Formula of Concord). Before the world began, God thought of me. On the cross Jesus thought of me. For my sake he refused to come down from that cross. For my sake he suffered, he died, he rose again. And now, for my sake, he still preserves his Word and sacraments. And he did and does all of this for the great and glorious end that "I should be his own, and live under him in his kingdom, and serve him in everlasting righteousness, innocence, and blessedness, just as he has risen from death and lives and rules eternally. This is most certainly true!" (Luther's Small Catechism, Second Article)[1]

The Great Commission

Shortly before his ascension Jesus gathered his disciples together and gave them what has come to be called his Great Commission. He said: "All authority in heaven and on earth has been given to me. Therefore go and make disciples of all nations, baptizing them in the name of the Father and of the Son and of the Holy Spirit, and teaching them to obey everything I have commanded you. And surely I am with you always, to the very end of the age" (Matthew 28:18-20).

So much is packed into these few words of the Savior! Precisely because he has all authority in heaven and on earth, the work he has given us to do cannot fail. He will be with his church, his royal priests, as they baptize and teach his gospel. He will be with them and by his power preserve his church. He will be with them; and by the power of grace inseparably attached to his Word and sacrament, he will make disciples. He will create faith and preserve it in the world until he comes again. Of that we can be sure because all power in heaven and on earth is his. Of that we can be sure because he will be with us until the very end of the age. Of that we can be sure because he who does not lie has promised it and will not fail to keep his promise. The very existence of the church from that day to this day is proof of it. The devil does all that he can to destroy the church. Tyrants have tried to drown the church in rivers of blood. Heretics and hypocrites have done their worst to corrupt the church by their false teaching or godless lives. But none of these have been able to destroy his Word or his church. Christ has been true to his Word!

And so, confident that he will remain true to his Word, Christians individually and in union with the church work to bring the gospel into all the world. They are most eager to do that

---

[1] For a consideration of the doctrine of election in a slightly different context, see chapter 5, especially pp. 103-107.

because of Christ's command. They are most eager to do it because of the great benefit, the benefit of salvation, that they have to share with a fallen world. After all, how can we help but share the salvation that Christ has given us in his Word? How can we withhold from those on the way to hell the one and only way of rescue from hell and for heaven? The apostles said as much when they were ordered to stop preaching Christ and him crucified: "We cannot help speaking about what we have seen and heard" (Acts 4:20). St. Paul impresses on us the urgency of the task when he reminds us of the sad plight of those who have not heard the gospel and of our corresponding obligation to bring it to them: "As the Scripture says, 'Anyone who trusts in him will never be put to shame.' How, then, can they call on the one they have not believed in? And how can they believe in the one of whom they have not heard? And how can they hear without someone preaching to them?" (Romans 10:11,14).

It is important to note that the apostles paid attention to all that Jesus said in the Great Commission. That is, it did not occur to them to water down the message and teach less than all he gave them to teach in his Word. To put it another way and to connect the Great Commission to the doctrine of election: they were confident that Jesus would gather all whom he had chosen through the teaching of all that he had taught. Paul makes the point in so many of his epistles: if he compromised any of the truth of God's Word, he could have escaped persecution, but then he would no longer be carrying out Christ's commission and would be found unfaithful to his Savior and Lord. He would show that he feared men more than he trusted God, or he would show that he didn't believe that the Lord could gather his church through the gospel means of grace; he would have arrogantly supposed that it was up to him to create the faith of the church, not up to Christ and the Holy Spirit working through the gospel.

Paul's zeal for mission work is beyond doubt, and it would be difficult for anyone to be more zealous in doing mission work than he was. We, therefore, will find no better example than Paul when we are confronted with the temptation that was foreign to his whole mission effort. The temptation is to let our zeal get out of bounds. The temptation is that we imagine that the success of our mission efforts depends on us—not on God's election, not on

God's promise to gather in those whom he has chosen by means of the faithful proclamation of his Word.

When that temptation gets the upper hand, we can start to get a sort of "Messiah complex," either individually or as a church body. We can see evidences of a Messiah complex when we torment ourselves over the seeming lack of success in proclaiming the gospel. "Since what I'm doing isn't working, I've got to find some new method (*a.k.a.*—gimmick) that will work. Maybe if sermons were more fun. Maybe if I didn't tell my neighbor that he really needs a Savior because he is a sinner; maybe if I left that part out until later. Maybe if our worship services were more entertaining, people would come. Maybe if we had more fun organizations. Maybe if we . . ." The list goes on and on and knows no end. As one approach yields the same apparent failure, a new one is attempted, and then another and another. Or still worse, if outward success seems to result from gimmicks, we imagine that we have really helped the message and served the purpose of the gospel.

Now someone is going to jump up and object: "But are we supposed to just repeat Bible passages in as tedious a way as we can find? Shouldn't we do our best with the gifts that God has given us in the proclamation of the gospel?" The answer is that of course we should employ the best means we can for the sharing of the gospel. It's not a question of trying to be as tedious as we can. It's not a matter of paying no attention to the way we invite, the way we worship, or even the order in which we present the truths of the Bible.

The point is not that methods don't matter. The point is that methods as such do not convert or preserve our faith. Only the gospel can do that. We need to make sure that when we are looking for methods, we don't imagine that if we just hit on the right method, then everyone will like the gospel (and us!). Jesus never told us to find the method that would take away the offense of the gospel and the scandal of the cross. And St. Paul assumed that there is no such method. What Jesus promised was that the gospel would work. What Jesus promised was that he would gather in the elect through the faithful proclamation of that gospel. That many, even most, will reject the message is not the fault of the gospel but of those who reject it. That the rejection of the gospel will be accompanied by hostility and even persecution is a fact of life that Jesus said would remain until the end of time (John 15:18-25). He doesn't threaten us with his judgment if outwardly we seem to fail; he warns against a success that is achieved by a compromise, really by a denial, of his Word.

St. Paul recognized that fact of life. For him, rejection and persecution were proofs of faithfulness, not indications that he had not yet hit on the right method of getting the message out so that all would believe it. That anyone at all believed it was proof that the gospel "worked," that it created faith and preserved faith in the face of the hostility and persecution he encountered when he was faithful to the Savior's Word. He tells the Thessalonian Christians, for example:

> You know, brothers, that our visit to you was not a failure. We had previously suffered and been insulted in Philippi, as you know, but with the help of our God we dared to tell you his gospel in spite of strong opposition. For the appeal we make does not spring from error or impure motives, nor are we trying to trick you. On the contrary, we speak as men approved by God to be entrusted with the gospel. We are not trying to please men but God, who tests our hearts. You know we never used flattery, nor did we put on a mask to cover up greed—God is our witness. We were not looking for praise from men, not from you or anyone else. (1 Thessalonians 2:1-6)

Paul's emphasis is clear: his goal was faithfulness to the message; he expected it to produce the result of faith, and he expected it to arouse hostility and opposition. No cleverness of his and no gimmick could produce the result; only the gospel could do that. And if he were looking for a gimmick that would take away all of the hostility and opposition, then he would be found unfaithful to the message.

So the point is not that looking for useful methods is bad. The point is not that we should be careless in the way we present the gospel. The point rather is that we should not imagine that methods will succeed where the message of the law and the gospel gets lost or is partially concealed by the method.

Paul says it—"we never used flattery, nor did we put on a mask to cover up greed"—not greed for money and not greed for souls either!

We need, therefore, to watch our hearts carefully when casting about for new methods of sharing the gospel. On the one hand, we do not want to despise the search with the thought that it doesn't matter at all how we present the gospel message. That would be akin to saying this to someone: "Why do you bother preparing a tasty meal for your family? You could get all the same benefit from fiber and minerals and vitamins in a simple and tasteless pill!" Paul often expressed his concern that neither he nor his coworkers do anything that would put an unnecessary obstacle in the way of the message. That was certainly a warning against a careless and indifferent presentation of the message. If a pastor just droned on in the pulpit, if the service was sloppy and conducted in an indifferent manner, those things would put unnecessary obstacles in the path of the gospel. If someone shared the gospel without ever bothering to consider the particular needs and circumstances of the one with whom he was sharing, that too would make the task of the Holy Spirit more difficult than it is already. If we are unmindful of the culture or indifferent to the society in which we share the gospel, we will come across as indifferent to those who hear us; they will close their ears before the gospel even has a chance to enter their hearts.

But, on the other hand, if we cover up some of God's truth because we are afraid of failure, then our methods do not advance the cause of the gospel; they become another hindrance to it. False doctrine converts no one, and silence about the whole truth of God's Word doesn't strengthen anyone either. Consider the sermons of Jesus in the gospels. Read the sermons of Peter and Paul in the book of Acts. In every case, Jesus and the apostles meet people where they are, with an understanding of their particular attitudes and needs. What will you always find in those inspired sermons and lessons? The sting of the law and the saving salve of the gospel are never far apart. And the sting can be as severe and biting as the gospel is saving and sweet (e.g., Matthew 11:20-28; Acts 2:14-41; 13:16-52).

The point is especially clear from the example of Paul's sermon in Athens (Acts 17:16-34). Paul was a well-educated man.

He knew how much the Greeks loved philosophy and their great poets. He knew that one of the bedrock assumptions in so much of Greek philosophy was that the material world was evil and the soul was good. For the Greeks, the goal of the soul was to escape from the prison house of the body and the material world.[2] Had Paul been concerned about not offending anyone, the last thing he should have brought up was the resurrection of the dead! But there it is, the one thing that would most easily shock and offend his hearers: "[God] has set a day when he will judge the world with justice by the man he has appointed. He has given proof of this to all men by raising him from the dead" (17:31). And what was the reaction of those who heard his sermon? Some quickly laughed, mocked, and dismissed everything that Paul had said. But at the same time, the gospel did its saving work too: "A few men became followers of Paul and believed" (17:34).

Whatever Paul's methodology, his guiding principle is clear: first, last, and always he wanted to be faithful to the message, trusting that it would save and taking it as a given that it would also be rejected. He expressed the matter so well in 2 Corinthians 2:14-17:

> Thanks be to God, who always leads us in triumphal procession in Christ and through us spreads everywhere the fragrance of the knowledge of him. For we are to God the aroma of Christ among those who are being saved and those who are perishing. To the one we are the smell of death; to the other, the fragrance of life. And who is equal to such a task? Unlike so many, we do not peddle the word of God for profit. On the contrary, in Christ we speak before God with sincerity, like men sent from God.

---

[2] It is interesting to note that such was not quite the message of the best of the Greek philosophers. But by Paul's day, much of Greek thought had been reduced to that caricature—it was a lot easier to deal with than the actual teaching of the philosophers. How everything changes only to stay the same: people still do that today, even to the teachings of the Bible (e.g., "Jesus loves me, this I know; and this is all I want to know").

Thus, any methodology that conceals truths from the Word of God is a methodology not in harmony with the Scriptures, with the practice of the apostles and of Christ himself. Any methodology that flatters the hearer by hiding from him his need and his guilt will end up hiding also the beauty of the Savior, who satisfies his need and removes his guilt. Any methodology that allows the hearer to think that he has some natural goodness left for making a right decision for Christ will end up obscuring the work of the Holy Spirit in creating the decision for Christ that comes only from the gospel.

In short, our methods must conform to the message, not the other way around. We find people where they are. We make use of the best tools we can find for reaching them. But in the process, we need always to remember that the assignment in the Great Commission is to be successful by "teaching them to obey everything I have commanded you" (Matthew 28:20). Hence, faithfulness to the message, not some quick popularity that comes from removing from the message things that people won't like, is the first mark of success. In the process of being faithful to the message, we can expect what the early church came to expect as "the Lord added to their number daily those who were being saved" (Acts 2:47).

And so, we come to the narrow middle road. The doctrine of election is not an excuse to be lazy in our seeking of the lost. The one who says to himself, "Why bother with sharing the gospel; the Lord will gather in his elect whether I share it or not?" is abusing the doctrine. And the doctrine of election is not an excuse to be sloppy in our presentation of the saving message. That's not the example we have in the preaching and teaching of the Savior. And it is not the example we have from the work of the apostles in the book of Acts.

But at the same time, the doctrine of election comforts us as we zealously seek to reach those lost in the dark night of unbelief. The success of the message we share is assured because the Holy Spirit is always present with his Word. But the success is his as he gathers in the elect. We do not know who the elect are. Only he knows that. And so, we do everything we can in conformity with the message to reach as many as we can. That the message often will be rejected will neither surprise us nor deter us. That some will hear and believe it for a time and then fall away will not surprise us either. But rejection will not move us to adopt methods that compromise the message in the vain hope that we can accomplish what only the message can accomplish. We will not presume to second-guess God's election. We will not imagine that we can improve on his Word by leaving some of it out in order to accomplish his goal of gathering in those he has chosen. Rather, in all things we will strive to be faithful to his Word. Then we will marvel at the miracle of faith that we have experienced ourselves; and as well, we will rejoice and give thanks that the same pure gospel still works and creates that life-giving miracle in others too, others with whom we share the message.

Finding the middle in the *Worship Wars*

We now enter on a short stretch of the narrow middle road that is fraught with dangers. We almost have to duck down low if we are going to avoid being hit by the grenades tossed from one side of the road to the other. It is a sorry spectacle indeed. Worship wars have to do with the way we worship, with the forms we employ in our worship services.

If we begin with a few principles that apply to our public worship services, we may more clearly see the middle of the road that avoids the extremes which are the essence of worship wars. What are the principles that we need to keep in mind when we arrange our worship services?

1. There are no divinely mandated forms of worship in the New Testament. In the Old Testament, there were. The forms of worship were clearly laid down in the ceremonial Law of Moses. That law prescribed set sacrifices for sins, rules for ritual cleanness and uncleanness, days of celebration and days of rest. But the chief purpose of the ceremonial law was to picture Christ and his work. When Christ came, he fulfilled all of those things pictured in the ceremonial law. He was the true sacrifice for the sins of the world. He brought perfect cleansing by the blood of the new and everlasting covenant. He gives us that cleansing in the Sacrament of Baptism. He brought us the true and everlasting rest that is ours in the mes-

203

sage of his work for our forgiveness. He himself is the one great and true Passover Lamb, whose body and blood we receive for our forgiveness in the Sacrament of the Altar. Since the ceremonial law has been fulfilled, the way we worship in the New Testament is an *adiaphoron*. That is, the forms we use in public worship are neither commanded nor forbidden in the Bible. We are free to adopt such forms as best serve the ultimate purposes of public worship.

2. And what is the ultimate purpose of public worship? It is first and foremost that we hear the Word of God in all its truth and purity and that we celebrate the sacraments in accord with Christ's institution. The goal in our worship services is that God the Holy Spirit should speak to us in the law to crush our pride. Once he has killed us with the law, the Holy Spirit then brings us again to life with the proclamation of the saving gospel of full and free forgiveness because of God's grace and Christ's merit. Thus, the ultimate purpose of our worship services is to let God do his thing; it's not so that we can do our thing. Christ in Word and sacraments is the center of the worship service—the center in the readings, the sermon, the hymns, the liturgy.

3. Public worship has then as its secondary purpose our response to that message of the gospel. That is a legitimate and proper purpose of the worship service, but it always follows the primary and ultimate purpose; the primary purpose must ever be the focus on Christ and what he has done, not on what we are doing. We don't read Robert Frost or Walt Whitman in church even though they have some nice things to say that make people feel good. We don't sing songs that are only about how we feel or even songs that focus exclusively on God's wonders in nature or in our hearts. We read his Word. We talk about its application to life. We confess our sins and the faith that his Word creates and preserves. We sing praises that focus on what Christ has done for us and for our salvation. We recognize our need for his mercy and help, and

we rejoice in the fullness of God's grace in Christ that satisfies our need. In short, whether in the readings, in the sermon, in the liturgy, or in the hymns, Jesus is everything. To the extent that our faith and feelings find expression, they are always in response to the clear Word of God with Jesus and his cross always at the center. Even when we are singing the psalms from the Old Testament, they are sung in the context of the message that focuses on our need and God's grace in satisfying that need—in a word, Christ is still the center.

4. Since the worship service is primarily God's service to us in the gospel, and since he is the God of our creation and the Lord of our salvation, it should be self-evident that the forms used in worship would have a measure of dignity, of reverence and respect for God and for his Word.[3]

5. Since God in his Word is always seeking to find us by means of his gospel, it should likewise be self-evident that we would not want to adopt forms of worship that would of themselves turn people away from listening to his Word. Forms of worship can turn people away from God when they are used to hide false doctrine or when they confuse people about the difference between false doctrine and true; a worship service that looks too much like a Roman mass or too much like a Reformed service may lead people to conclude that there is no difference between the doctrines those services are designed to reflect and the true doctrine. Such confusion can easily be the case even if not the intentions of those designing or

---

[3] Some have rightly observed that perhaps we as worshipers should give a bit more thought to this matter of the dignity of God's house and the dignity of worship there than is common these days. Given the One who is there and what we come to do there, perhaps we should appear in his presence with some dignity too. It may well be that God does not care much what we wear to church. But maybe we should care enough to look our best. Tattered jeans or short-shorts when something better is available to us do not bespeak respect. If you wouldn't go to court or to an afternoon wedding looking that way, why would you want to bow low before the judgment seat of God in confession and hear him embrace you as the bride of Christ in absolution looking that way?

conducting the service. (Cf. in this regard especially Article X of the Formula of Concord.)

In applying these basic principles to the forms of worship we use, we need to remember what the Bible teaches us about *adiaphora* in general. With things that are *adiaphora,* that is, with those things that are neither right nor wrong in and of themselves, the "rule" is Christian love. That love seeks the building up of our brothers and sisters in Christ, not the bold and bald and loveless exercise of my rights or my freedom or my opinions and preferences.

St. Paul set the example for us in the way he dealt with the problem of food. In the Greek world of Paul's day, often the priests at the pagan temples doubled as butchers. People would go to the temple to buy their meat, meat that usually had been previously sacrificed to a false god. That presented a problem for many Christians. They had once been participants in those sacrifices. After their conversion, many of them had a bad conscience about eating meat; they feared that by buying and consuming meat which had been offered to idols, they were again participating in those pagan sacrifices. And so, they refused to eat meat, lest they sin against their conscience.

Paul understood the problem. He knew on the one hand that eating or not eating meat is an *adiaphoron.* To eat meat is not a sin, and to abstain from the eating of meat is not a virtue. But if someone's conscience is bothered by eating meat offered to idols, then he should not eat it. And those whose conscience was not bothered should be left free to eat it as they pleased, since eating or not eating is in itself neither sin nor a virtue. But neither side should look down on the other. Those who understood that they were free to eat meat should not have tried to force those who were troubled by it to violate their conscience. At the same time, those who were troubled by eating meat should not have tried to force their own scruples on everyone else. To force someone to act against his conscience is to force him to sin, since to act against conscience is a sin. That's true even when the conscience may be in error. And, likewise, to bind someone else's conscience, to make a sin out of something that is free, is just as wrong. So each should respect the other. With time the one whose conscience is in error may come to understand better the freedom that he has in matters of *adiaphora*. But that is not something that should be forced (cf. Romans 14).[4]

The matter of circumcision was likewise a problem. Some of the Jewish converts to Christianity thought that circumcision should still be treated as the necessary sacrament that it was in Old Testament times. They tried to bind the consciences of the gentile converts, insisting that circumcision was necessary for salvation. From insisting on the necessity of circumcision, they then went on to insist as well on the necessity of following the Old Testament dietary laws. Much of the epistle to the Galatians is a strong, even a vehement condemnation of such a teaching and of such teachers. To make anything other than the grace of God and the saving work of Christ a condition for pleasing God or for salvation is to deny the heart and core of the gospel. Paul says of them, "Let [them] be eternally condemned" (Galatians 1:9). So then, when someone tries to bind the conscience of another over what started out as an *adiaphoron,* it ceases to be an *adiaphoron.* Earlier, Paul, when he was working among the Jews, had his coworker Timothy (whose father was Greek) circumcised; that would make it easier for Timothy to work among the Jews. But once Jewish Christians insisted that circumcision was necessary to salvation, Paul condemned the practice in the strongest possible terms. What had been an *adiaphoron* ceased to be one when it was turned into a law or made necessary in any way for a true Christian life or for salvation.

Thus, those who think themselves strong and sure and certain in what they are doing give up their freedom to do what they think best in love for those they consider weak. And at the same-

---

[4] It's important to keep in mind that we are here talking about legitimate *adiaphora;* we are not talking about things clearly commanded and forbidden by the Word of God. A person might say, "Well, my conscience doesn't bother me if I occasionally get drunk or if I have a sexual relationship outside of marriage; and since my conscience doesn't bother me, for me it is no sin." That's a gross misuse of the principle of respect for a person's conscience in matters of *adiaphoron.* Such things are not *adiaphora* at all; the Word of God clearly calls them sins; and sins they are, whether someone's conscience is bothered or not. The principle of *adiaphoron* does not do away with the clear law of God.

time, those who have a particular sense that their own way is the only right way are not free to bind the conscience of anyone else when it is a matter of an *adiaphoron.*

Indeed, St. Paul told Timothy not to let himself get bogged down in quarrels about *adiaphoron* but, as a good pastor, to concentrate on what really matters, namely, on the law and gospel of salvation (1 Timothy 4). It is sad to see how many seem to miss St. Paul's good advice when it comes to forms of worship that are neither commanded nor forbidden in the Scriptures. It is a sorry spectacle to see one side insisting that it has found the only really correct way to worship and the other side with equal vehemence waving a flag of liberty that they think gives them the right to do whatever they please. It is doubly strange to see that happening in Lutheran circles, given the clarity with which the Lutheran Confessions deal with the matter of freedom in forms of worship (cf. Articles XV and XXIV of the Augsburg Confession and of the Apology, and Article X of the Formula of Concord). Luther too knew of no law when it came to forms of worship. Each Lutheran territory adapted existing forms as it thought best. It cleansed the existing forms of those things that promoted false doctrine (e.g., the worship of the saints, transubstantiation and the veneration of the elements of Holy Communion, the mass as a sacrifice for the sins of the living and the dead, etc.). Then they retained much of what remained; some kept more, some less. Luther's own *Deutsche Messe* (his German Mass) was neither a slavish following of the liturgies of the past nor a freewheeling rejection of what had been inherited from earlier centuries.

The point is that there should be a narrow Lutheran middle road when it comes to forms in worship. The extremes of excessive ceremony that make the Lutheran service appear no different from a high form of the Roman mass would best be avoided. We do not want to give anyone the impression that there is no difference between the Lutheran teaching concerning the Sacrament and the Roman false doctrine of transubstantiation (the doctrine that the priest transforms the bread and wine into Christ's body and blood when he recites the Words of Institution). Freedom in establishing forms of worship should not be exercised in such a way that people become unclear about the difference between false doctrine and true.

At the same time, the rejection of all the historic forms of worship to the point that Lutheran worship services seem to be the same as the services of so-called mega-churches may well be an abuse of freedom. For again, people may get the impression that the doctrine of the one is the same as the doctrine of the other when they see no real difference in the content of the services. Is the focus of the mega-service to get people in the right mood to "make their decision for Christ" or "invite King Jesus into their hearts" or just teach them how to live better lives? We certainly would not want to adopt words or forms, music, or sermon styles and content that would give people the impression that that's what our services are all about.

In the worship wars one side shouts: "We know that this is *the* right way to worship, and so that's the way we're going to do it. We don't care what anyone else thinks about it; and we certainly don't want to have anything to do with the 'tent meeting' approach to worship so common among false teachers in Protestantism." And the other side with equal vigor cries out: "We're free to worship any way we want to; and besides that, we think our way will be more appealing to outsiders who are 'turned off' by any kind of formalism."

Where is the middle between these two extremes? In his epistles to the Corinthians, Paul gives us some useful reminders that apply well to the way we worship. In 1 Corinthians 14 he admonishes the Corinthians to conduct their worship service in an orderly manner. But what, finally, is an orderly form for worship? Is it not that in our worship we hear the beautiful summary of the whole gospel message in 2 Corinthians 5:20–6:1?

> We are therefore Christ's ambassadors, as though God were making his appeal through us. We implore you on Christ's behalf: Be reconciled to God. God made him who had no sin to be sin for us, so that in him we might become the righteousness of God. As God's fellow workers we urge you not to receive God's grace in vain.

The form of a worship service that conceals our desperate need for such a reconciliation has missed the ultimate point of the worship service. Such services tend to leave out as a matter of course a confession of sins or talk about the need for true repentance. Rather, the main use of the law in such a service is what we generally call its third use. The first use of the law is that it shows us our sin and our desperate need of a Savior; the third use of the law is that it shows us those works which are pleasing to God. But without the first use, the third use easily degenerates into moralizing or self-improvement instruction. It misses the point that the very first purpose of a worship service is to present Christ as the one and only Savior of sinners.

That very basic first purpose of worship can also be missed where the form, the ceremony, has become an end in itself. The ceremony itself and the emphasis on doing everything "right" may fail to confront any and all with their need of a Savior. Then, as in the service with no apparent form, we will give people little reason to focus on the solution that Jesus is and that Jesus provides for that need.

In sum, one sometimes fears that Jesus as the Savior of sinners can get lost in an excess of ceremony, in spite of the intention of those concerned with the proper form of the ceremony. One fears equally that in the interest of not offending the visitor, the need that they have for the Savior of sinners can disappear in a service that is more entertaining than edifying.

A consideration of the members of our congregation and of our sister congregations simply should not be ignored. It would be good if we all recognized that there are certain parameters within which freedom and variety can be a good thing. Inside of those parameters, the two most important purposes of the worship service should always be kept clearly in view. We want always to show visitors and members alike their need and Jesus as the solution to their need. If our own members are so uncomfortable with the forms that the message gets lost, then there is something wrong with the forms—even if someone has decided that this is really the right way to do things. Likewise, if in the interest of appealing to the outsiders the service ignores the offense of our sinfulness and the only way of salvation, then our exercise of our freedom from forms is getting in the way of the real purpose of the service.

Yes, it can happen that the ego of the one in charge of the service gets in the way: "I know that this is the best way, and so this is the way we're going to do it!" Where is the love for members weak and strong in that kind of an attitude? Where is the heart of a servant to the servants of God in that kind of thinking?

And it can happen as well that a lack of trust in the power of the law and the gospel gets in the way. If I'm not really sure that the law will crush and the gospel bring to life again, then the service can easily degenerate into something other than this appeal: "Be reconciled to God!" It can become an attempt to bring people in by making Christianity seem easy and entertaining. The one so tempted needs to remember that faith is always a miracle in which the truth of the gospel wins the victory over fallen reason and emotion. Yes, the one so tempted needs to remember that the gospel has already won that victory in him! Why is he afraid that it won't or can't win the victory in others too? Of course, there will always be those who reject the gospel; Christ told us that from the start. Our forms will not change that fundamental reality. But the gospel will also always have its fruit. Christ promised that too. His Word will not return to him empty (Isaiah 55). The pure Word, the "all things" of the Great Commission, is what we want to present in whatever forms we adopt. The forms, after all, are means to an end, not ends in themselves.

We cannot here prescribe the exact form that we should use in worship if we are to be on the narrow middle road. We cannot do that precisely because the forms are *adiaphora*. But we can hope that the emphasis of those arranging our worship services would always be on "speaking the truth in love" (Ephesians 4:15). Then our unity in the faith will be evident. Then those who worship with us will from week to week be built up in that faith "until we all reach unity in the faith and in the knowledge of the Son of God and become mature, attaining to the whole measure of the fullness of Christ. Then we will no longer be infants, tossed back and forth by the waves, and blown here and there by every wind of teaching and by the cunning and craftiness of men in their deceitful scheming" (Ephesians 4:13,14).

But now it is time to run the final stretch of the narrow middle road.

9

The Final Stretch
on the Narrow Middle Road

The road is long, but it finally comes to an end. That is true whether we are speaking of the road of life or the road through the truths of the Bible. While the stretches of the road that we have traveled in the chapters of this book by no means portray the whole of the journey, it is time to bring our wanderings in this work to a close. We will leave for others and for another time the consideration of other parts of the journey that we have neglected or skipped over.

It is on the final stretch of the road that the two—the road of life and the road through the truths of the Bible—become one. The ultimate goal of both life and of the truths revealed in the Bible is the glory of God. And that goal is finally reached when at the end of days, we come to enjoy the beatific vision of Jesus enthroned in glory. The goal is finally reached when in heaven we join with all the saints and angels to sing forever their song of praise:

> "Worthy is the Lamb, who was slain, to receive power and wealth and wisdom and strength and honor and glory and praise! . . . To him who sits on the throne and to the Lamb be praise and honor and glory and power, for ever and ever!" (Revelation 5:12,13)

> "Hallelujah! For our Lord God Almighty reigns. Let us rejoice and be glad and give him glory! For the wedding of the Lamb has come, and his bride has made herself ready. Fine linen, bright and clean, was given her to wear." (Revelation 19:6-8)

As always with the truths of God's Word, there is no end of delight in listening to what God has to say and in pondering the import of his words for our life here and our life there in the endless bliss of heaven.

Poor Aristotle! He knew nothing of the joy of life with Christ here. He was altogether unaware of the blessed state of the saints in the full light of the eternal day with Christ in heaven. So Aristotle and his god, human reason (the *logos* of Greek philosophy), will not help us on this final stretch of the road. Indeed, many of the philosophers of his day and since have thought that the greatest gift that the gods gave to men was the ability to end one's own life. They considered it a virtue and a duty to commit suicide once life no longer afforded one the pleasures of the flesh. Montesquieu, for example, one of the most famous of the French *Philosophs* of the 18th century, published his *Persian Letters* in 1721. In the *Persian Letters* Montesquieu's correspondent argues that the church shouldn't object to suicide. After all, if God loves all that he has created, then what difference does it make to him whether one becomes dust now or later; whether dust or a live human being, anything God has made should be equally loved by him, or so Montesquieu argued. That's the best that reason could do for him! It does not occur to him that the same reasoning should make murder, mass murder, and genocide likewise matters of indifference to God.

These days our culture seems to be forsaking whatever thin veneer of Christian truth may have covered it. It seems to be returning to that attitude of the philosophers guided by blind reason alone and then adopting attitudes which are as unreasonable and horrific as those of Montesquieu. Societies devoted to assisting people who want to commit suicide are multiplying in Europe and now in North America as well. How sad! How tragic that so many would find in death the ultimate proof of the meaninglessness of life and a vainly hoped-for escape from its burdens into nothingness!

The opposite attitude in the world is no better. An opposite and equally faithless opinion is that death is the ultimate horror: fearing what may lie beyond, people struggle against death with all their might and all their resources and the resources of their family and even of the state. When their vain struggles finally fail, they die in despair.

Oh, how blessed the lot of the Christian! He neither longs for death as an escape from the supposed meaninglessness of his life nor clings to life in terror of a vast abyss into which he will fall when death claims him. The Christian has walked along the narrow middle road, with Christ as his light and Christ as his goal. He has had God's Word as his map and faithful guide. The road often has been rough. Often the climb has been steep and the path watered by tears. But at length it comes to an end. For both the journey and its end, the Christian is profoundly, yes, eternally grateful.

This stretch of the road too has a narrow middle to it. It is the middle between an eager anticipation of our future in heaven on the one hand and, on the other hand, our delight in serving Christ in the here and now. To spend too much time with eyes fixed on heaven can make people lax and lazy in the joyful carrying out of the service that Christ wants from them here and now. That to some extent was the problem of the church in Thessalonica; Paul wrote 2 Thessalonians in part to deal with just that problem. But an exclusive attention to the here and now can get very depressing when the days are long and the road is hard. Many places in the New Testament address that problem. Especially the book of Revelation was inspired to encourage patience and to give us hope when the journey seems long and its crosses heavy.

As we bring the journey that is this book to a close, let us then spend a little time considering what the Bible has to say about our future in heaven. And then let us consider also the middle between an excessive longing for that happy day that knows no end and the joyful service to God in the here and now, a service that we are eager to render until God himself brings it to an end.

Our blessed future in heaven

"What will heaven be like?" "What will we do in heaven?" Who hasn't asked those questions a hundred times? The little child asks them out of curiosity. The sufferer asks seeking comfort for troubles of the moment. The aged ask with longing and in anticipation of their entry into its peace and joy. And what does the Bible have to say to all of us in answer to the questions? The answers are filled with comfort for the aged, hope for the suffering, and much food for thought for the young.

Most of the passages that speak of heaven are surprisingly short. Jesus tells us that in heaven there will be no more death (Luke 20:36). St. Paul tells us that heaven is a reward so great for the blessed that none of earth's sorrows are worthy to be compared to its glory (Romans 8:17,18). He tells us that there we will find rescue from every form of evil (2 Timothy 4:18). St. Peter tells us that heaven's blessings can never be spoiled or come to an end (1 Peter 1:4).

Jesus, knowing that his brothers and sisters would want a little more, gave us the most touching description of heaven in his final words to the church on earth. The description is in the book of Revelation. That book was written at a time when the church was suffering one devastating persecution after another. All of the apostles except for St. John were dead; and if we accept tradition, they had died horrible deaths as martyrs. St. John himself was about 90 years old and living in exile on the salt mine prison island of Patmos. To underscore Paul's words in Romans 8:18 and the echo of prophet Isaiah (Isaiah 25:8; 35:10; 49:10; 60:20), Jesus encouraged the faithful to patiently endure. This is what awaits them after this short time on earth and what those already in heaven experience and enjoy even now:

They are before the throne of God and serve him day and night in his temple; and he who sits on the throne will spread his tent over them. Never again will they hunger; never again will they thirst. The sun will not beat upon them, nor any scorching heat. For the Lamb at the center of the throne will be their shepherd; he will lead them to springs of living water. And God will wipe away every tear from their eyes. (Revelation 7:15-17)

[God] will live with them. They will be his people, and God himself will be with them and be their God. He will wipe every tear from their eyes. There will be no more death or mourning or crying or pain, for the old order of things has passed away. (Revelation 21:3,4)

How tender! How cheering! Though heaven will be inhabited by thousands upon thousands of the saints and angels, Jesus nevertheless pictures it for us in such a personal way. "[God] will wipe every tear from their eyes!" That's lifetimes worth of tears! He has counted them—the tears of childhood, tears from the hurts of the teenage years, tears from the disappointments of middle age, tears caused by the pains of old age. God will not be too busy for any of them. He never was too busy while we were in the midst of those tears here on earth; it's just that we weren't always as aware of his kind and personal attention as we should have been. In life Jesus taught us to call God our Father. And there in heaven God, like a tender father, will take each one of us to himself. God will show each of us in such a personal way how well he understood us. Even in heaven, not one of us will be some nameless, faceless blot in a crowd. Not one of us will be cringing in a corner, hoping that no one will notice that we are there and point to us and cry out: "There's been a mistake! What's that one doing here?" No, each one will be the dearly beloved child of God. Each one will see most fully, most beautifully, that when Jesus was born, when he suffered, when he died, he was thinking about me, even me. Each one will see how God really did already in eternity desire my salvation, yearn for it, plan for it, and rule all of history so that I would be with him forever. And thus, heaven will be, for the whole church and for each individual believer, the great wedding feast of the Lamb that Jesus speaks about in Revelation 21.

But what do we notice even in this most beautiful picture of heaven? It and the other passages that we cited earlier speak of heaven almost entirely in negatives. That is, they tell us what heaven will not be and will not have. It will not have death or pain or sorrow or tears. To put it most simply, these passages tell us that sin and all of its consequences will have no place in heaven. Death and sadness, tears and the impermanence of every earthly joy are all the results of sin, be they the results of our own sins, the sins of others, or simply the consequences of the fall of Adam and Eve.

It is certainly comforting to know that in heaven our sins will not only be fully forgiven but that also their causes and their effects will be completely gone. There will be no more temptations that caused us here such struggle. There will be no more shame and guilt buried so deep in our memories. There will be no more of the ravages of our sinful condition so evident in sickness and sorrow of every kind and finally in death itself. All of that will be gone, gone forever. To the extent that we remember any of it, the memory will only be a cause of rejoicing and thanksgiving that Jesus has rescued us from it and replaced it with eternal peace and joy.

But still we are left with questions about the positives: what will there be in heaven for us once temptations, sin, and all its terrible effects are gone? St. Paul gives us a bit of a clue as to why the Bible says so little in answer to that question. He tells us in 1 Corinthians 13:12 that here we look up to heaven through a smoky glass; we can only see intimations of heaven's glory. Once we get there, it will all become clear and bright as day; we will know and understand there, just as God knows and understands us perfectly here. Then in 2 Corinthians 12 he speaks of a man (probably himself) who was snatched up into heaven before death. But there he saw and experienced things that have no point of reference on earth, things that he just wouldn't or shouldn't even attempt to describe. That's how wonderful it will be!

We can understand the difficulty. Here on earth we know of no moment when we are not to one degree or another affected by sin. Here on earth we know of no moment when we are not completely hemmed in by the limitations of time and space. We cannot even begin to imagine a time or a condition where such is not the case. How can we even begin to picture what it will be like never to be tempted again, never to suffer frustration or sorrow again, never to be even capable of sickness or death? It is simply unimaginable for us. Even the notion of being completely and perfectly happy forever, without becoming bored by such a state, is unimaginable to us.

The best way that the Bible has of summing up such a state, such a place, such a condition, is perhaps in the words of St. John: "How great is the love the Father has lavished on us, that we should be called children of God! . . . Dear friends, now we are children of God, and what we will be has not yet been made known. But we know that when he appears, we shall be like him, *for we shall see him as he is*" (1 John 3:1,2).

"We shall see him as he is!" And just how is he? He is always our gracious God and our perfect Savior. He is always ruling over events in our lives, over things great and small, to accomplish the blessed end that we should be forever with him in heaven. He is always surrounding us with the protection of the holy angels, without ever leaving us just to their care, as sufficient as that would be. But that's not how we see him now. Now we see him under the burden and weight of the cross. Now we often view him only through the prism of tears. Now we wonder why he permits this to happen and allows that. Now we have occasion often to say deep down inside, "When I get to heaven, when I see him, there are a few bones that I'm going to have to pick with him! There are a few things that I'm going to want him to explain!"

Job thought that way too in the midst of his suffering. But read the closing chapters of Job's book. When God finally does visit him, Job is overwhelmed both by God's glory and his goodness; he raises not one of the questions that he had for God in his moments of weakness and suffering. That is no doubt the way it will be for us too. That's what it means: "We shall see him as he is!" No more questions, no more doubts about his grace and his goodness as he exercised them from the moment of our conception to the second of our last breath. We will see perfectly that he always was what he told us he was in his Word, in his sacraments: our gracious God, our Refuge and Help in every need, our Redeemer, our mighty King, our Brother! Thus, our first words in heaven will probably not be, "How come . . . ?" Instead, in wonder and awe and profound thanksgiving we will simply say, "Oh!" For then and there, as Paul said in 1 Corinthians 13:12, "Then we shall see face to face. Now I know in part; then I shall know fully, even as I am fully known."

But we still haven't answered the question of what we will actually be *doing* in heaven. If the reader will pardon one personal reference, the author remembers his aged mother thinking out loud one time. She said, "I wonder if someone will have to do the dusting in heaven; if so, I'd be happy to do it." The child asks, "Can I play with my puppy in heaven?" One of our seminary professors speaks of the little boy he had in confirmation class. The boy lived for fishing and would often show up for class smelling of fish and the river bank. And just as often the boy would ask, "Will we be able to go fishing in heaven?" He just could not imagine that he would be happy there if he couldn't go fishing.

For all of these queries and musings, the good seminary professor had perhaps the best answer when he told the boy in his confirmation class, "I don't know exactly what we will be doing in heaven; all I know is that whatever we are doing, *we will not wish that we were doing something else!*" What an excellent answer! Does the baby at birth have even the foggiest notion of what its life will be like outside of the womb? Of course not; the baby simply has no point of comparison of the former state to the latter. So for us too when we consider our passing from the temporal to the eternal, from being always stained by sin to being ever free from it. The Bible tells us that we will worship God perfectly and forever. The Bible tells us that we will be forever with the Lord and will see him as he is. That should be enough for us. After all, if our best moments here in time were those when we felt closest to him, surely when we perfectly see and experience him in the fullness of his grace and glory, we will not be disappointed!

Our life here and now

So the Bible does not go much beyond the largely negative descriptions that tell us what heaven will not be like. We just don't have the vocabulary for more than that. But we may surmise still another good reason why the Bible is relatively sparse in its descriptions of heaven, namely this: We have work to do in the here and now before we get there! If the picture of heaven's glory were complete in the Bible, how could we stand it to stay here a minute longer? God tells us enough of the glory that awaits us in heaven to comfort and encourage us here and now. He tells us enough so that even on good days here, we may long for the perfect and endless day there. He tells us enough so that we don't fall too much in love with this world and what it offers while we wait for the perfect world and what it contains. He tells us enough so that in union with the church, the bride of Christ, we hear Jesus in the last verses of the Bible promise to come and take us to himself; and we sigh in answer: "Amen. Come, Lord Jesus!"

The narrow middle road then is to have both feet firmly planted on the ground as we are about our Father's business in the here and now. The narrow middle road is that our vision nevertheless looks ahead, looks up, looks eagerly forward to the end of the road where we will see Jesus as he is.

Under the inspiration of the Holy Spirit, St. Paul more than anyone else tells what his own thoughts were on the middle road between eagerness to serve and a longing for heaven. While in prison in Rome, unable to serve the way he had for so many years and with the possibility that he would be put to death after his trial, Paul had this to say on the middle road:

> I eagerly expect and hope that I will in no way be ashamed, but will have sufficient courage so that now as always Christ will be exalted in my body, whether by life or by death. For to me, to live is Christ and to die is gain. If I am to go on living in the body, this will mean fruitful labor for me. Yet what shall I choose? I do not know! I am torn between the two: I desire to depart and be with Christ, which is better by far; but it is more necessary for you that I remain in the body. Convinced of this, I know that I will remain, and I will continue with all of you for your progress and joy in the faith, so that through my being with you again your joy in Christ Jesus will overflow on account of me. (Philippians 1:20-26)

One thing stands out above everything else: Christ! If Paul dies and goes to heaven, there he will have blessed peace and life with Christ. If he lives and can still be useful here on earth, then Christ will be exalted and Christ's elect will be served. And so, whether here or in heaven, Christ is all in all; Christ is everything! When Paul faces trial in the imperial court, he will be faithful to Christ and make a good confession of his faith in accord with the Word of God that he had taught. If he dies, he will cling to Christ, who promised to deliver him at last and give him the reward of grace earned by Christ on the cross (2 Timothy 4:8). If he lives, such service as he is still able to offer will have the Word and work of Christ as its center; that's how faith and joy are born and sustained in a believer's heart.

What a perfect model for us as we travel the last stretch of the narrow middle road. Jesus has made it clear that our time here is not to be wasted. He does not want us to spend our days gazing up into heaven in lazy longing. He made that clear to the disciples on the day of his own ascension. They looked up, no doubt stunned by what they had just witnessed. But Jesus did not let them spend much time in idle gazing. He had told them shortly before that they had work to do (Matthew 28:18-20). And then at his ascension he told them to get ready to do it (Acts 1:9-11). At the same time, he assured them that he would not forsake them but would return and take them to himself when the time had fully come. He has given us this time of grace for service that he considers important and of eternal significance. So we will not despise our time in the here and now the way the ungrateful steward did (Matthew 25:14-30). Nor will we be like the foolish virgins who seemed to think that their Lord would never really come at all and thus were unprepared when he did come (Matthew 25:1-13).

The time here is a busy time for us indeed. In the strong words that he uses to describe his life, the apostle Paul tells us, when his journey is about to end, just how busy it was: "I have fought the good fight, I have finished the race" (2 Timothy 4:7). One cannot fight a good fight or run a race with his eyes gazing lazily into the sky. No, the fight and the race required all of Paul's attention and all his energy, even as he was focused on the prize at the end. We are heirs of all his labors. It was through Paul that the gospel spread so far and wide. And it was through Paul that the Lord inspired so much that is so useful to us on our journeys along the middle road and even on this final stretch of that road.

Each of us in his day has reason to consider this final stretch of the middle road. When we are young, we perhaps think of the end of the journey less than we will when we are old. We in our youth should have our attention fixed on the work that the Lord may yet place in front of us in the various stations of life. We think about the possibilities of a future vocation, of a future as a husband or wife, as a parent. We think about all the doors that we have yet to pass through. There is so much excitement, so much of anticipation, so much energy and eagerness. And that's all well and good. It should be that way. Mindful of the focus on the here and now and of the greater attention to the immediate future, the church has always prayed: "For all swift and young and happy things, we thank thee, O Lord." But even the young and the very young do well to remember that the present and its possibilities are all gifts for use and usefulness. Even the young do well to think from time to time that the greatest joys await them still in heaven, and the greatest joy of the here and now is service to the One who won heaven for them at so great a price.

For the rest of us, thoughts of heaven too will come and go with varying degrees of intensity. We want to see our children grown and with children of their own. We would like to tell even our grandchildren the story of Jesus that we taught our children. We should be happy to show both our children and our grandchildren that our reason for living is to love and serve him who loved us and gave himself for us. So our thoughts of the end of the journey may not be many or even thoughts of eager anticipation. But still, on our best days, we do not live for the here and now. We live to serve. And there is no greater joy than such service. In the needs of those around us, whether dear friends and family or even enemies, we see the lowliness of Christ. We see the opportunity to give him a cup of water, to offer a piece of bread to the Man of sorrows on the way to the cross, a cloak or a blanket against the cold to the Child in the manger. We see the opportunity to share the Bread of Life in the message of the gospel that saves for time and for eternity. It is all so worthwhile. It is all so blessed. It is all made holy and an eternal fruit of the passion of the Savior.

But when the time comes that such service is severely constricted or made almost impossible by the infirmities of sickness or age, well, then we think of heaven more often and with greater longing. And there is nothing wrong with that. We see that our journey is coming to an end. We may wish that the end would come sooner rather than later. But it may be that the Lord still wants to use us as examples of patience and devotion for those we will soon leave behind. It may be that the Lord is taking his time in order to cut better the ties that bind us to the earth or the ties even that bind others to us; he may be blessing them by giving them the time they need to adjust to our leaving and even to be happy for us when we do leave. Whatever the case may be, we are grateful for the journey. We are grateful for the gospel that made it worthwhile. We are grateful for the opportunities we had to reflect our love for Christ and his Word and his people. We are grateful for it all—but really, we don't want to do it over again. And so with the saints of every age, we may say often, "Come, Lord Jesus!" Our greatest task has become a striving for patience. Our hardest work is that of not making the work of those who care for us harder than it needs to be. Our holiest efforts at service are our prayers for them and our efforts to be grateful to them when we are more inclined to be grumpy.

But still there is Christ. Still there is the promise that he will come for us at just the right time. Still there is that faith which clings to his promises, no matter how hard that may be in times of pain and suffering. Gone are the relatively idle questions about degrees of glory in heaven. Gone are speculations about states of the soul here and there or in between. Questions about what we will do when we get there fall to the side. Now there is only the very practical desire to *see him as he is*. The knowledge that we shall see him thus is near at hand. That remains our comfort and our encouragement.

And so, we come to the close of our journey along the narrow middle road. All along the way there have been ditches on the right and the left of that narrow middle road. All along the way there have been temptations from fallen reason to turn a truth into an error by forgetting the rest of the truth. All along the way there have been temptations to take our eyes off of the map, the sacred Scriptures, and off of Christ, the center. To the extent that our eyes wandered, we stumbled and fell. But Christ in his compassion pulled us back again to the middle by the sign of the cross. He held before us his pierced hands and side. He showed us the marks of his love and the price he willingly paid to redeem us. He is the source in Word and sacraments, the content and the goal of our faith. Had it not been for his grace and its creating and sustaining power in the Word and sacraments, we would have perished long ago. And when we finally attain to our blessed end, we will spend an eternity in the company of the saints, worshiping and giving thanks for so great a salvation. As the hymnist sang, "What joy awaits us there!"

Will there be dusting to do in heaven? Can we go fishing there or play with a puppy? Will there be seminars with the apostles and prophets and the great church fathers where we can ask questions and listen to the fascinating accounts of their lives of service? Will there be endless reunions with loved ones who will tell us how great the grace of God was to them in events from their lives about which we knew nothing here on earth? Will we take walks with Jesus in a forest of trees ever green and along streams of living water?

Imagination runs wild. And whatever it is that we imagine heaven to be like, it will be a thousand times better. Look at the perfection and the power of the One who won it for us! Yes, and even consider how much better life here is than you ever imagined it would be. Oh, yes, how blessed we are to live with Christ here. How blessed we will be to live with him there!

We have reached the journey's end. To God be all praise and glory!

Appendix

A Portion of a Sermon
by C. F. W. Walther

(Translated from *Licht des Lebens—Ein Jahrgang von Evangelien-Predigten aus dem Nachlass des seligen D. Carl Ferdinand Wilhelm Walther, gesammelt von C. J. Otto Hauser;* Concordia Publishing House, St. Louis, Missouri, 1905; pp. 351,352)

Here, however, perhaps many say in their hearts: "How can I believe that God will certainly listen to me when I see that God nevertheless does not give so much prayed for in faith?" To this we answer: "If we ask God for that for which he has given us a promise, then God most certainly keeps his Word. But he has certainly not promised that it should always go well for a Christian according to the flesh. Only this he has promised, that he at the Christian's prayer wants to give him grace to help him through every need, to grant him what is necessary in temporal things, and one day to make him eternally blessed in Christ."

If we now ask something according to God's will and promise, then he hears us; when, however, for example, the mother of John and James asked the Lord to let her sons sit in his kingdom, one on his right and the other on his left, this petition failed; she had no promise for that sort of thing. If, therefore, anyone would want

227

to ask for a great sum of money or for a high position of honor, then also this request would fail.

When, however, Peter at Christ's command jumped into the waves of the sea and cried when death threatened: "Lord, help me, I'm sinking!" then Christ quickly extended his hand to him. When accordingly now a Christian prays for spiritual goods necessary for salvation, then God listens to him; yes, also if he asks for something temporal—that God would give him food and clothing, would not let him be tempted beyond his ability to resist, and would not let him be ruined in time of need.

If, however, the Christian prays for other temporal goods for which he does not have a promise, he should, if the request does not contradict the Word of God, pray in firm faith. But he should leave it to God how he may wish to fulfill his petition; he should prescribe to God neither the time nor the measure nor the place but always with Christ add to his prayer: "Still not my will but your will be done." You know best of all, dear Father, what is good and beneficial for me; only let me have your grace, only make me blessed [i.e., save me]. Such a petition is never left unheard. If God also does not do as we think he should, nevertheless he does what agrees with his honor and our well-being.

Now then, recognize from all this the shoals on which your prayer can easily be shattered. Never forget it: God has commanded that you pray; second, he wills that your prayer be acceptable in the name of Jesus; and finally, he has promised also that he will certainly listen to it. Do not believe that you will ever truly be able to pray without a battle; when you pray, you are fighting against your flesh, the world, and Satan; therefore, grab hold always of the weapons of God and confidently dare even to wrestle with God as Jacob did. Just don't give up; pray, sigh, seek, knock, and think of nothing other than: "I will not let you go until you bless me!" God will gladly let himself be overcome by you; and when you close in faith with Amen, then God will always answer in heaven: "Yes, yes, thus shall it be." Amen.

Scripture Index

19—99
22—17, 101
50:15—19
51—28, 63
51:17—151
66—65
68:6—164
73—172
90:2,4—97
90:10—61
91—151
91:11,12—2
91:15—151
103—65, 170
103:22—66
115:3—99
127:3-5—170
130—28, 63
136—65, 66
139—63, 97, 100
139:1-3—97
139:2,4—98
139:15,16—98
139:17,18—98, 120
139:18—98
143—63
147:11—145

Proverbs

16:1,9,33—114
28:9—39

Isaiah

1:18—vi, 37
9:8–10:19—64
25:8—216
28:19—49 (footnote)
35:10—216
40:12-31—97
49:10—216
49:15,16—16
52:5—63

53—17, 101
54:10—16, 21
55—211
55:8,9—vi
60:20—216
63:1-6—17
63:3—102
64:6-9—43

Jeremiah

10:23—114

Lamentations

1:12,13—39
3:22-24—39

Ezekiel

18—35
18:31,32—36
36:22,23—63

Daniel

9:4-19—111
12:3—155

Joel

2:12-14—173

Malachi

3:8-14—149

Matthew

4:5-7—2, 27
5–7—150
5:1-11—148
5:16—144, 157, 163, 183
6:25-34—99, 148 (footnote)
6:30-33—60
6:33—84

Mark

Luke

John

Acts

Romans

Other books in the
Impact Series

Order online at **www.nph.net**, or call **1-800-662-6022**
(Milwaukee area 414-475-6600 ext. 5800),
8:30 A.M. to 4:00 P.M. CT weekdays.